SCL

TŌNOHARU

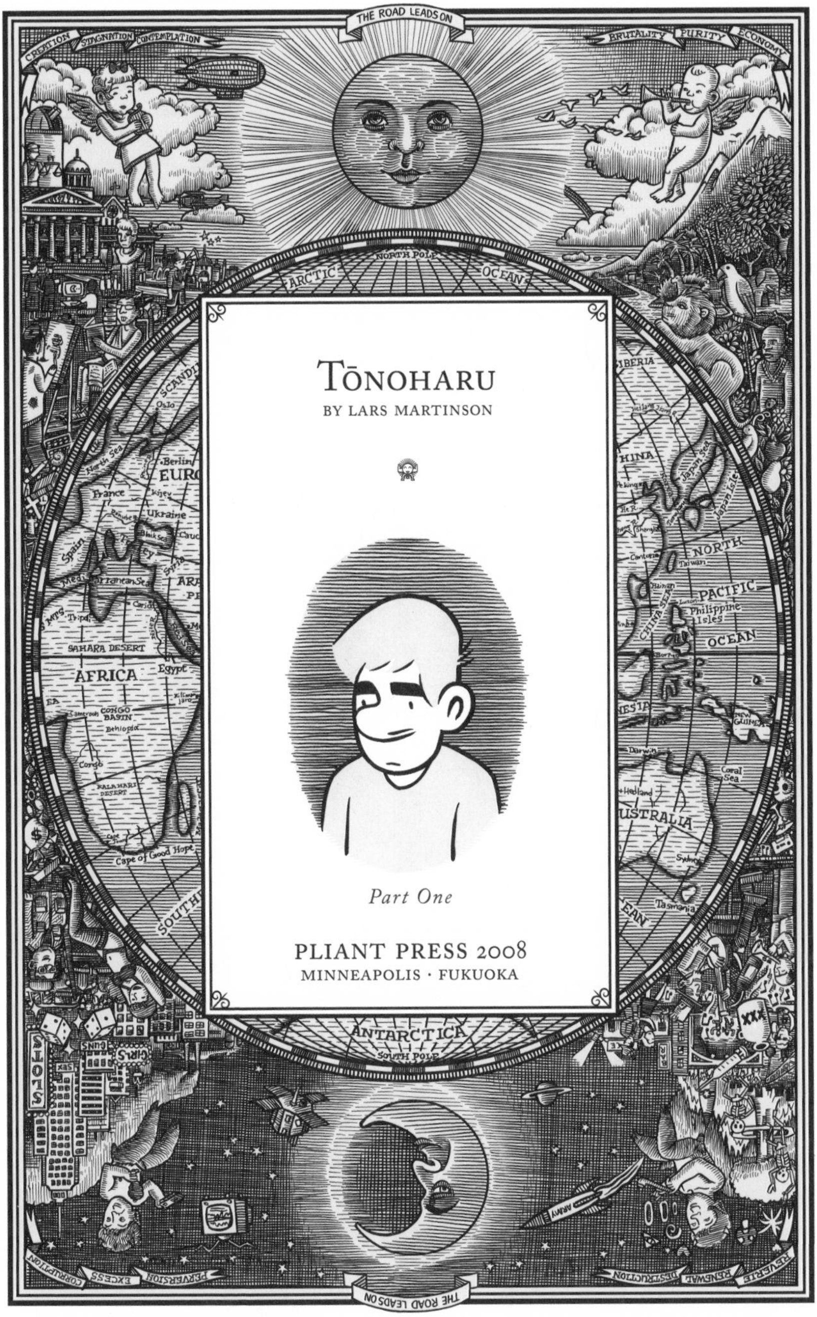
THE ROAD LEADS ON
CREATION
STAGNATION
CONTEMPLATION
BRUTALITY
PURITY
ECONOMY
ARCTIC
NORTH POLE
OCEAN
AFRICA
SAHARA DESERT
NORTH
PACIFIC
OCEAN
ANTARCTICA
SOUTH POLE
CORRUPTION
EXCESS
PERVERSION
DESTRUCTION
RENEWAL
REVERIE
THE ROAD LEADS ON

TŌNOHARU

BY LARS MARTINSON

Part One

PLIANT PRESS 2008
MINNEAPOLIS · FUKUOKA

to Naoko

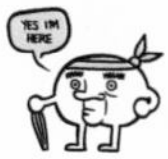
YES IM HERE

PROLOGUE

A COUPLE OF DAYS ago my supervisor asked me about renewing my contract for another year.

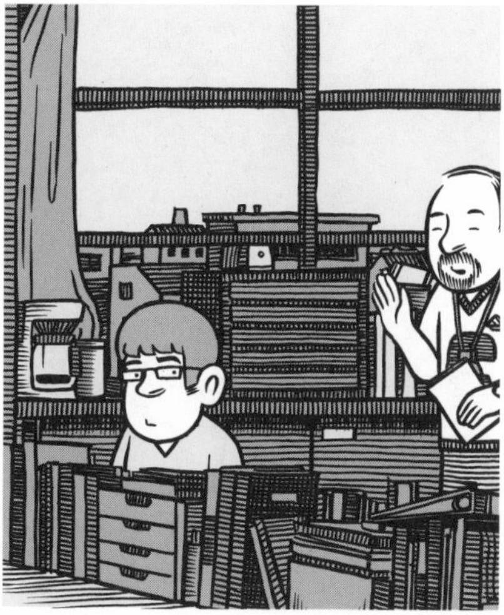

My decision wasn't due for another month, but he thought he'd get the paperwork out of the way if I'd made up my mind.

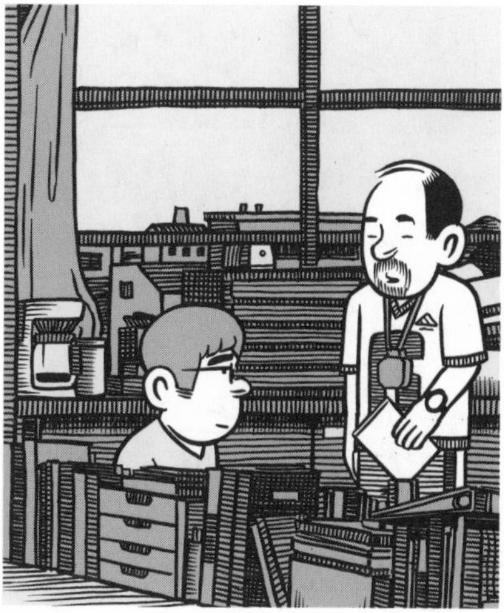

I told him I was still mulling it over but would try to let him know within a week or two.

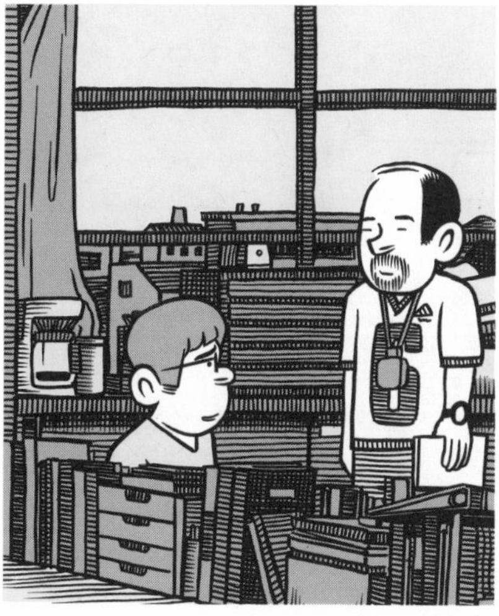

After he left I took out a calendar and did the math. I've been in Japan for almost exactly eight months now.

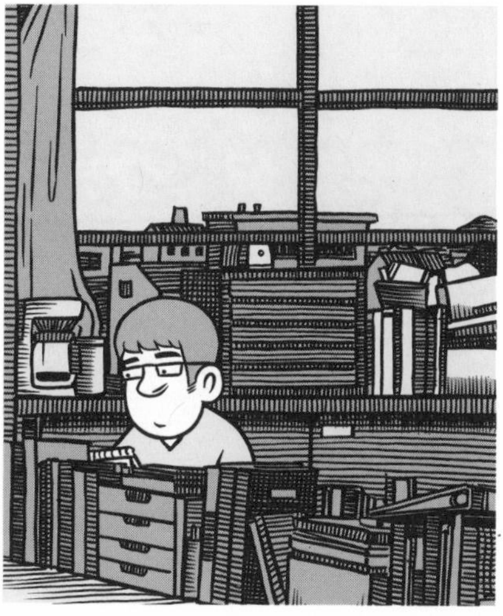

In the back of my mind I knew it was something like that, but it still felt weird to attach a number to it.

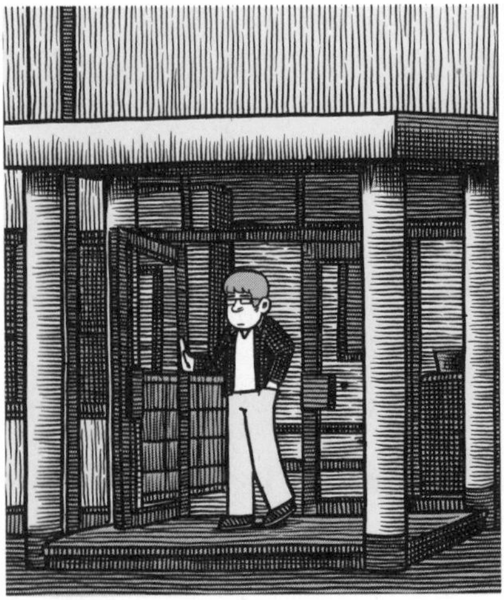

Sometimes it feels like I've only been here for a couple weeks. Other times it feels like it's been years.

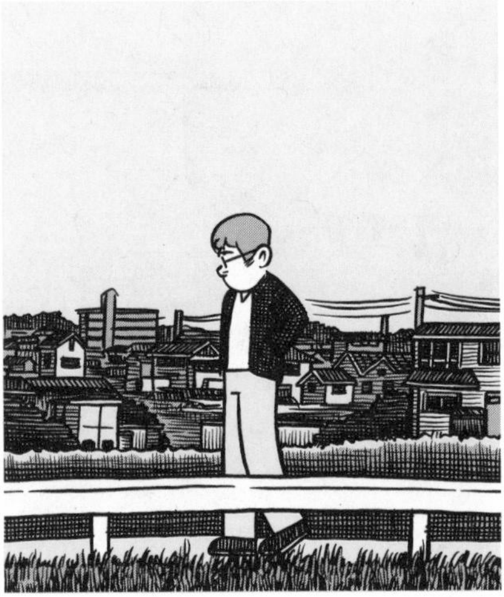

I never imagined that the passage of time could be so nuanced before I came here.

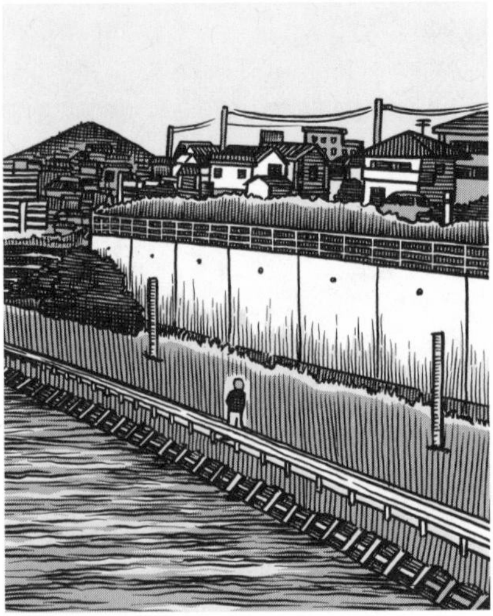

But I guess I've come to question a lot of things I used to take for granted.

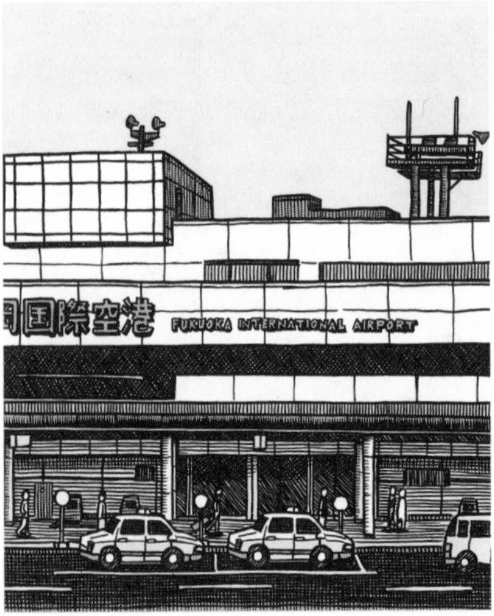
国際空港
FUKUOKA INTERNATIONAL AIRPORT

Like renewing my contract. I thought I had it all figured out. I was going to renew twice, for a total of three years.

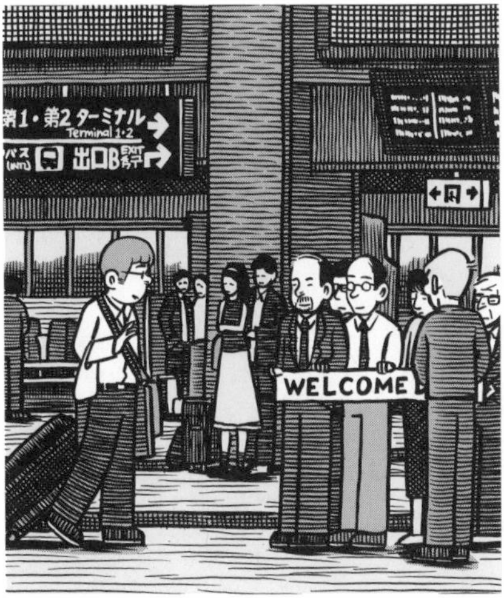

第1・第2 ターミナル
Terminal 1・2
バス
出口B
EXIT
WELCOME

My legacy was to be monumental. Fluency in Japanese, adoring students and colleagues, a revolutionized curriculum…

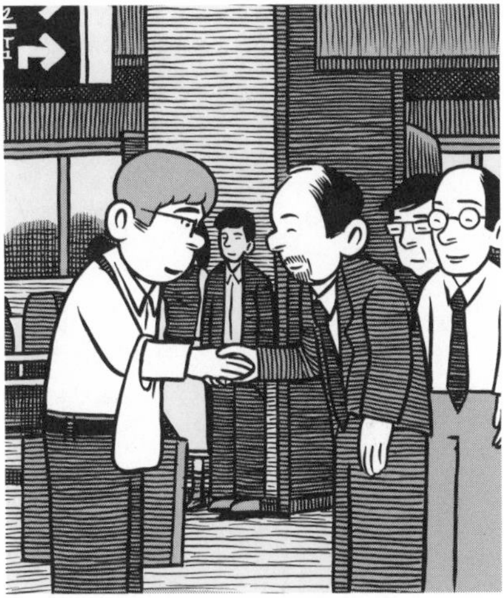

I think there were signs even then that things wouldn't work out so idyllically.

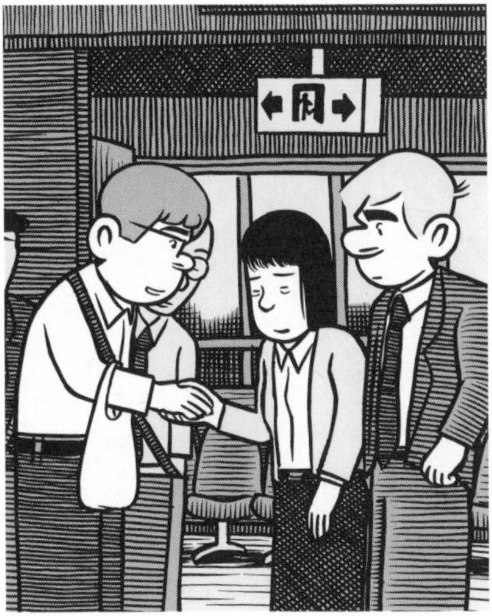

Like my predecessor for example. The red flags seem so obvious in retrospect.

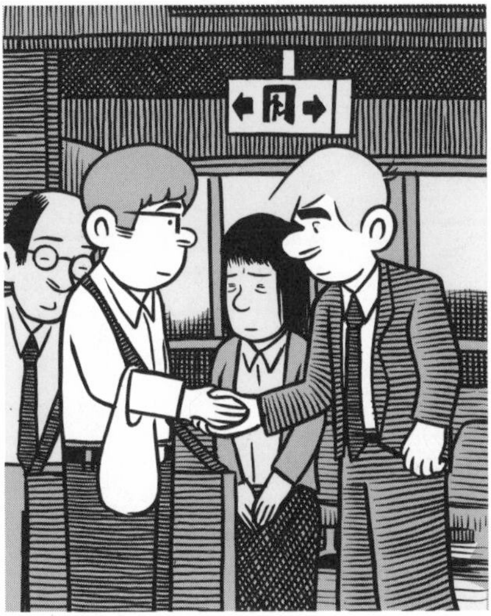

There was his reluctance to discuss his experience, or the fact that he was quitting after just a year, or that ever-present look of defeat on his face…

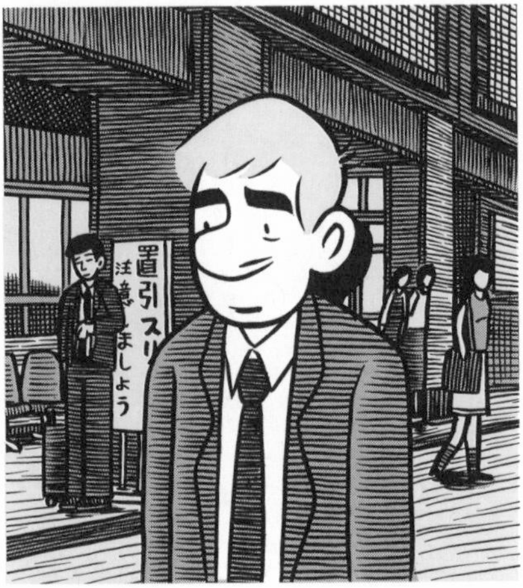
置引スリ
注意
ましょう

His last night in Japan he assured me that his reasons for leaving were personal and had nothing to do with the job I was about to inherit.

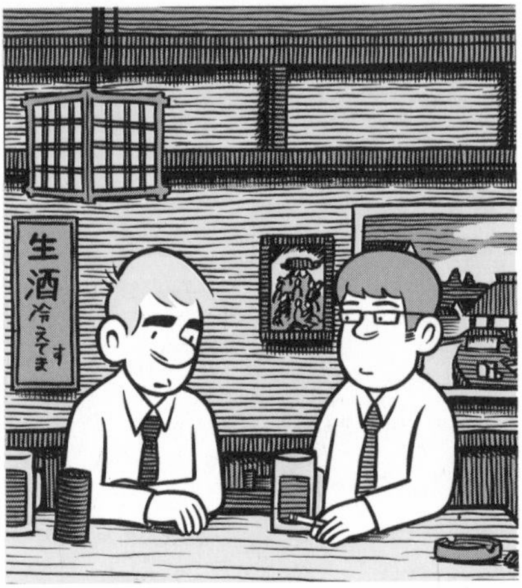
生酒
冷えてます

It didn't occur to me then that he might have just said that so I wouldn't start off on the wrong foot. Now I wonder…

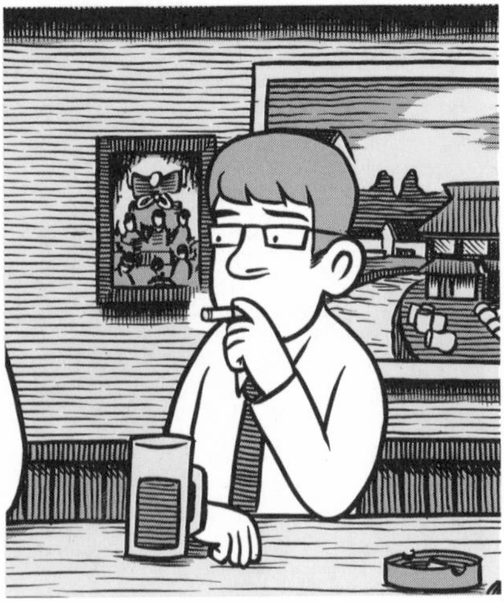

But I might just be imagining significance where it doesn't exist. My mind has plenty of time to wander.

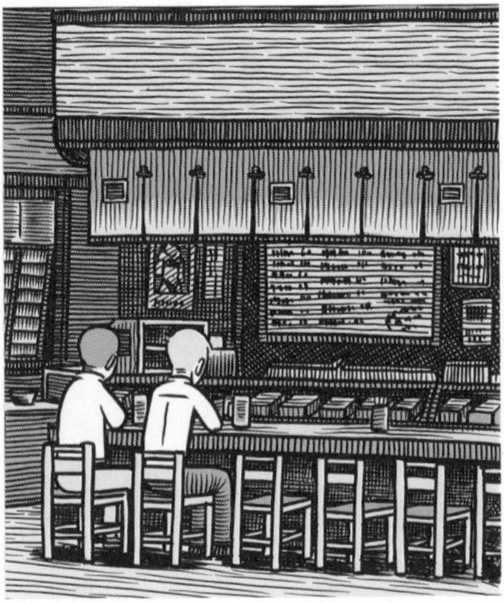

I am employed at a junior high school as an Assistant English Teacher, or an "AET".

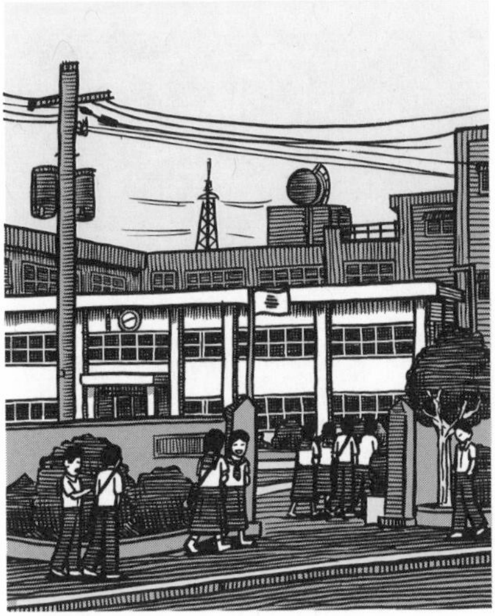

Exactly what form my assistance takes is largely at the discretion of each of the six English teachers that I work with.

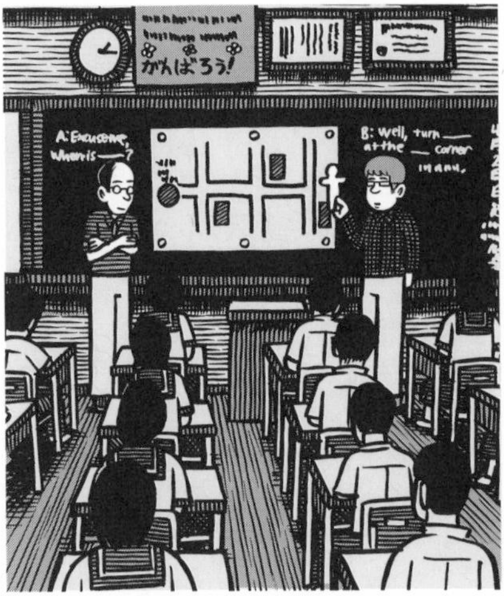
がんばろう!

On one end of the spectrum is Mister Sato. He's a passionate teacher and one of the friendliest people I've ever met.

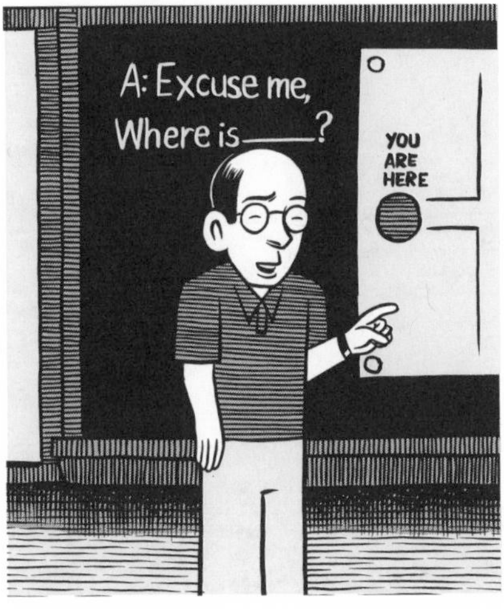
A: Excuse me,
Where is____?
YOU ARE HERE

He has me in class as often as possible, and is always open to trying new things. Just a great guy all around.

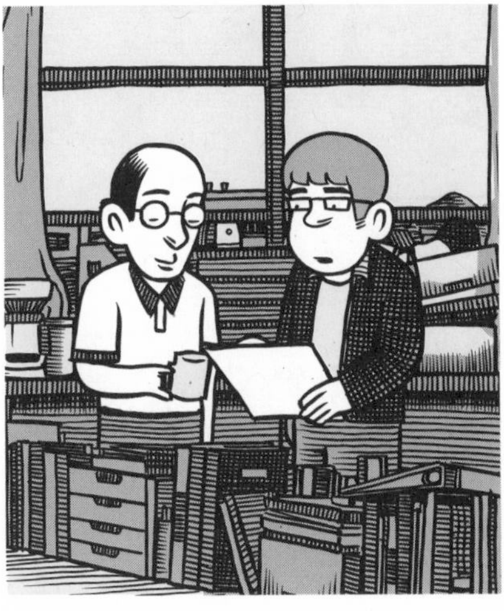

Mister Sato's polar opposite is Miss Mori. Never in my life has someone gone to such lengths to steer clear of me.

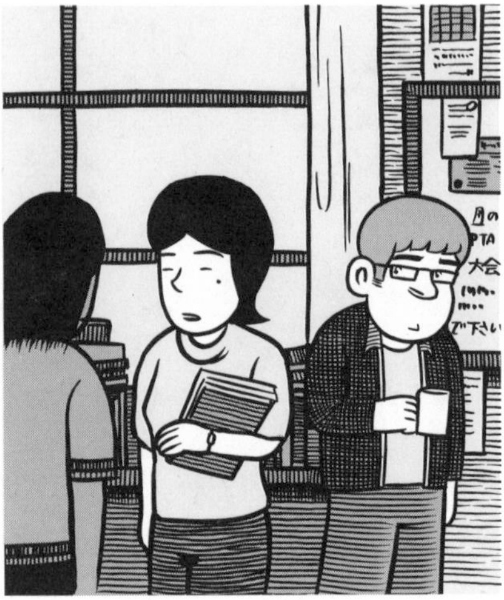
PTA
大会

As the only English teacher who didn't even bother coming to my welcome party, she's literally avoided me from day one.

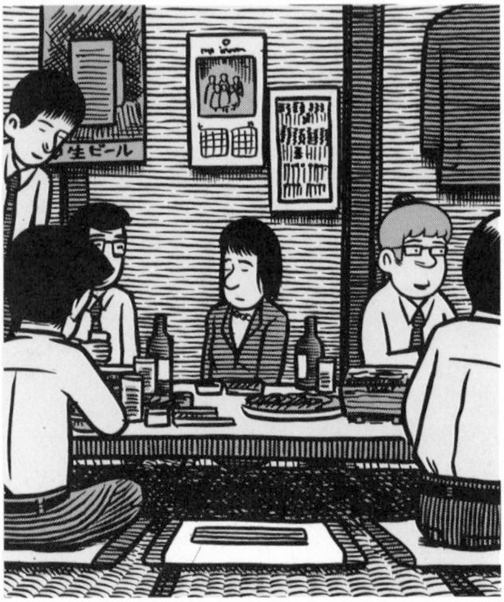
生ビール

She's cancelled classes with me on all but three occasions. "I need to concentrate on the textbook" is her eternal excuse.

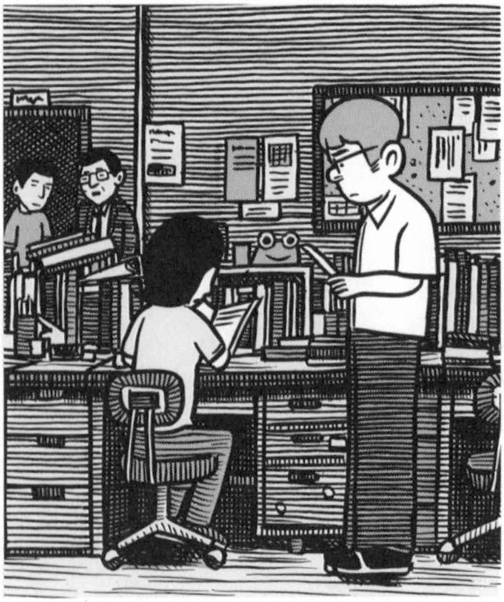

The other four teachers fall somewhere in between. They interact with me and have me in class, but only as much as they're strictly obligated to.

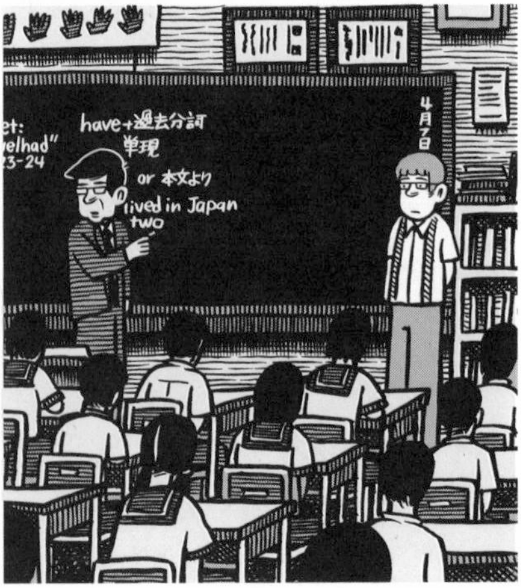
lived in Japan
two

The work is pretty easy. It's telling that no prior training or experience is required.

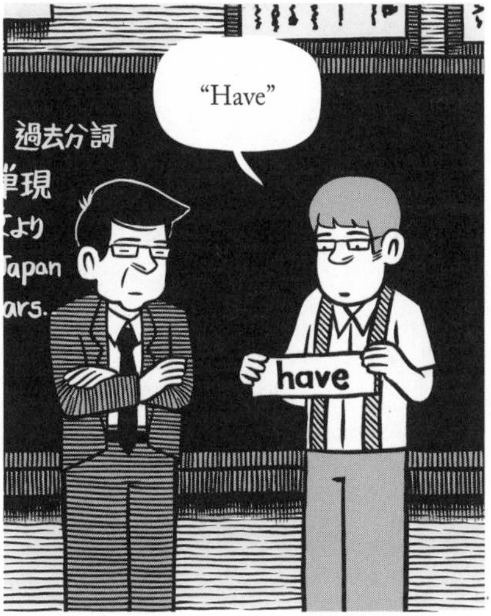

過去分詞
"Have"
have

My job could easily be done on a part-time basis. I rarely have more than two or three hours of work on any given day.

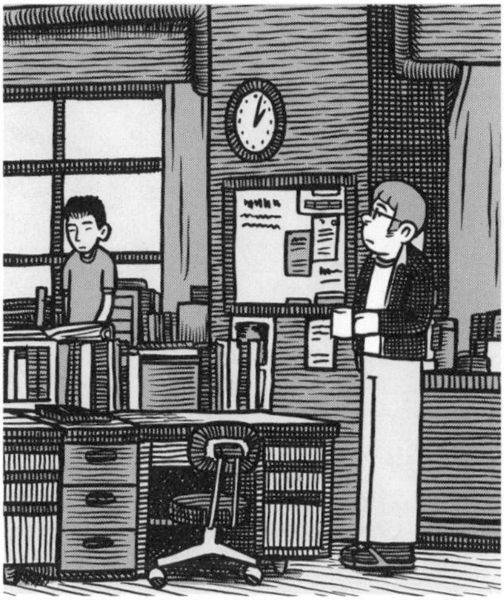

No one seems to care what I do for the rest of the time as long as I am physically present at school for eight hours a day.

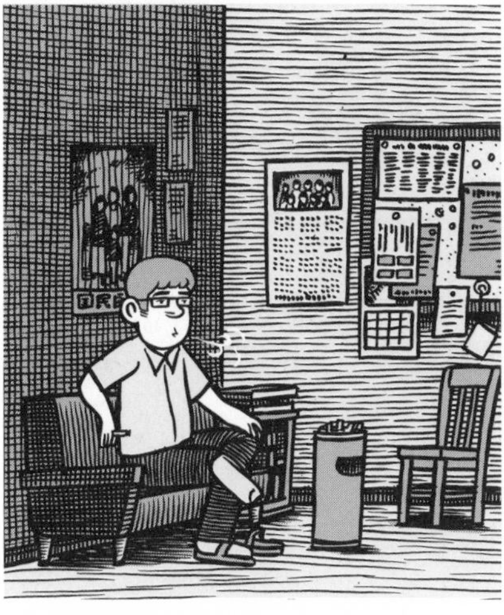

I stopped pretending to work outside of class a long time ago. I could probably set up a hammock and no one would say anything.

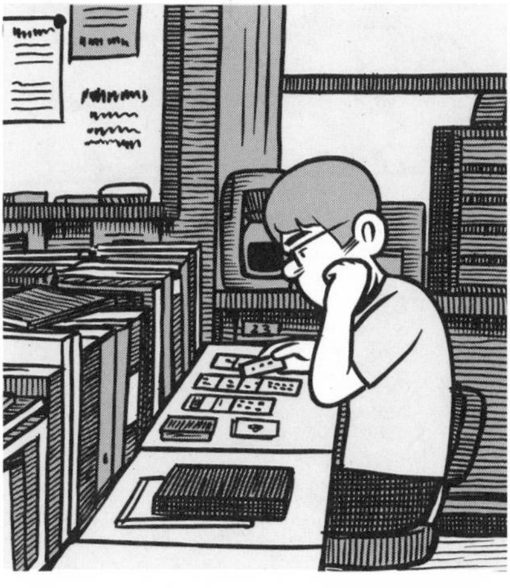

My friends back home can't understand why I'd even consider quitting at the end of this year's contract.

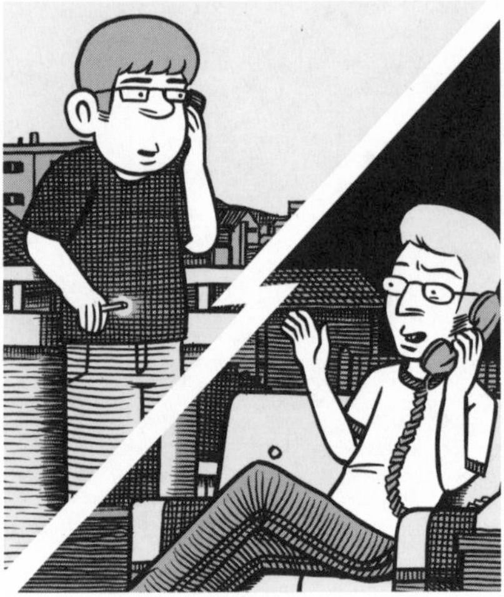

Most of them are working grueling jobs for slave wages, so I can see how my job must seem ideal from their point of view.

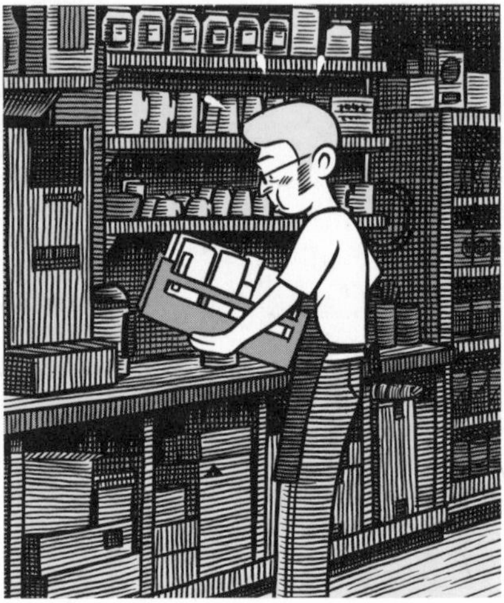

High pay, low stress, an abundance of free time…on paper it sounds great.

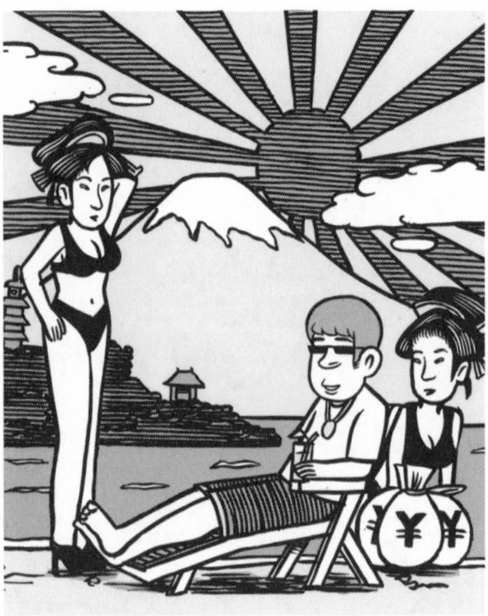

But the reality of it isn't so pristine. The devil is in the details.

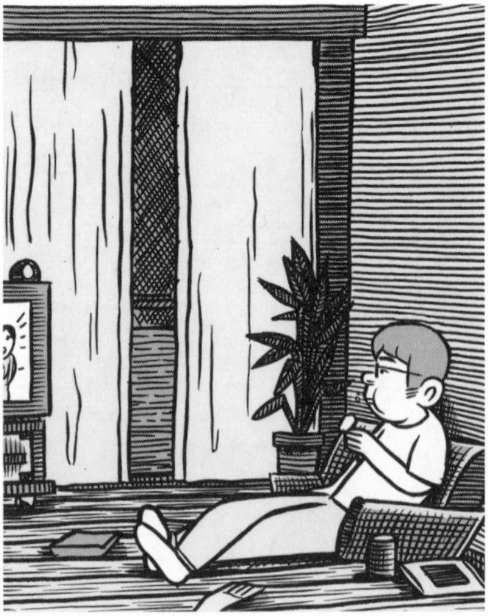

Never knowing what the hell is going on gets old pretty quick, for example.

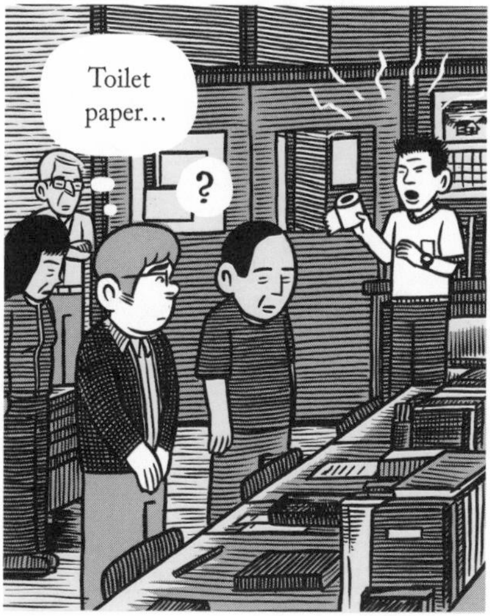
Toilet paper...
?

After eight months of blood, sweat and tears, my Japanese still amounts to little more than caveman talk.

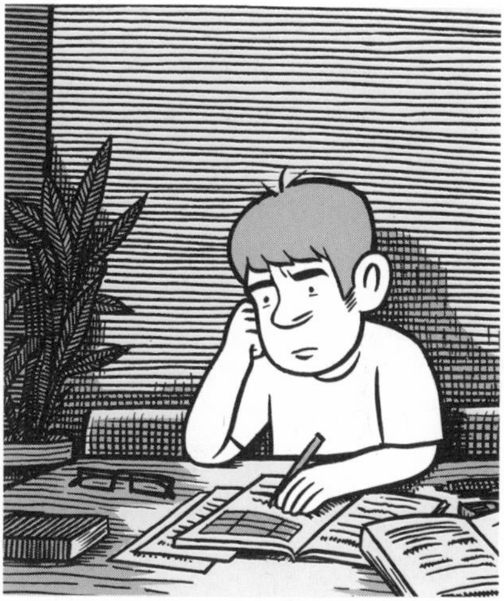

If I want to ask someone about the weather or their favorite color, I can grunt out something that will be understood.

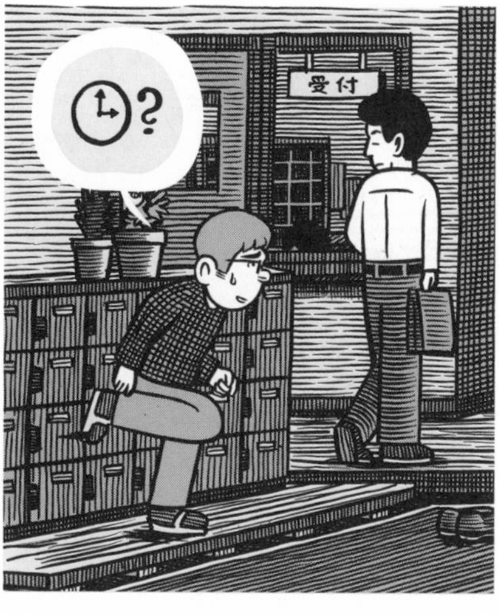
?
受付

Unfortunately, even small talk requires more sophistication than that. The nuances of conversation are deceptively complex.

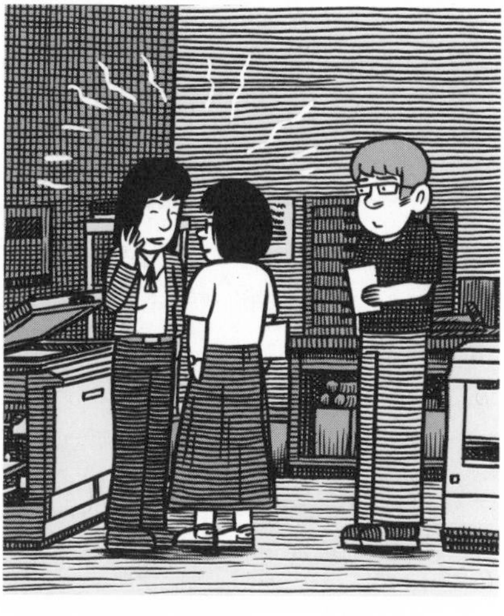

What really kills me is when some nice, shy teacher works up the courage to strike up a conversation with me.

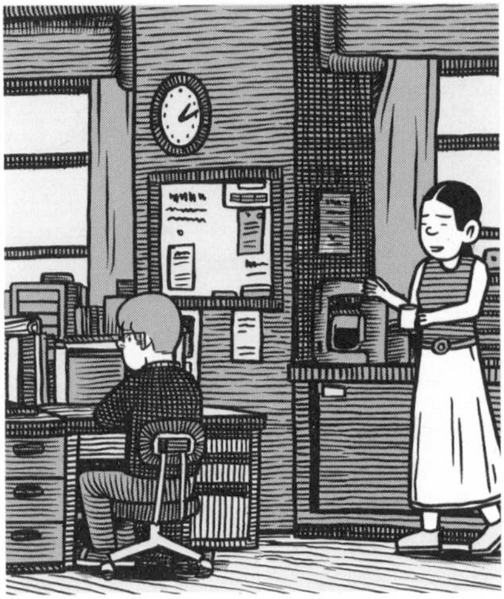

As the conversation moves beyond the initial pleasantries, unknown words and phrases begin to pop up and my Japanese starts to fail me.

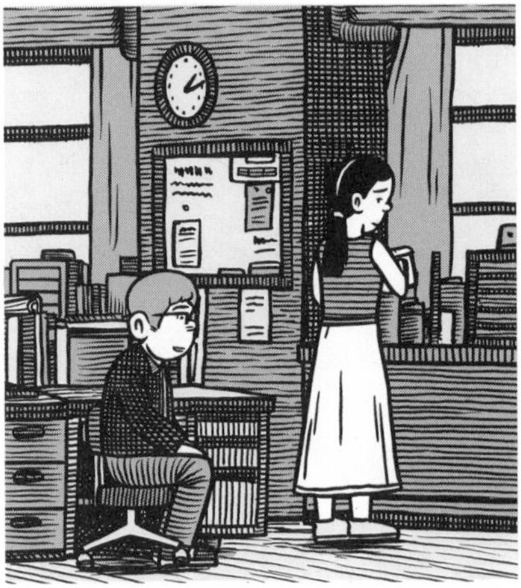

They'll rephrase something that I didn't understand, but I won't understand that either. We laugh uncomfortably, and look down at our shoes…

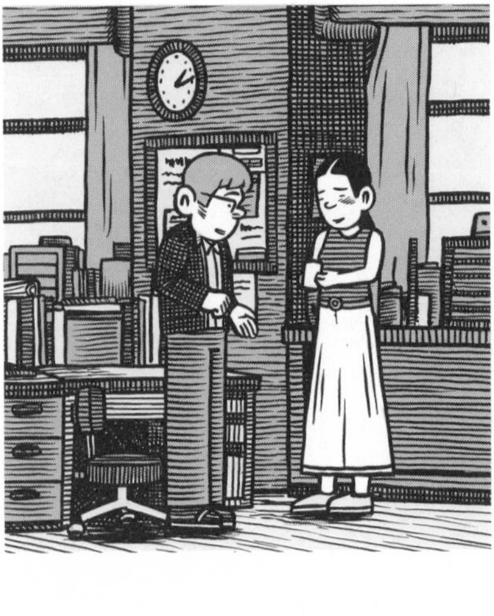

The pauses are painful. I can actually see the conversation dying before my eyes, unresponsive to all attempts to save it.

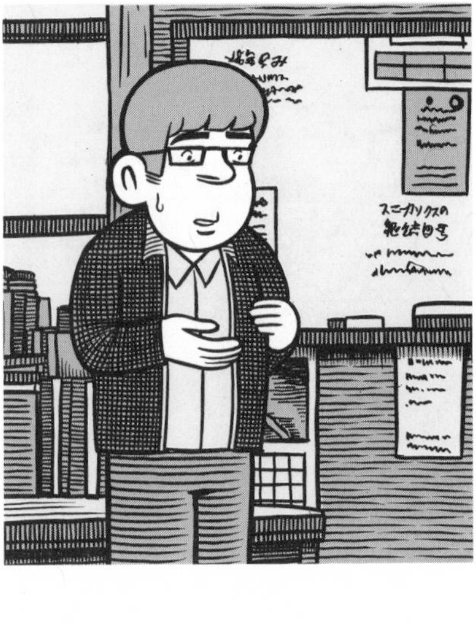

We struggle for a bit, but after a couple minutes it becomes clear that we just don't have the means to communicate in a meaningful way.

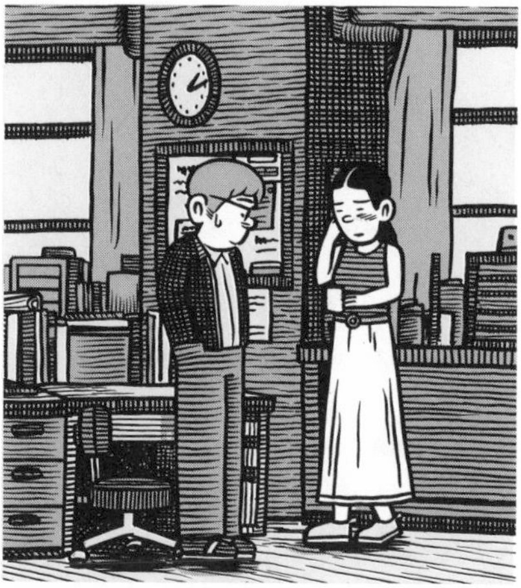

So with an abrupt nod, our conversation ends and they walk away, never to return.

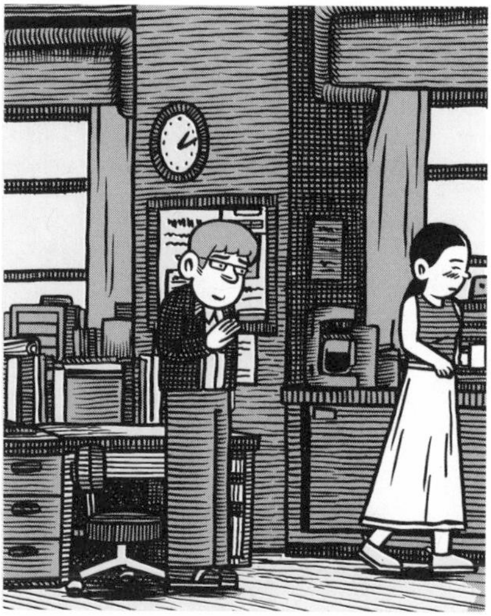

The isolation might be a little more tolerable if I had more to occupy my time.

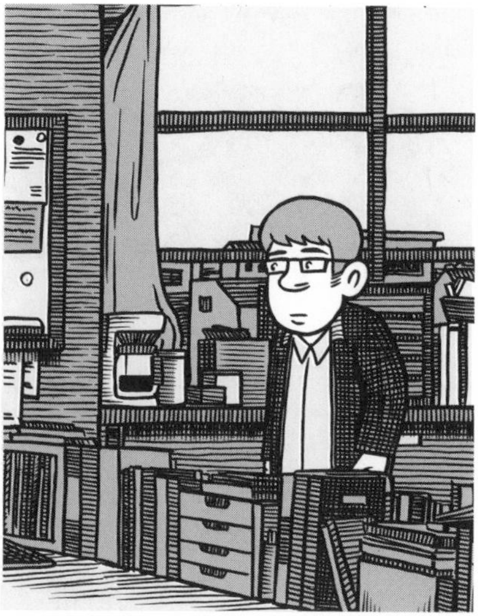

But my job offers no help in this regard, and outside of work my options aren't much better.

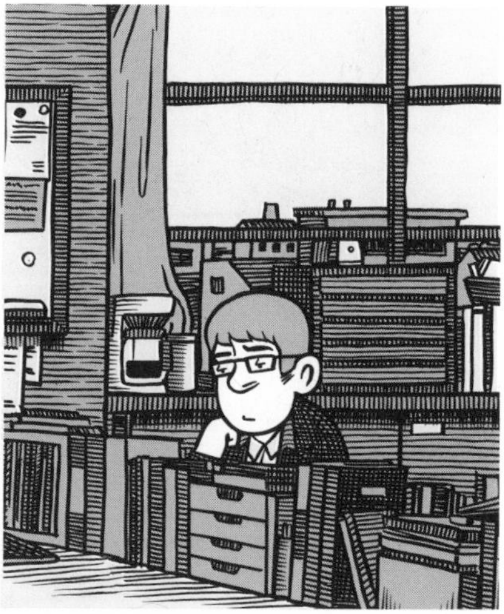

I live in the sticks. The nearest real city is an hour away and the trains going there stop early.

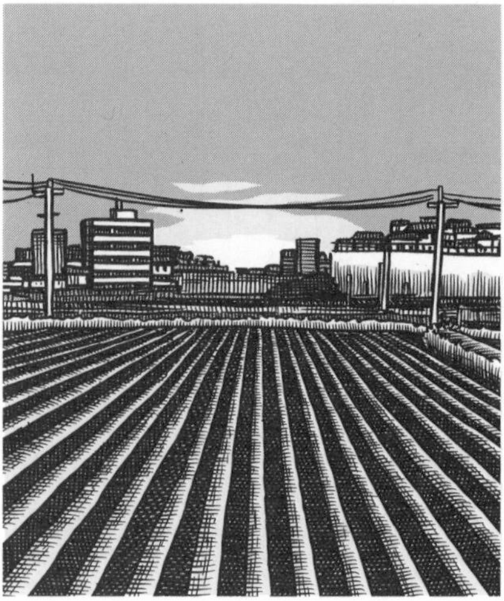

My little town has its charm, but cosmopolitan it ain't. I am currently the only non-Japanese resident.

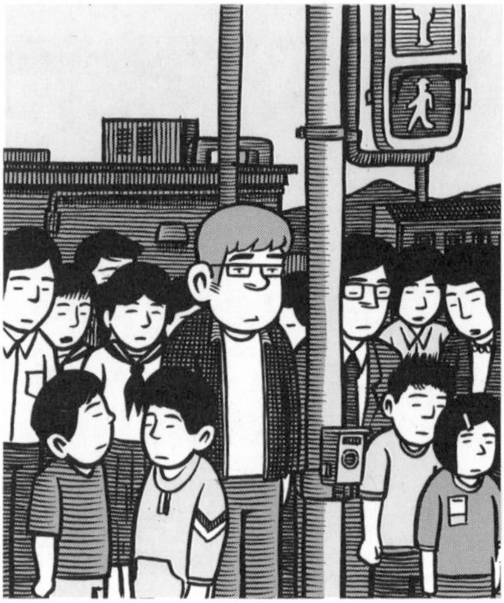

A family from Eastern Europe used to live here for some reason, but they left a few months before I got here.

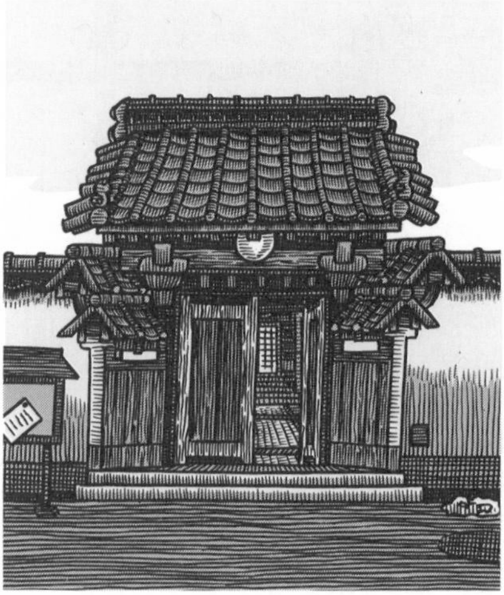

From the sound of it, they didn't make too many friends. The events surrounding their departure are still discussed in hushed tones.

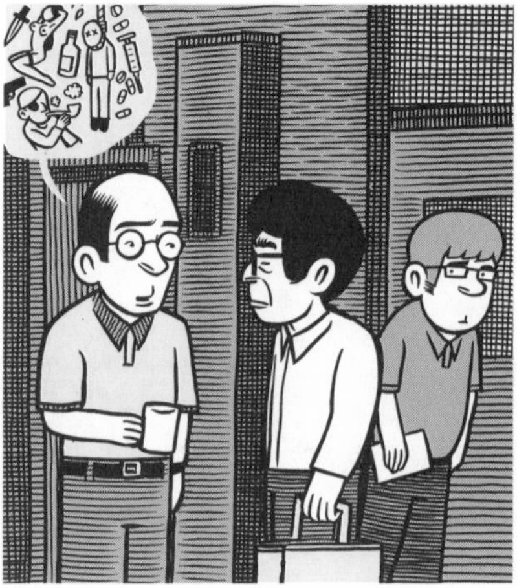

The only expat I ever met in my neck of the woods didn't seem like he'd win too many popularity contests either.

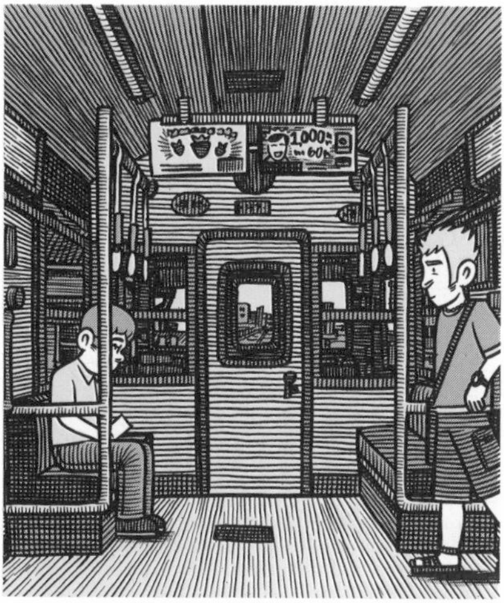

It was about a week after I arrived. He had been working as an AET a few towns down the line.

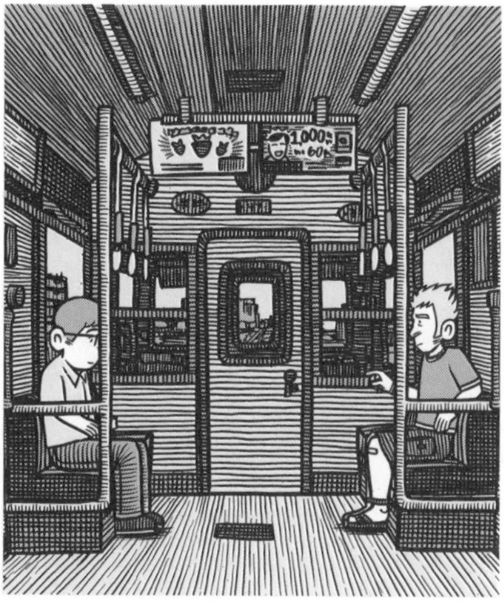

I asked if he had any insights for someone new to the job. His response was light on advice and heavy on anger and self-pity.

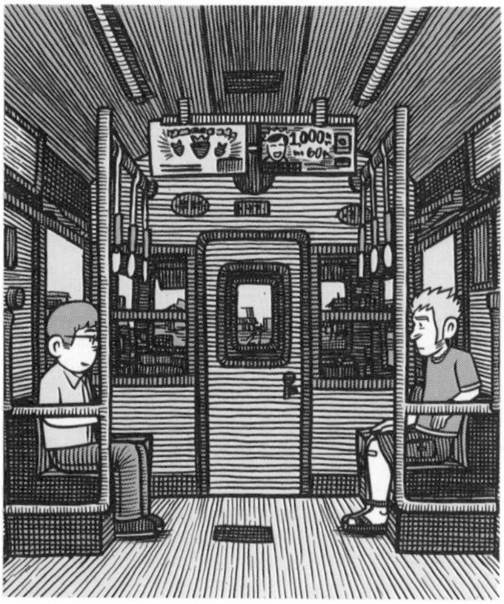

Every word out of his mouth was dripping with venom. Japan was shit, his job was a joke, all the other teachers were incompetent jerks…

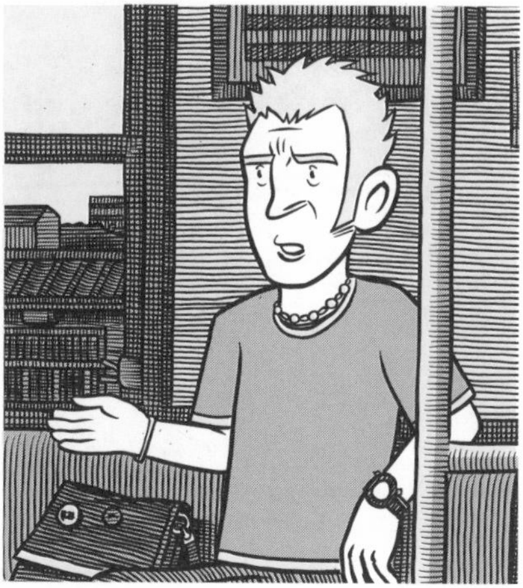

Granted, his situation did sound pretty dismal. His predecessor broke her contract and left several months early, leaving behind loose ends and bitter colleagues.

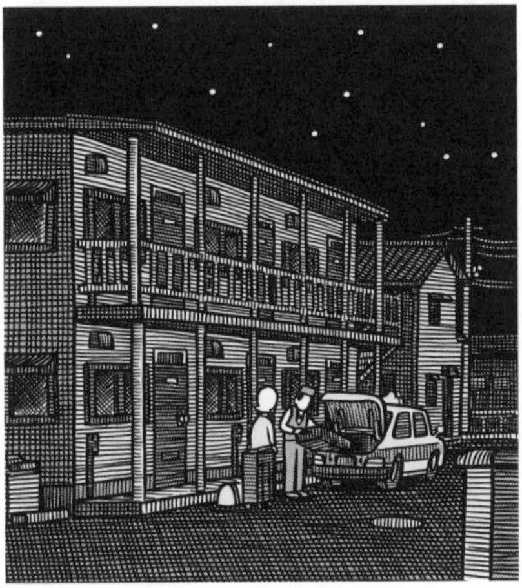

In any case, I was quick to dismiss him. He was just an asshole that was using Japan and a crappy job as scapegoats for his own issues.

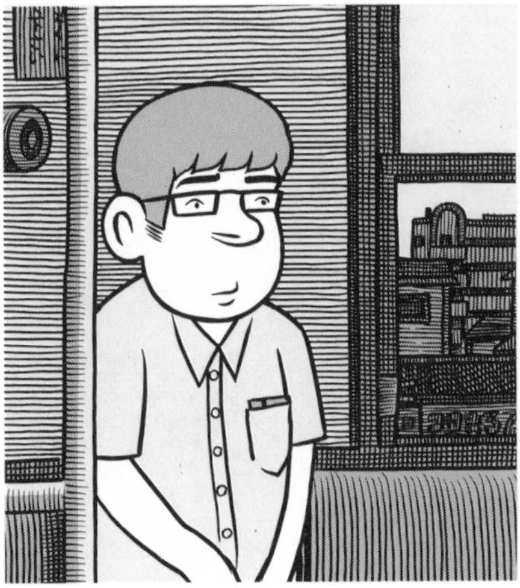

After listening to him for forty minutes, we finally got to my stop and I could make my escape. I never saw him again.

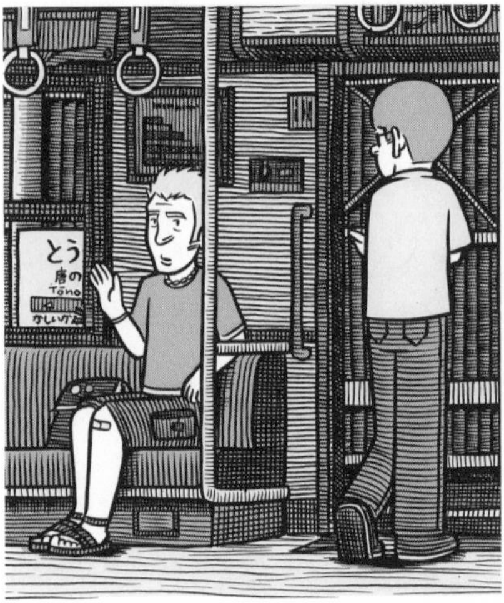
とう

I still suspect my knee-jerk assessment of him was more right than wrong, but since then my own experience has made me a little more sympathetic.

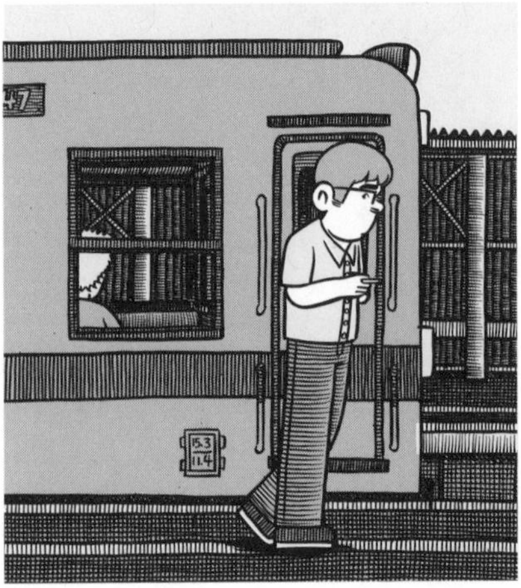

Sometimes it feels like the AET program was designed to ensure discontent. There's the countless hours of idle time…

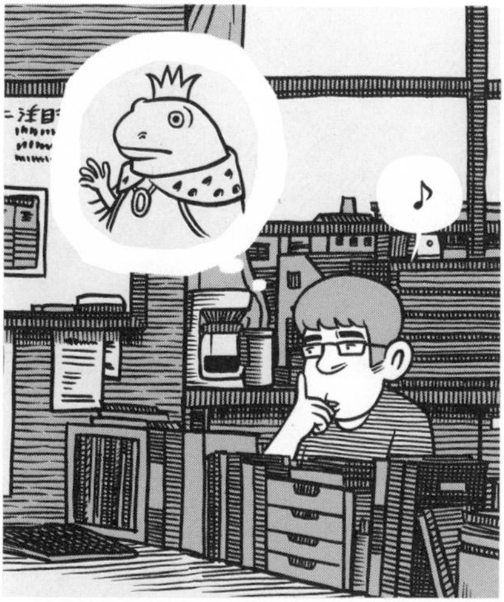

The geographical remoteness, the language barrier, the thousand little cultural differences…

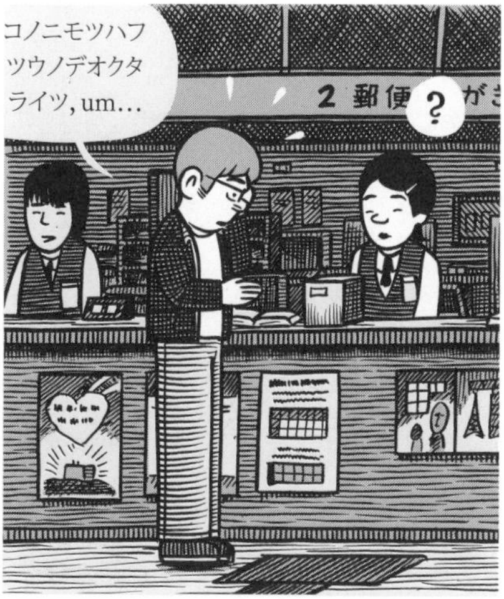
コノニモツハフツウノデオクタライツ, um…
2 郵便
?

Allow all this to stew for a few months without an outlet for release, and it's enough to drive anyone a little crazy.

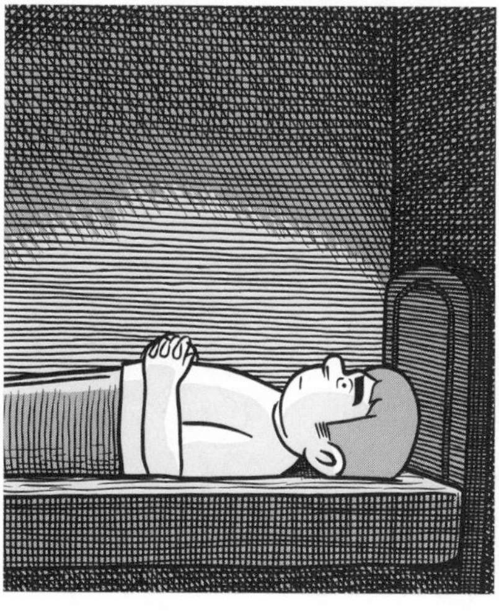

Sometimes I wonder if it's just a matter of time before I become that guy on the train, spewing bile at whoever is unfortunate enough to cross paths with me.

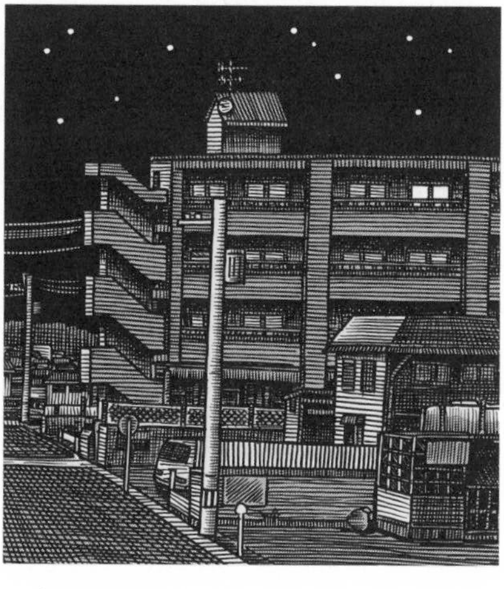

But I don't want to paint too bleak a portrait of life here. There's plenty to be thankful for, too.

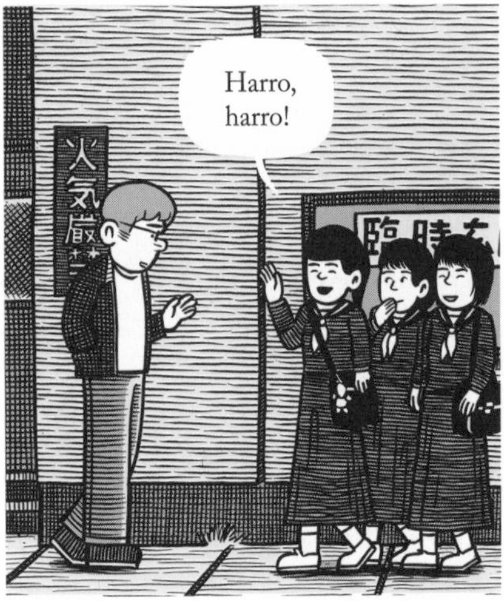
Harro, harro!

There's my students. Mister Sato. The food. High-tech toilets. The drunken reverie of the teacher parties, where the language barrier temporarily becomes a non-issue.

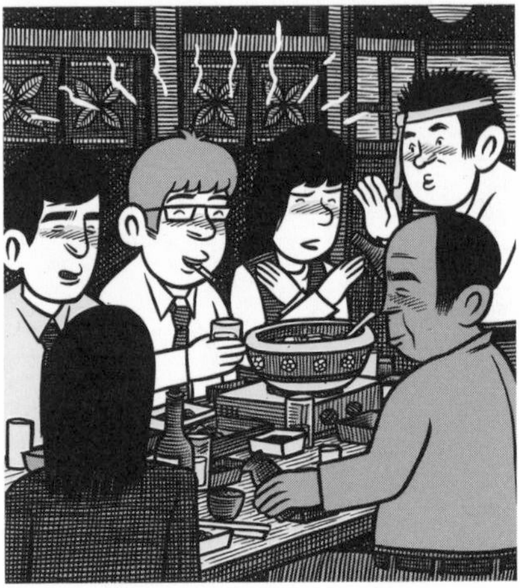

Getting to see the Spring Festival floats alone would have made everything else worth it.

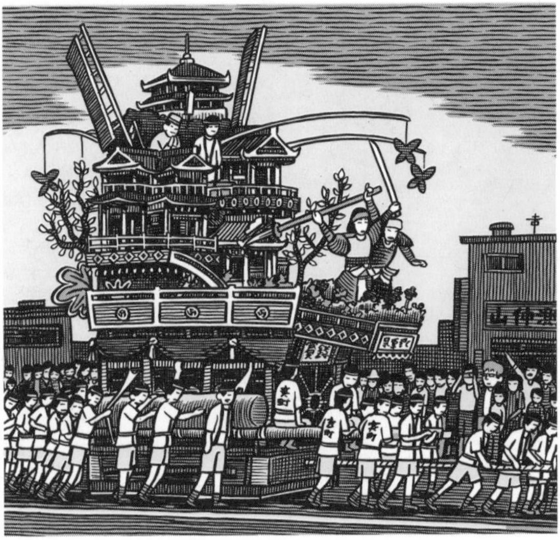

And actually, every experience I've had here, even the unpleasant ones, have deepened my understanding both of myself and of the wider world.

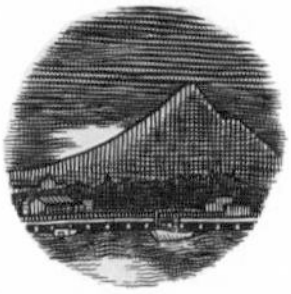

I feel privileged to have had the opportunity. In no way do I regret spending a year here.

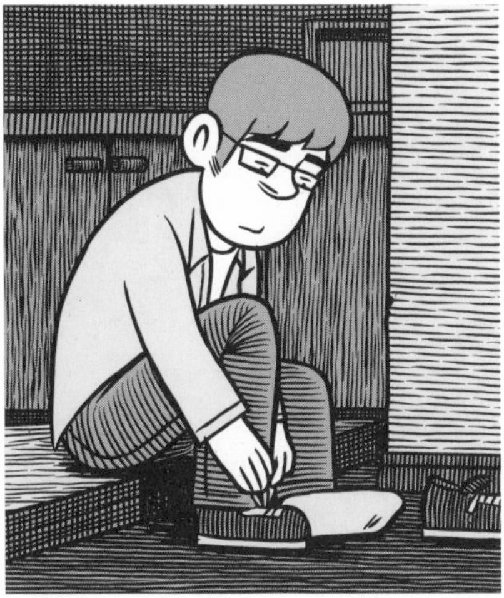

If I was sure I'd see improvement in just a few key areas, I'd renew my contract in a heartbeat.

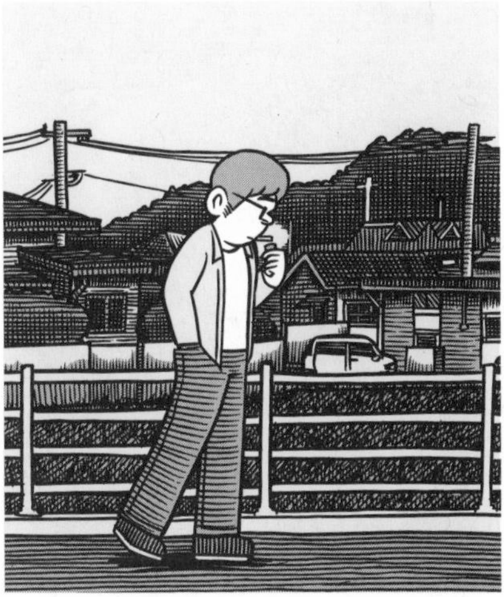

But if a second year was just more of the same, then the law of diminishing returns would apply and it would be a waste of time.

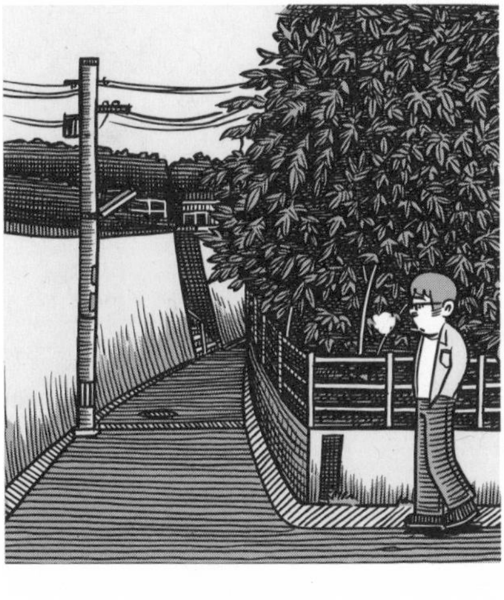

As much as I hate to admit it, I think the second scenario is more likely. I've worked myself into a pretty deep rut.

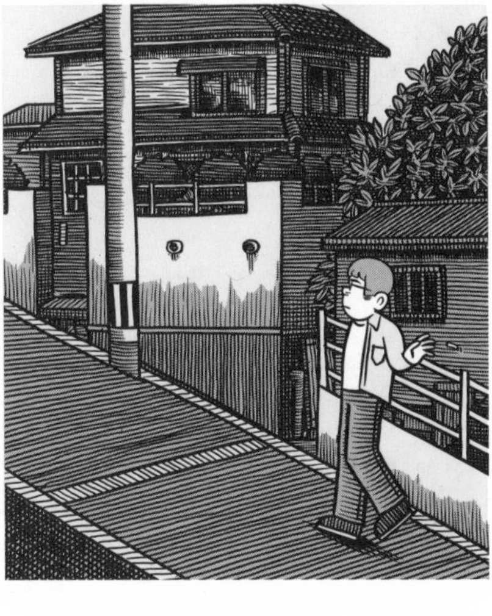

But the idea of giving up just rubs me the wrong way. My foolish pride tells me to struggle on, consequences be damned!

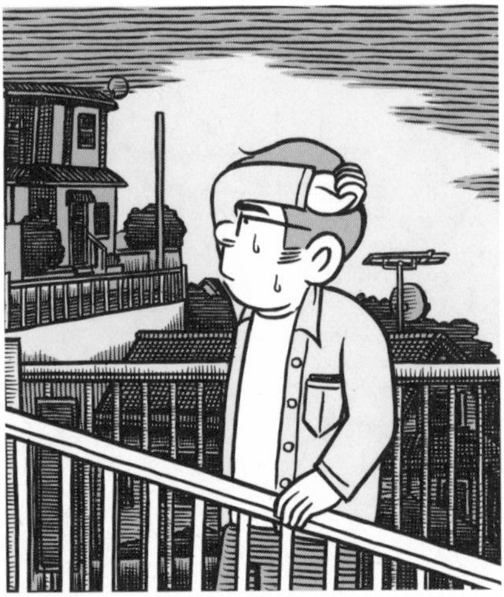

The question is, is it still possible to turn things around? Or would I just be wasting a year to satisfy my ego?

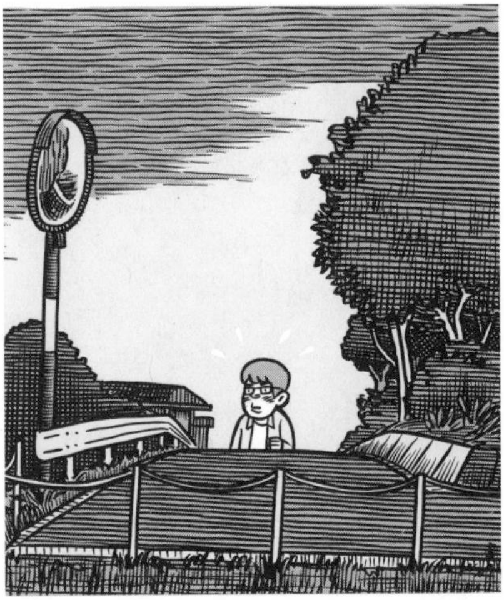

I only have a few days to decide, and frankly, I have no idea what I'm going to do.

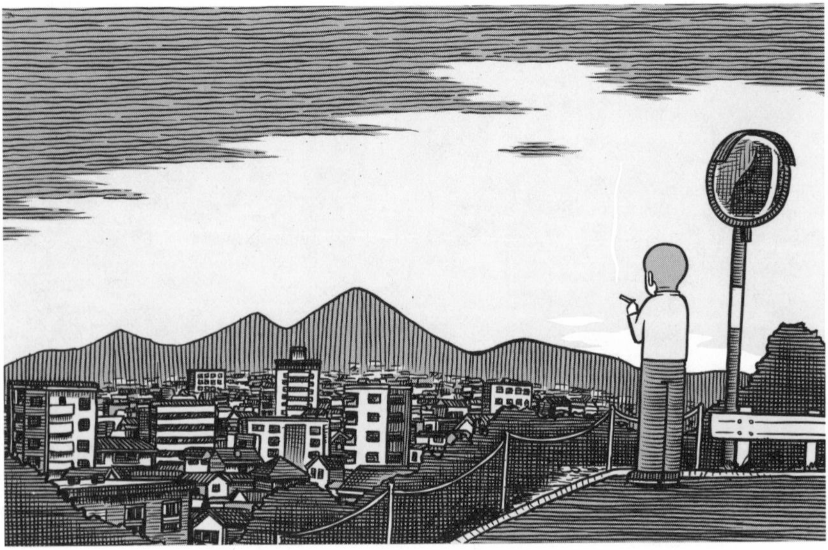

PART ONE

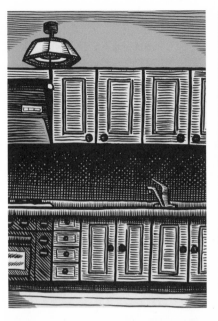

And the kitchen.

Rice cooker's over here, toaster oven, microwave…

So that's pretty much the grand tour

Looks good!

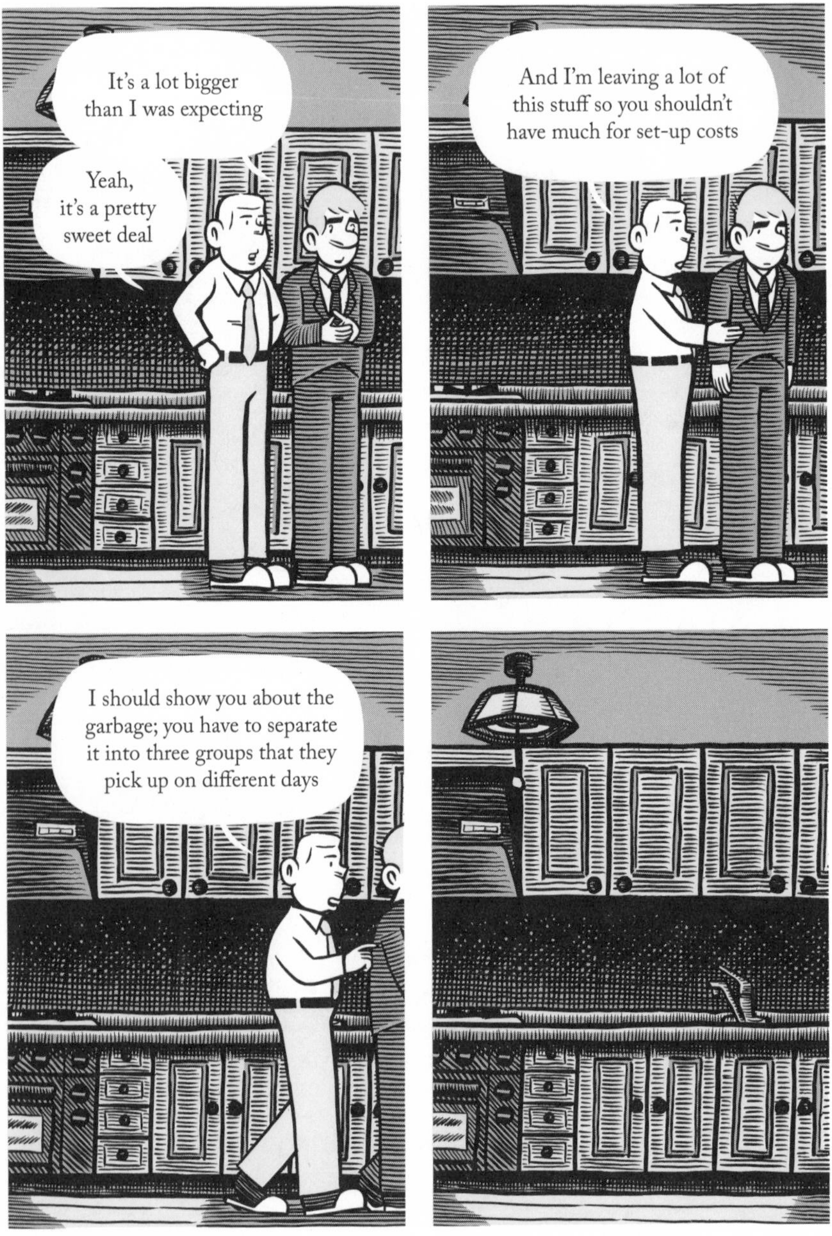
It's a lot bigger than I was expecting
Yeah, it's a pretty sweet deal
And I'm leaving a lot of this stuff so you shouldn't have much for set-up costs
I should show you about the garbage; you have to separate it into three groups that they pick up on different days

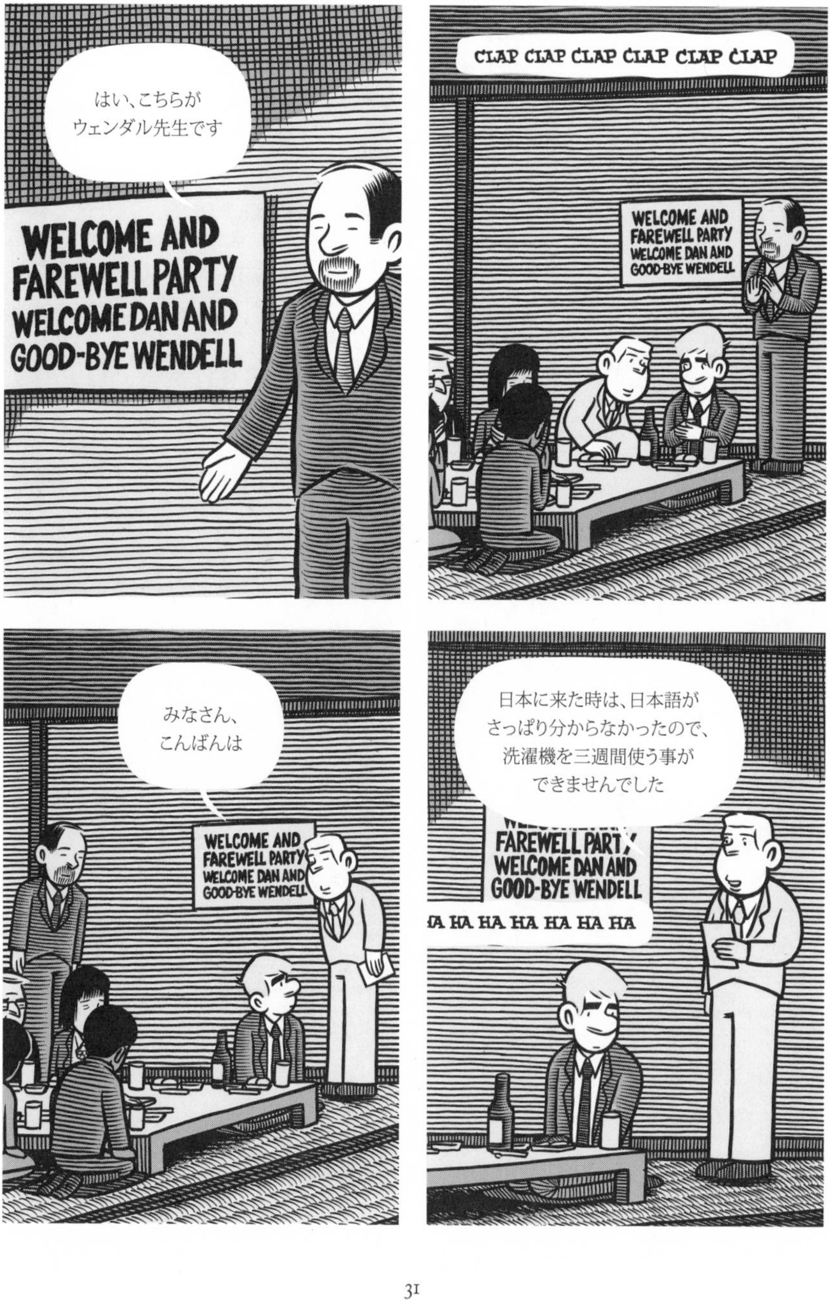
はい、こちらが
ウェンダル先生です
WELCOME AND
FAREWELL PARTY
WELCOME DAN AND
GOOD-BYE WENDELL
CLAP CLAP CLAP CLAP CLAP CLAP
WELCOME AND
FAREWELL PARTY
WELCOME DAN AND
GOOD-BYE WENDELL
みなさん、
こんばんは
WELCOME AND
FAREWELL PARTY
WELCOME DAN AND
GOOD-BYE WENDELL
日本に来た時は、日本語が
さっぱり分からなかったので、
洗濯機を三週間使う事が
できませんでした
FAREWELL PARTY
WELCOME DAN AND
GOOD-BYE WENDELL
HA HA HA HA HA HA

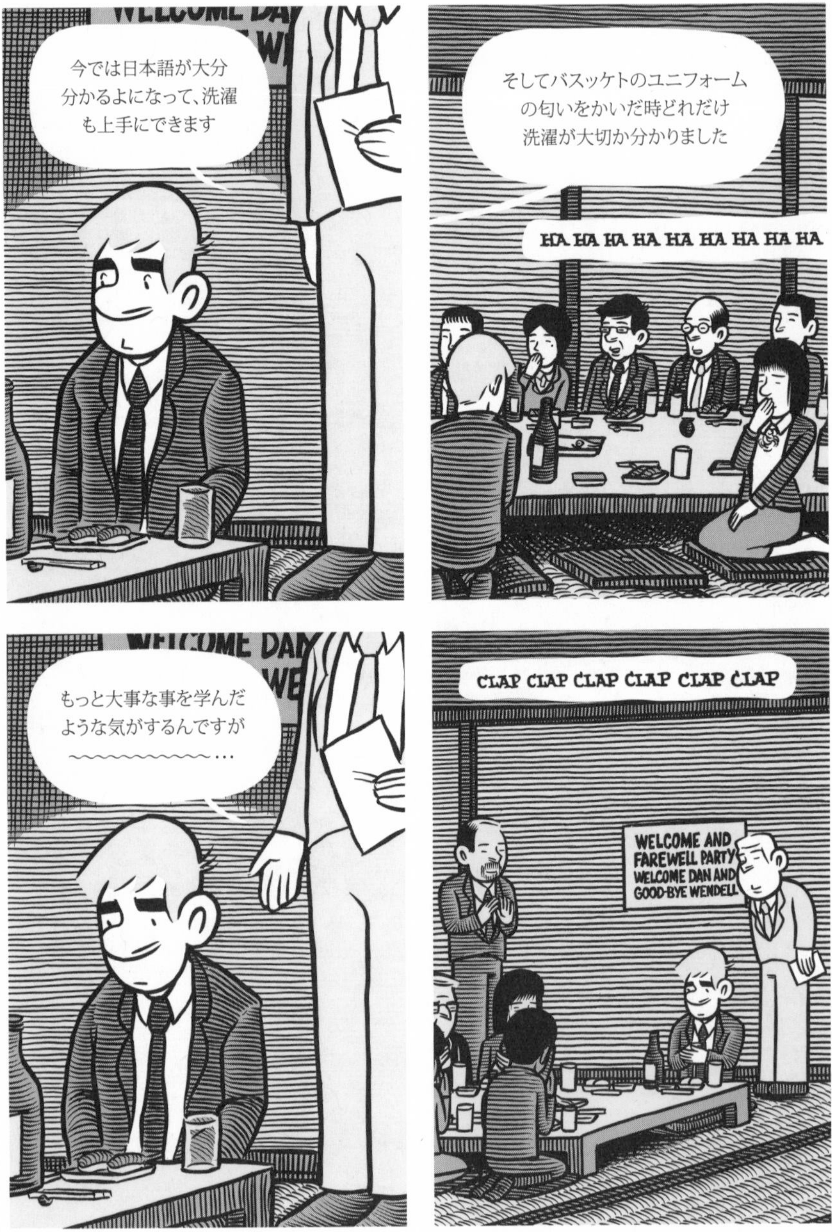
今では日本語が大分
分かるよになって、洗濯
も上手にできます
そしてバスッケトのユニフォーム
の匂いをかいだ時どれだけ
洗濯が大切か分かりました
HA HA HA HA HA HA HA HA HA
もっと大事な事を学んだ
ような気がするんですが
～～～～～～～～…
CLAP CLAP CLAP CLAP CLAP CLAP
WELCOME AND
FAREWELL PARTY
WELCOME DAN AND
GOOD-BYE WENDELL

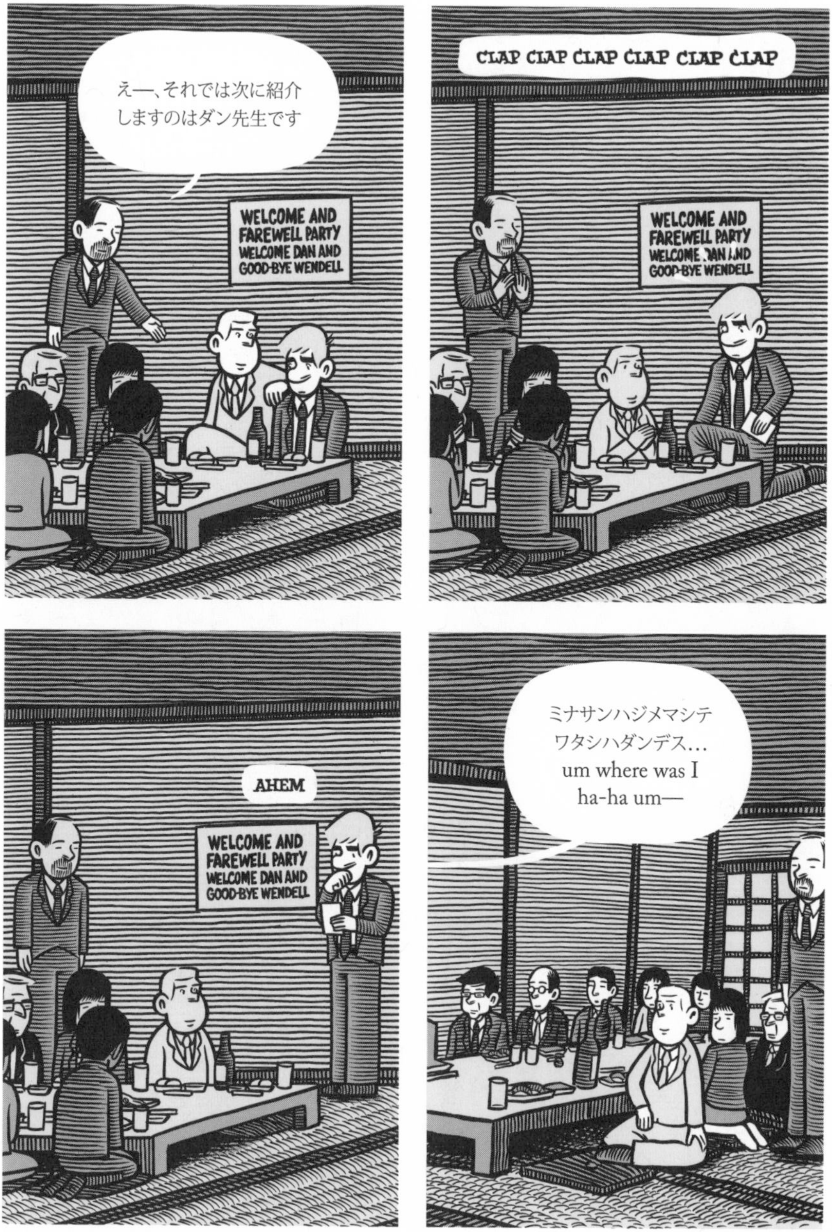
え—、それでは次に紹介
しますのはダン先生です
WELCOME AND
FAREWELL PARTY
WELCOME DAN AND
GOOD-BYE WENDELL
CLAP CLAP CLAP CLAP CLAP CLAP
WELCOME AND
FAREWELL PARTY
GOOD-BYE WENDELL
AHEM
WELCOME AND
FAREWELL PARTY
WELCOME DAN AND
GOOD-BYE WENDELL
ミナサンハジメマシテ
ワタシハダンデス...
um where was I
ha-ha um—

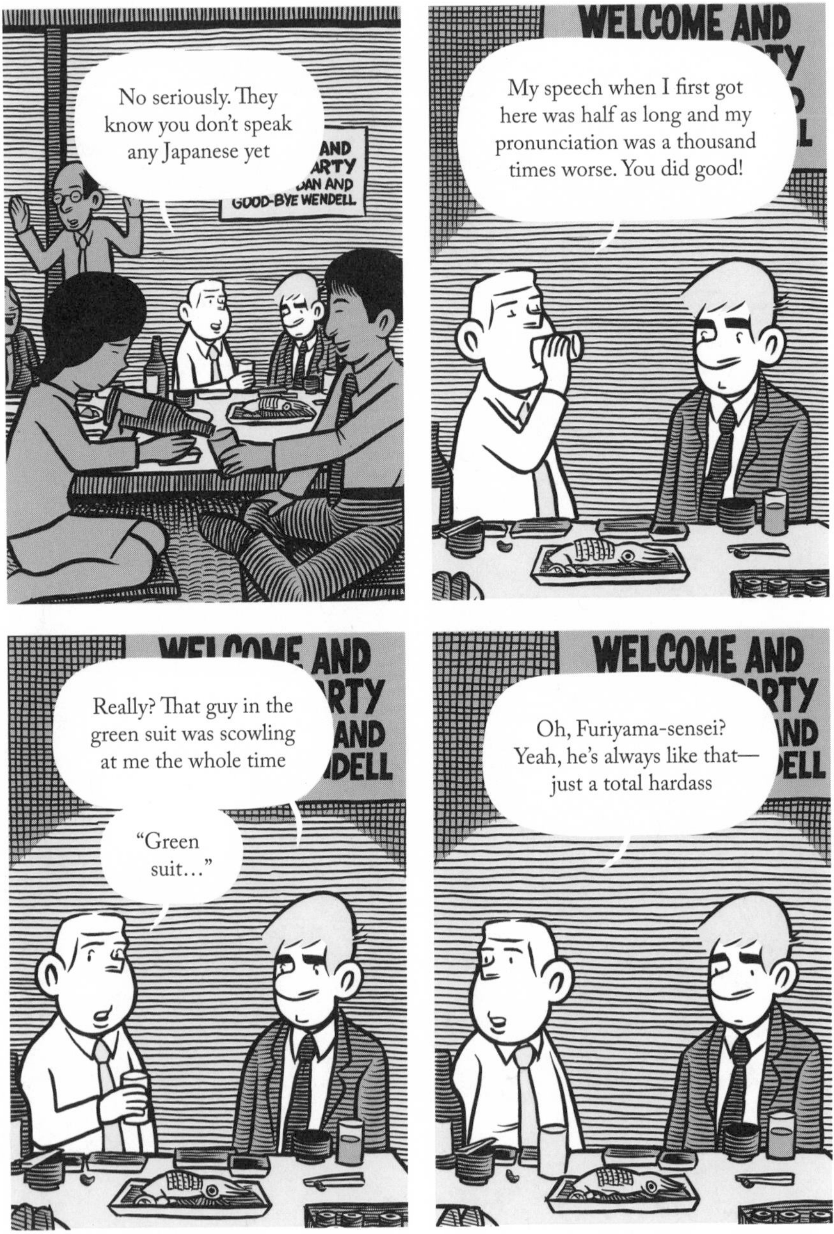
No seriously. They know you don't speak any Japanese yet
DAN AND
GOOD-BYE WENDELL
WELCOME AND
My speech when I first got here was half as long and my pronunciation was a thousand times worse. You did good!
Really? That guy in the green suit was scowling at me the whole time
"Green suit..."
WELCOME AND
Oh, Furiyama-sensei? Yeah, he's always like that—just a total hardass

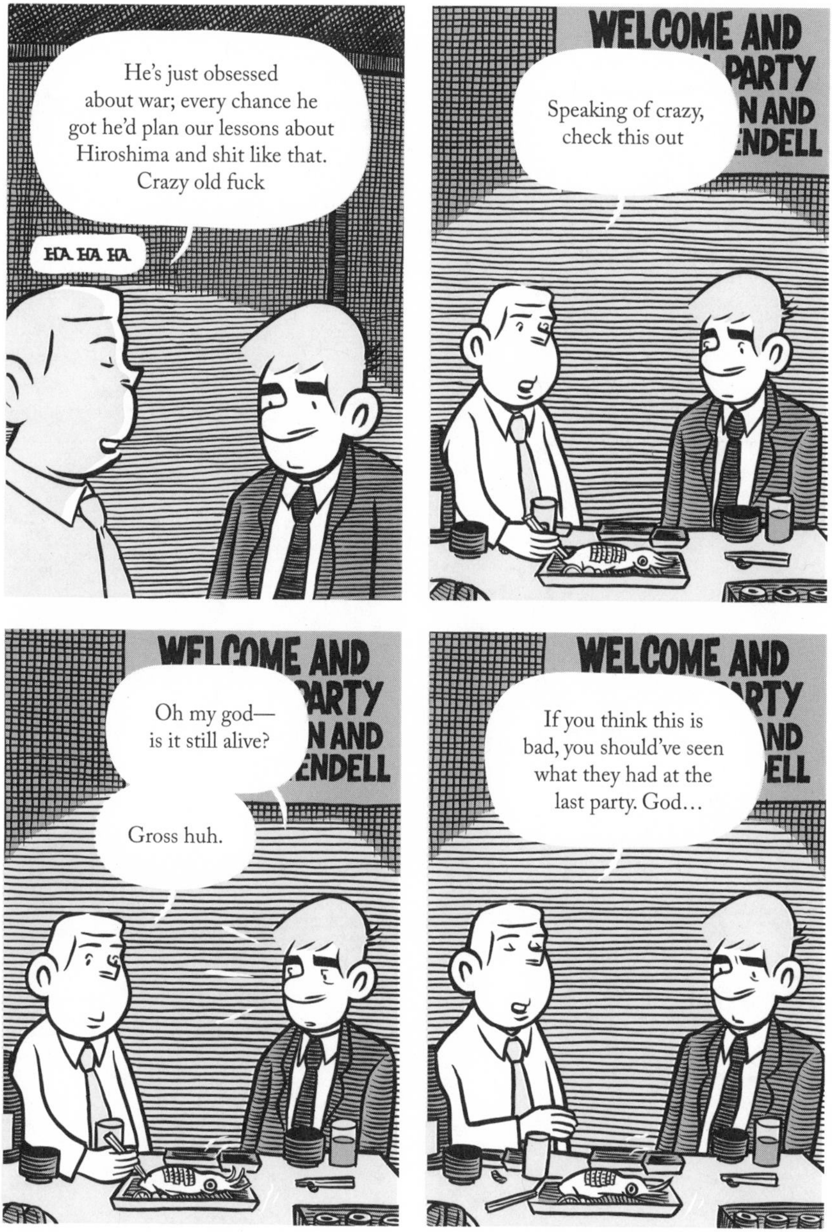
He's just obsessed about war; every chance he got he'd plan our lessons about Hiroshima and shit like that. Crazy old fuck
HA HA HA
Speaking of crazy, check this out
Oh my god—is it still alive?
Gross huh.
If you think this is bad, you should've seen what they had at the last party. God…

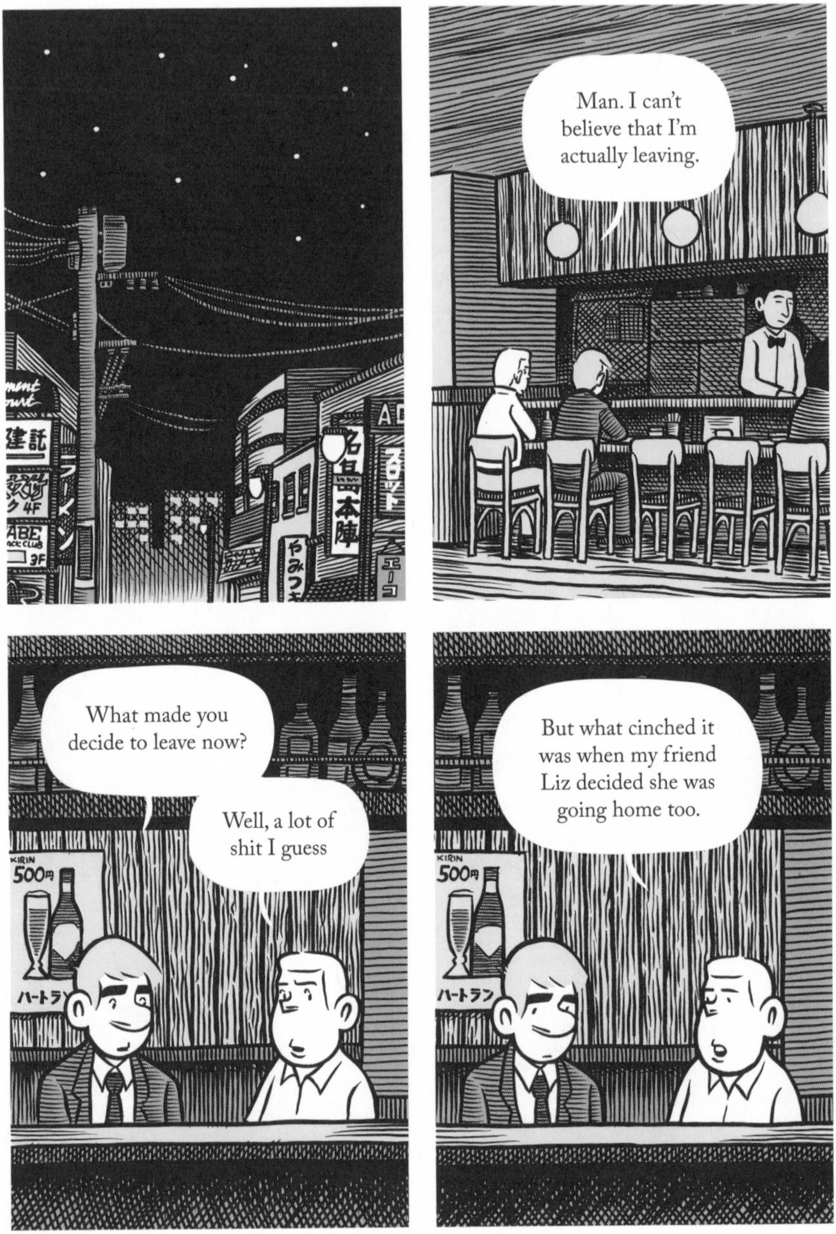
Man. I can't believe that I'm actually leaving.
What made you decide to leave now?
Well, a lot of shit I guess
KIRIN
500円
ハートラン
But what cinched it was when my friend Liz decided she was going home too.
KIRIN
500円
ハートラン

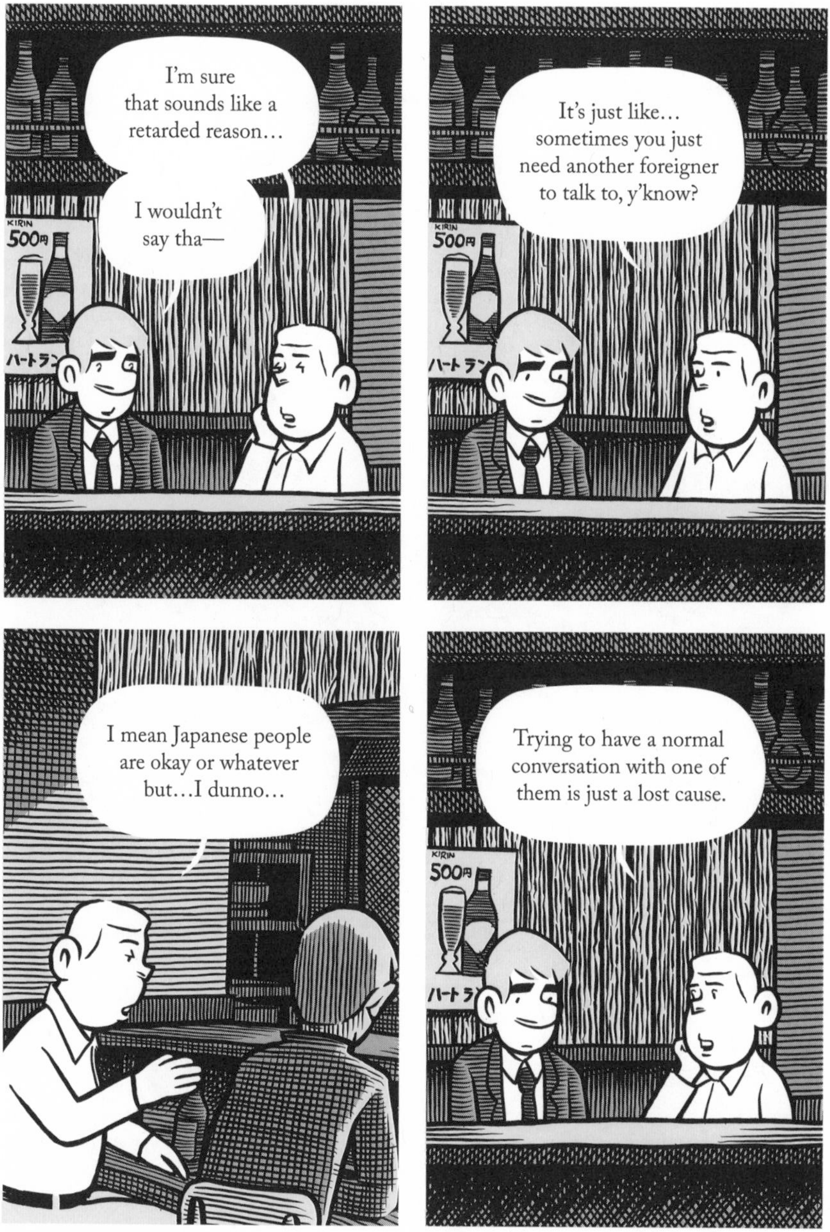
I'm sure that sounds like a retarded reason...
I wouldn't say tha—
KIRIN
500円
ハートラン
It's just like... sometimes you just need another foreigner to talk to, y'know?
I mean Japanese people are okay or whatever but...I dunno...
Trying to have a normal conversation with one of them is just a lost cause.

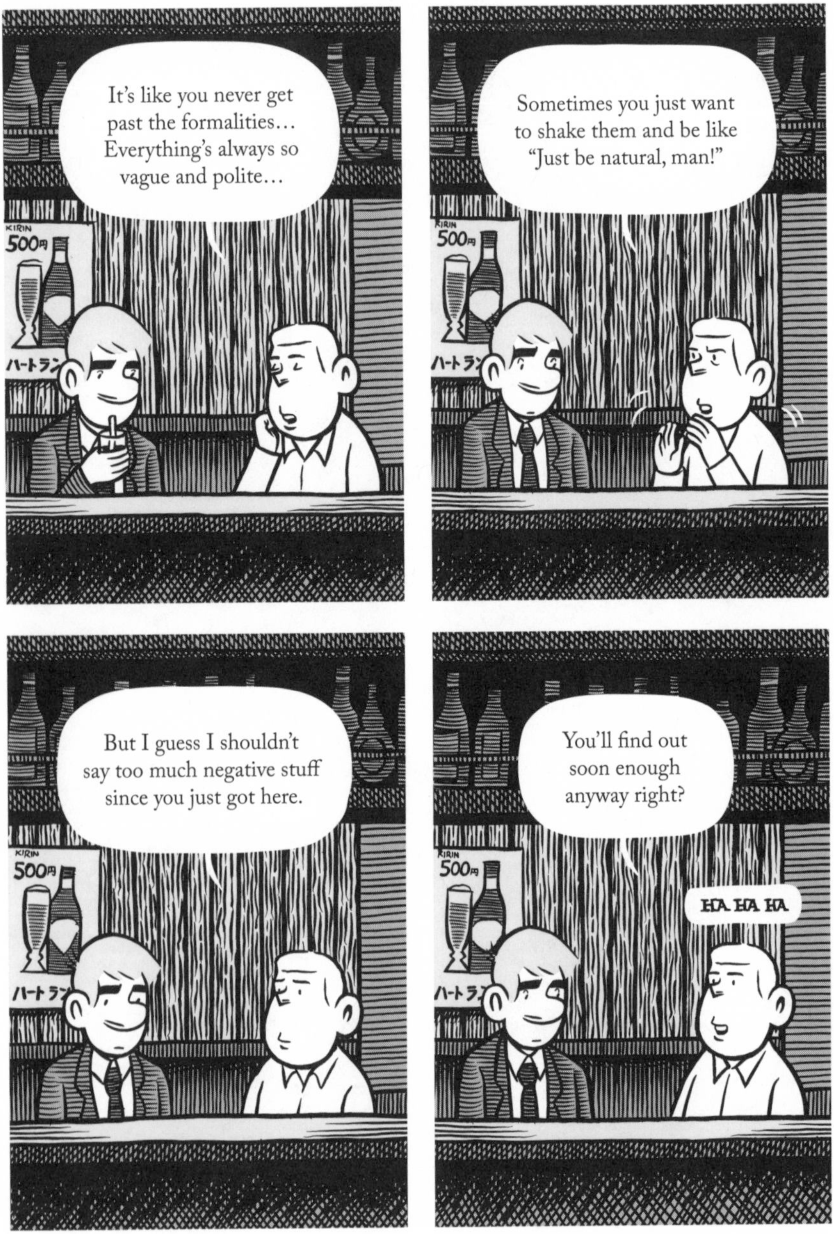
It's like you never get past the formalities… Everything's always so vague and polite…
KIRIN
500円
ハートラン
Sometimes you just want to shake them and be like "Just be natural, man!"
But I guess I shouldn't say too much negative stuff since you just got here.
You'll find out soon enough anyway right?
HA HA HA

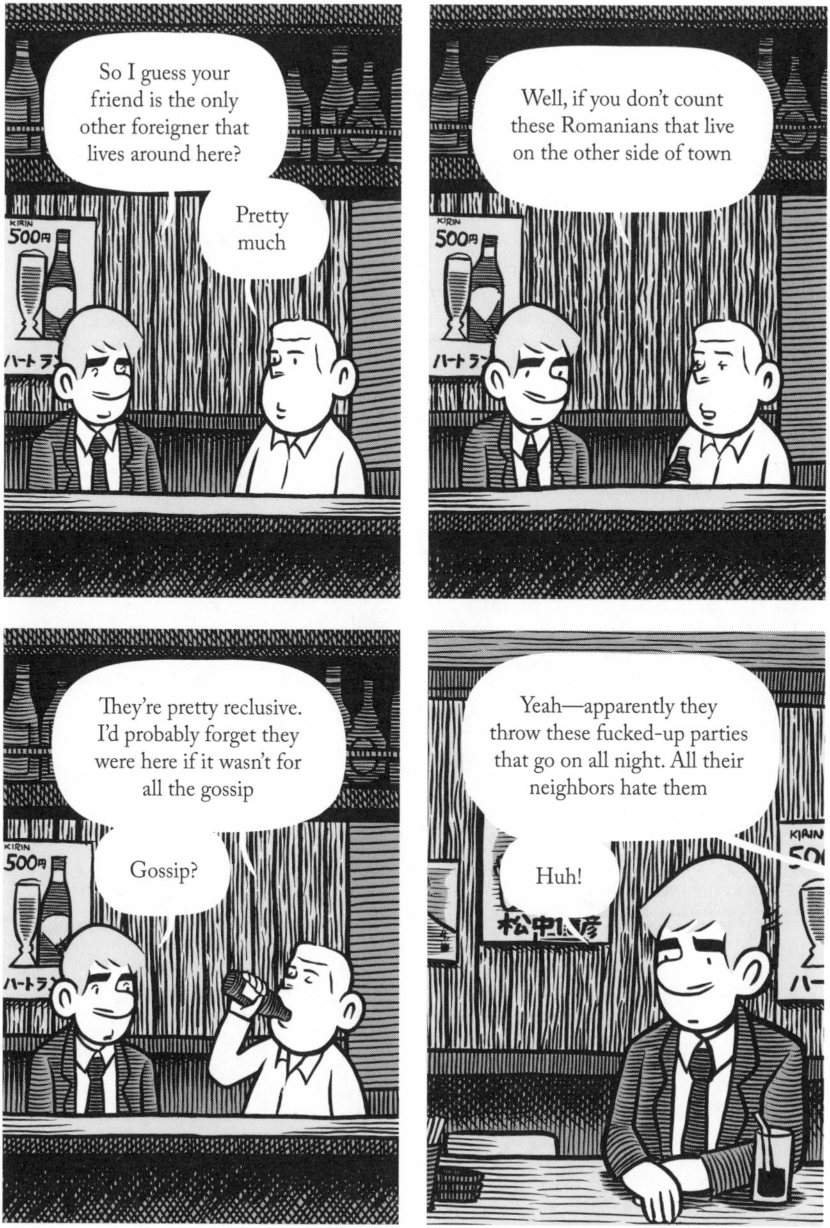

So I guess your friend is the only other foreigner that lives around here?
Pretty much
KIRIN
500円
Well, if you don't count these Romanians that live on the other side of town
They're pretty reclusive. I'd probably forget they were here if it wasn't for all the gossip
Gossip?
Yeah—apparently they throw these fucked-up parties that go on all night. All their neighbors hate them
Huh!

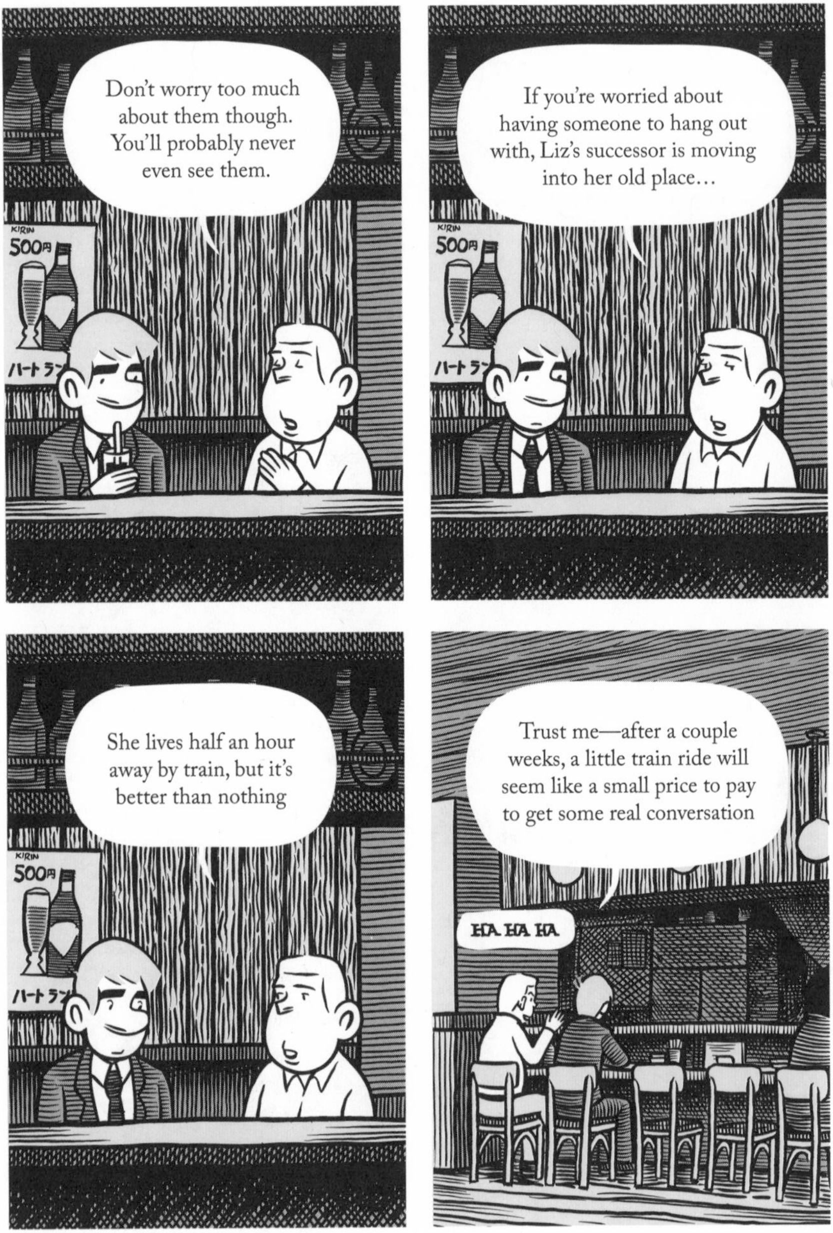
KIRIN
500円
Don't worry too much about them though. You'll probably never even see them.
If you're worried about having someone to hang out with, Liz's successor is moving into her old place...
She lives half an hour away by train, but it's better than nothing
Trust me—after a couple weeks, a little train ride will seem like a small price to pay to get some real conversation
HA HA HA

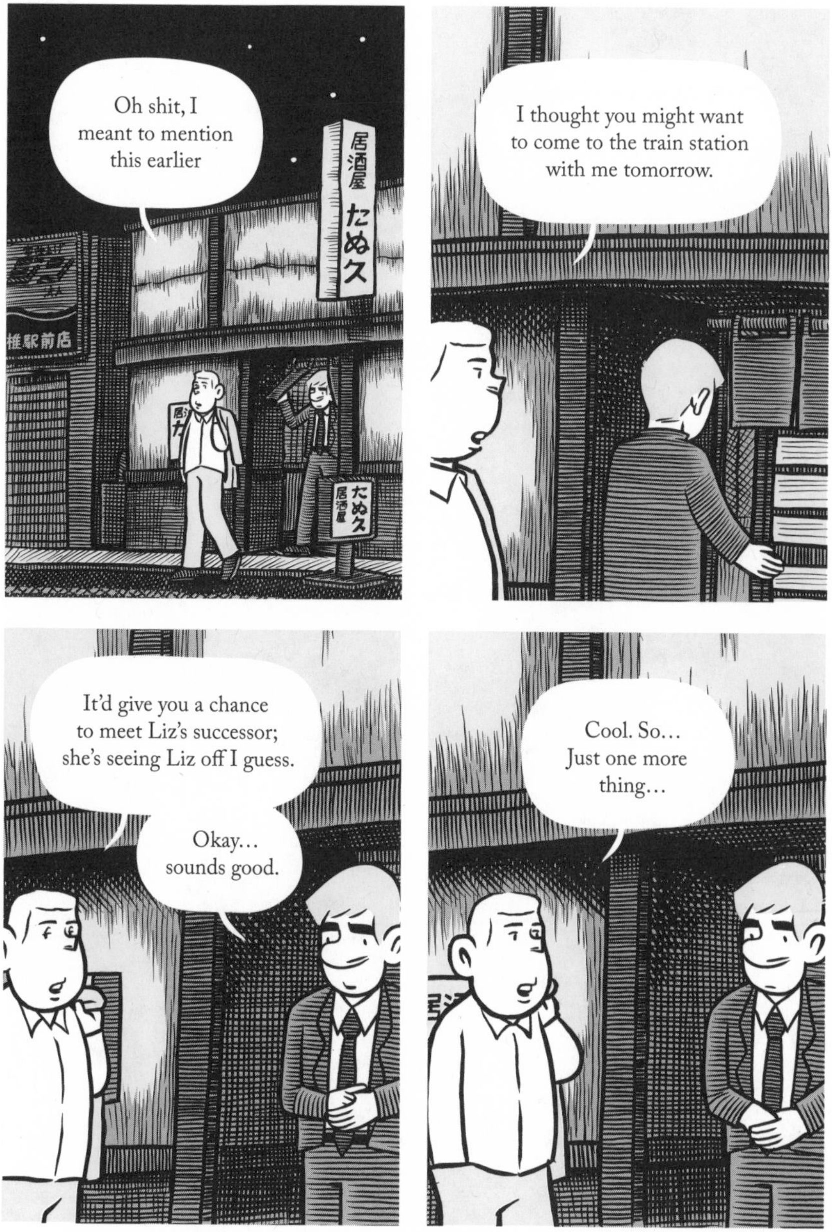
Oh shit, I meant to mention this earlier
居酒屋 たぬ久
I thought you might want to come to the train station with me tomorrow.
It'd give you a chance to meet Liz's successor; she's seeing Liz off I guess.
Okay… sounds good.
Cool. So… Just one more thing…

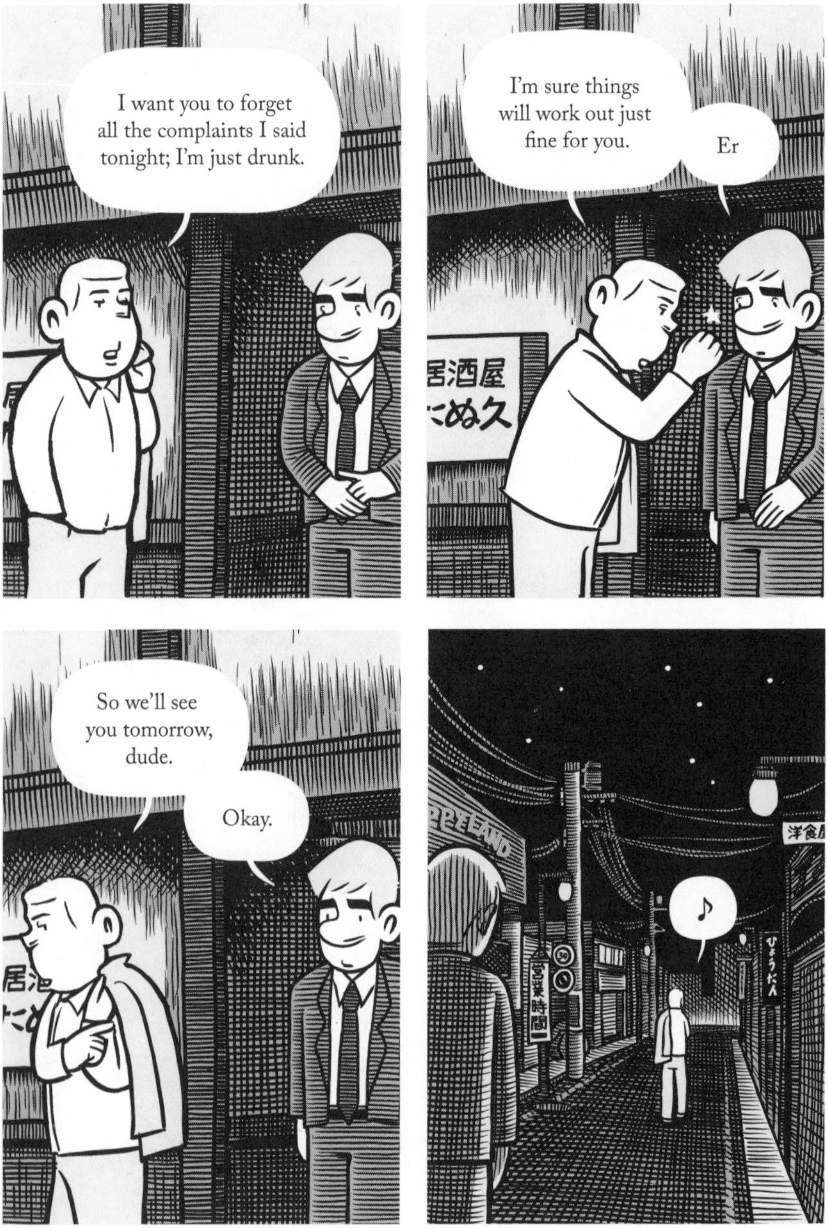

I want you to forget all the complaints I said tonight; I'm just drunk.
I'm sure things will work out just fine for you.
Er
居酒屋
So we'll see you tomorrow, dude.
Okay.
♪
営業時間
ひょうたん

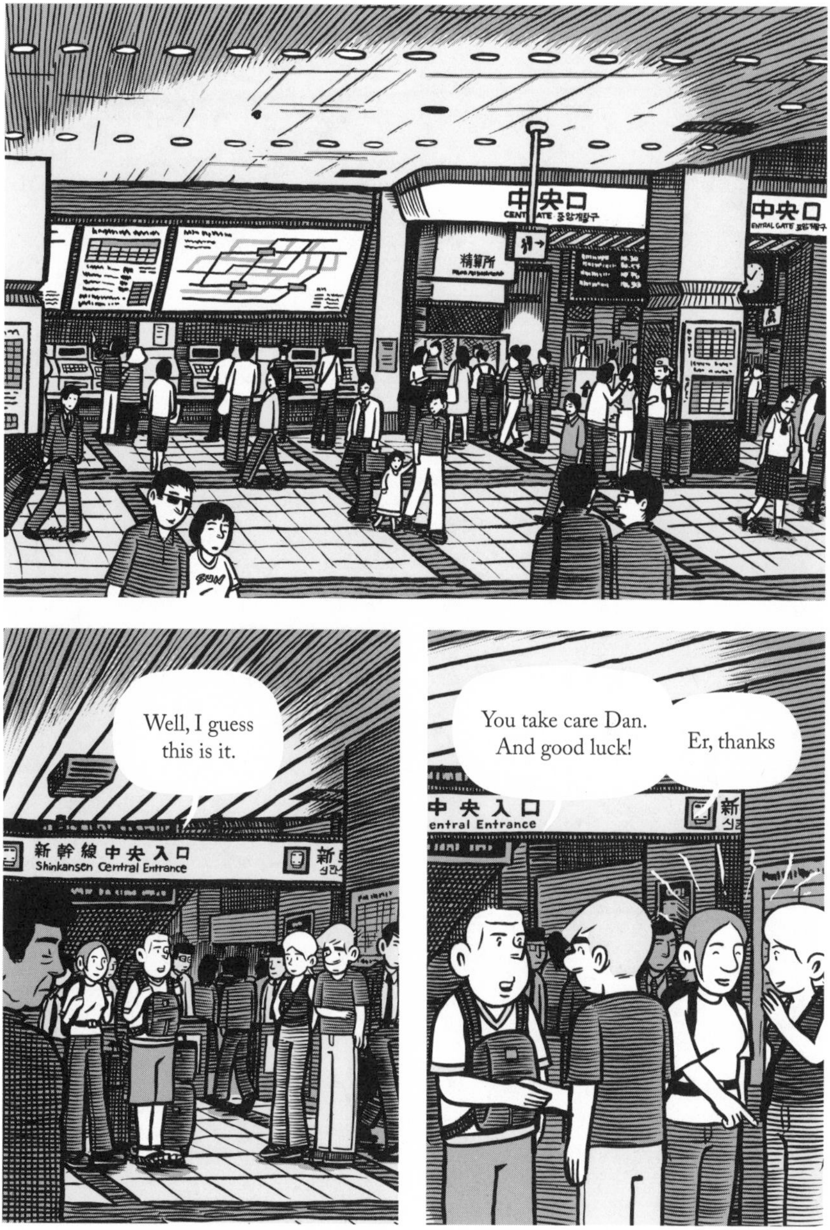
中央口
精算所
中央口
Well, I guess this is it.
新幹線中央入口
Shinkansen Central Entrance
You take care Dan. And good luck!
Er, thanks
中央入口
entral Entrance

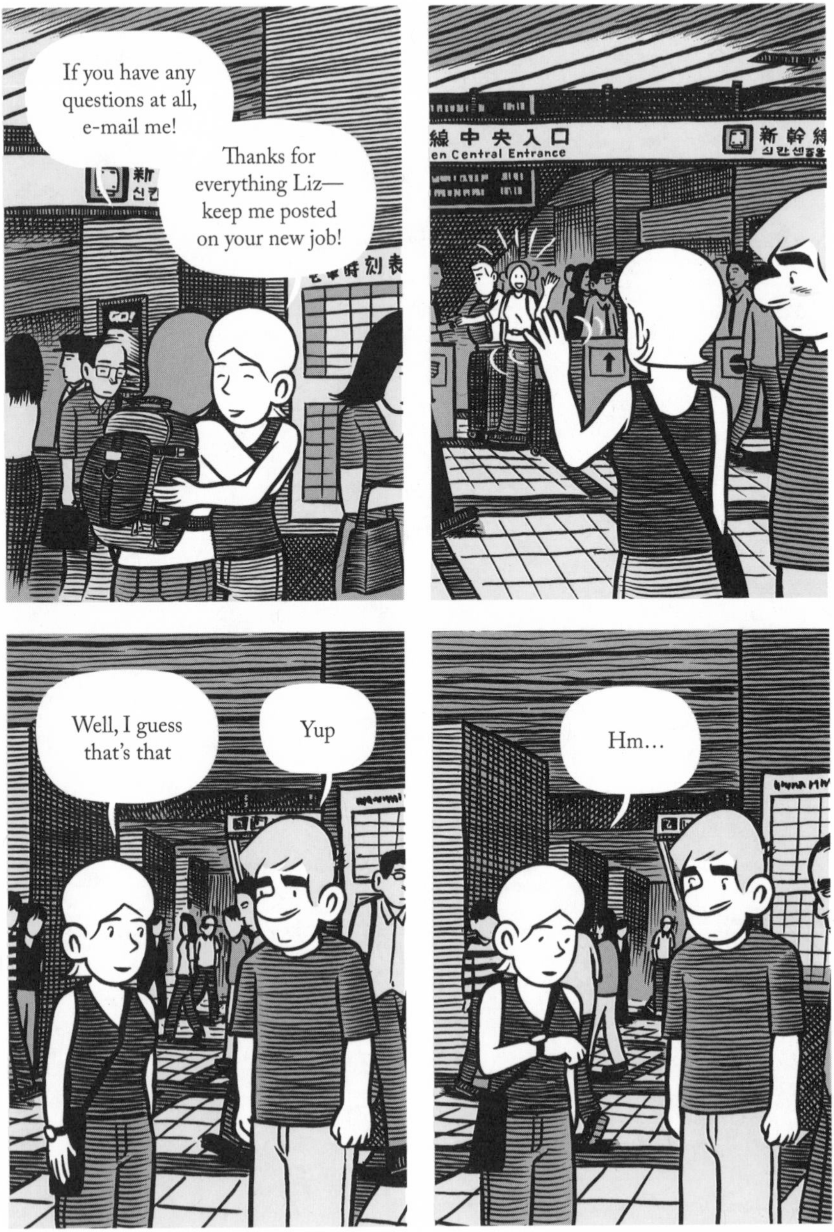
If you have any questions at all, e-mail me!
Thanks for everything Liz— keep me posted on your new job!
線中央入口
en Central Entrance
Well, I guess that's that
Yup
Hm…

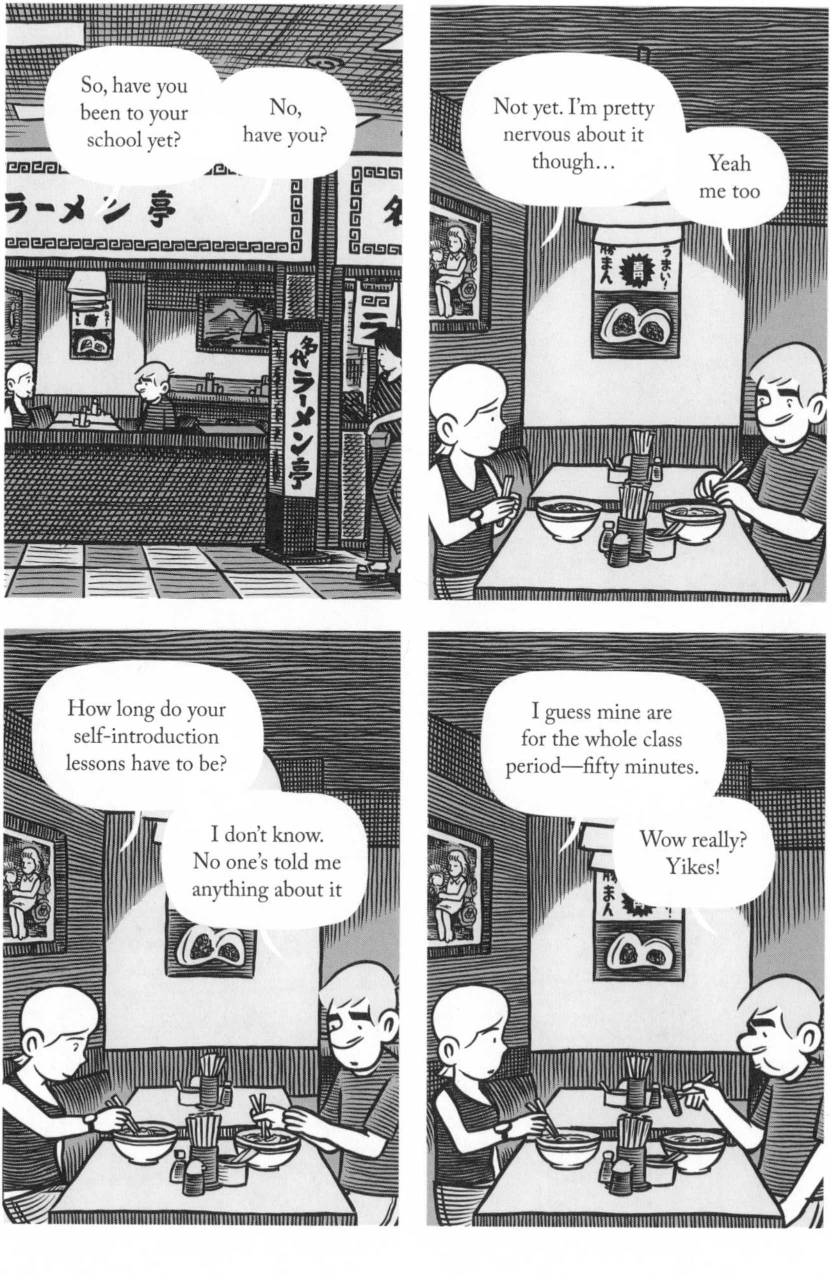
So, have you been to your school yet?
No, have you?
名代ラーメン亭
Not yet. I'm pretty nervous about it though…
Yeah me too
How long do your self-introduction lessons have to be?
I don't know. No one's told me anything about it
I guess mine are for the whole class period—fifty minutes.
Wow really? Yikes!

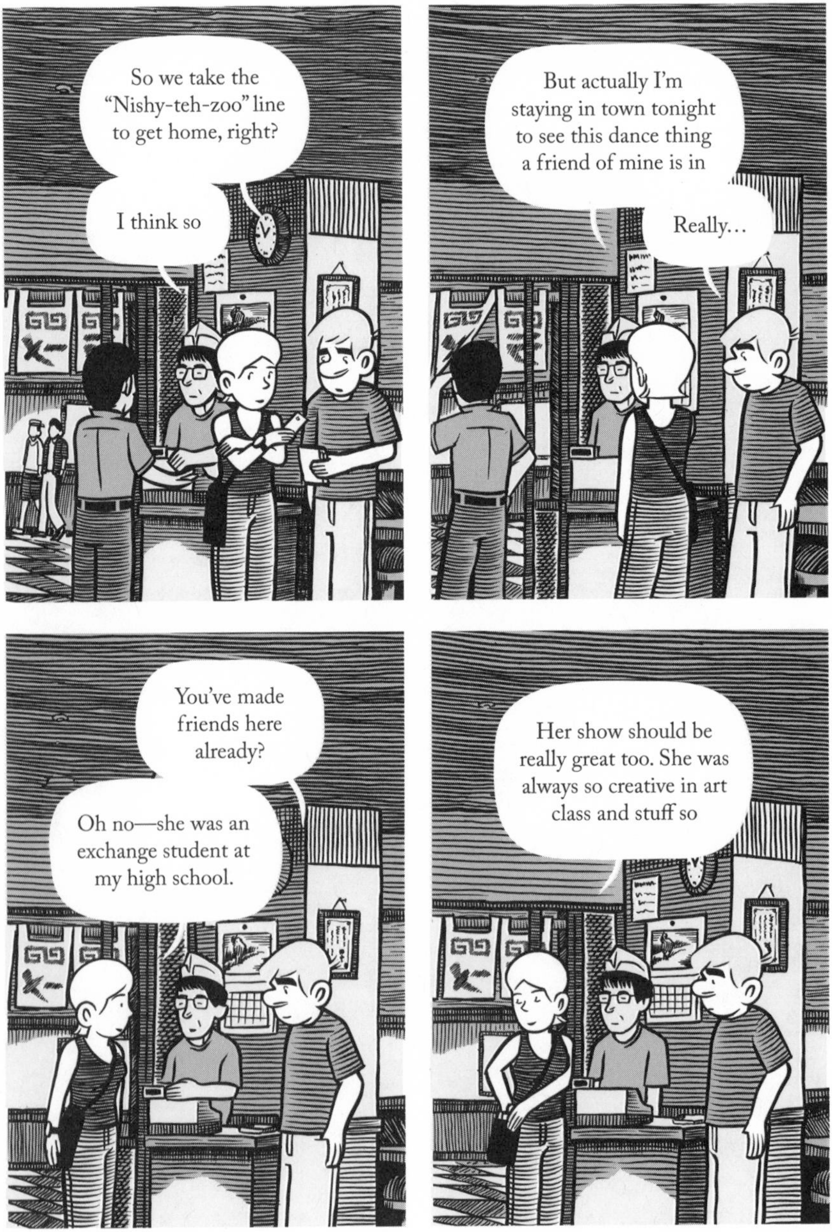
So we take the "Nishy-teh-zoo" line to get home, right?
I think so
But actually I'm staying in town tonight to see this dance thing a friend of mine is in
Really...
You've made friends here already?
Oh no—she was an exchange student at my high school.
Her show should be really great too. She was always so creative in art class and stuff so

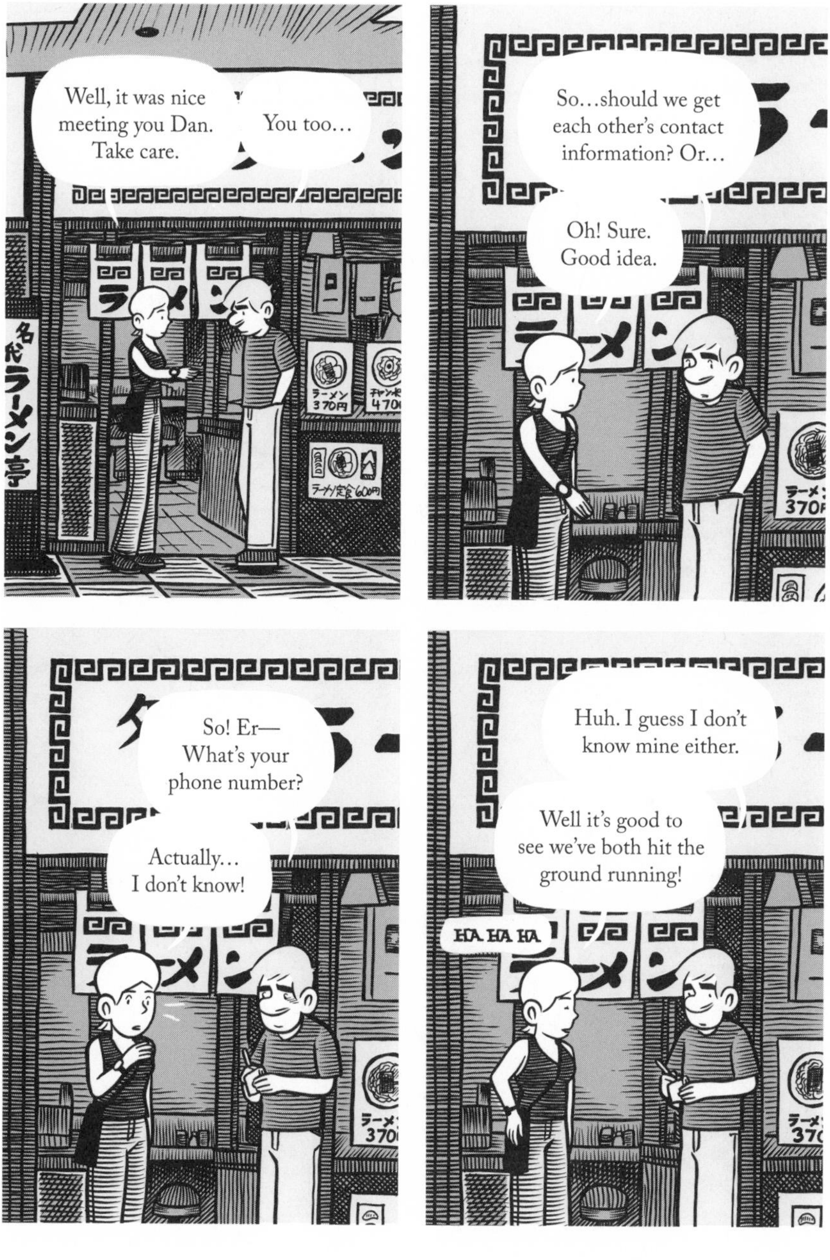
Well, it was nice meeting you Dan. Take care.
You too...
名代ラーメン亭
ラーメン 370円
ラーメン定食 600円
So...should we get each other's contact information? Or...
Oh! Sure. Good idea.
So! Er— What's your phone number?
Actually... I don't know!
Huh. I guess I don't know mine either.
Well it's good to see we've both hit the ground running!
HA HA HA

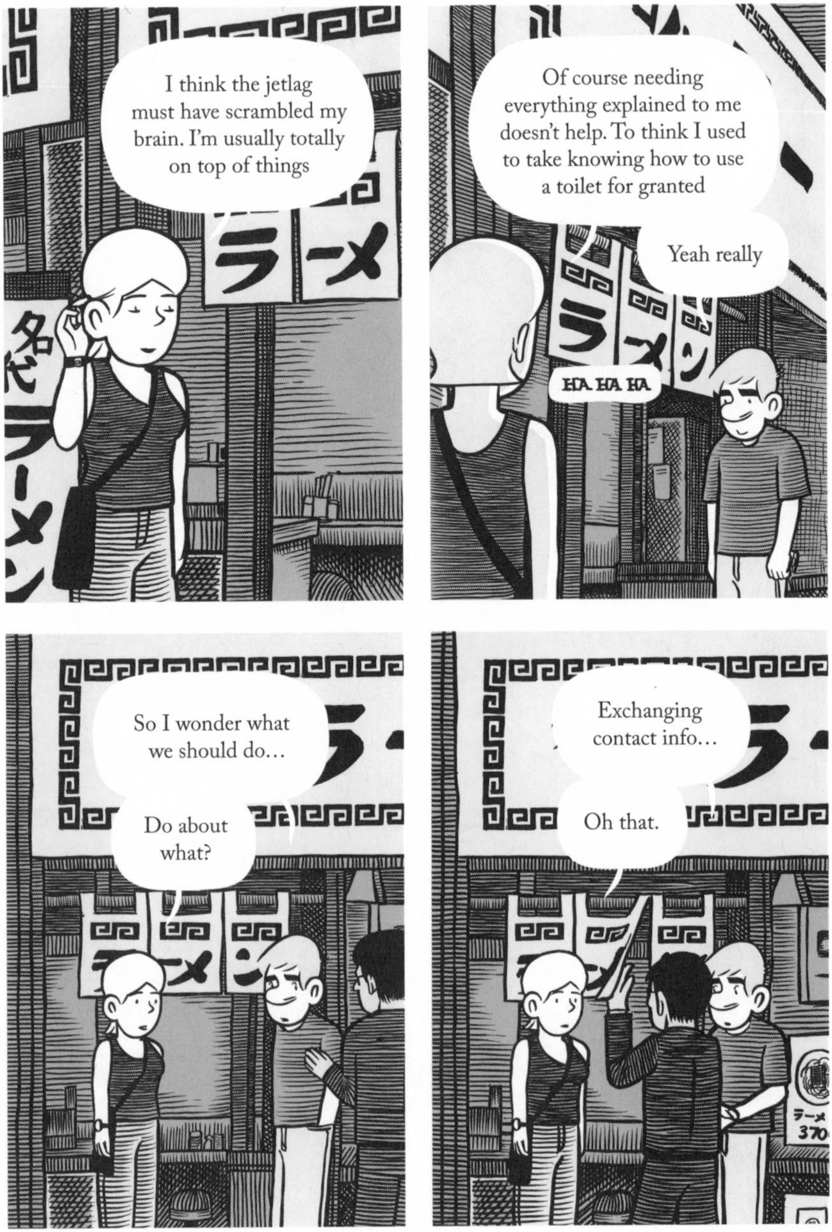

I think the jetlag must have scrambled my brain. I'm usually totally on top of things
Of course needing everything explained to me doesn't help. To think I used to take knowing how to use a toilet for granted
Yeah really
HA HA HA
So I wonder what we should do…
Do about what?
Exchanging contact info…
Oh that.

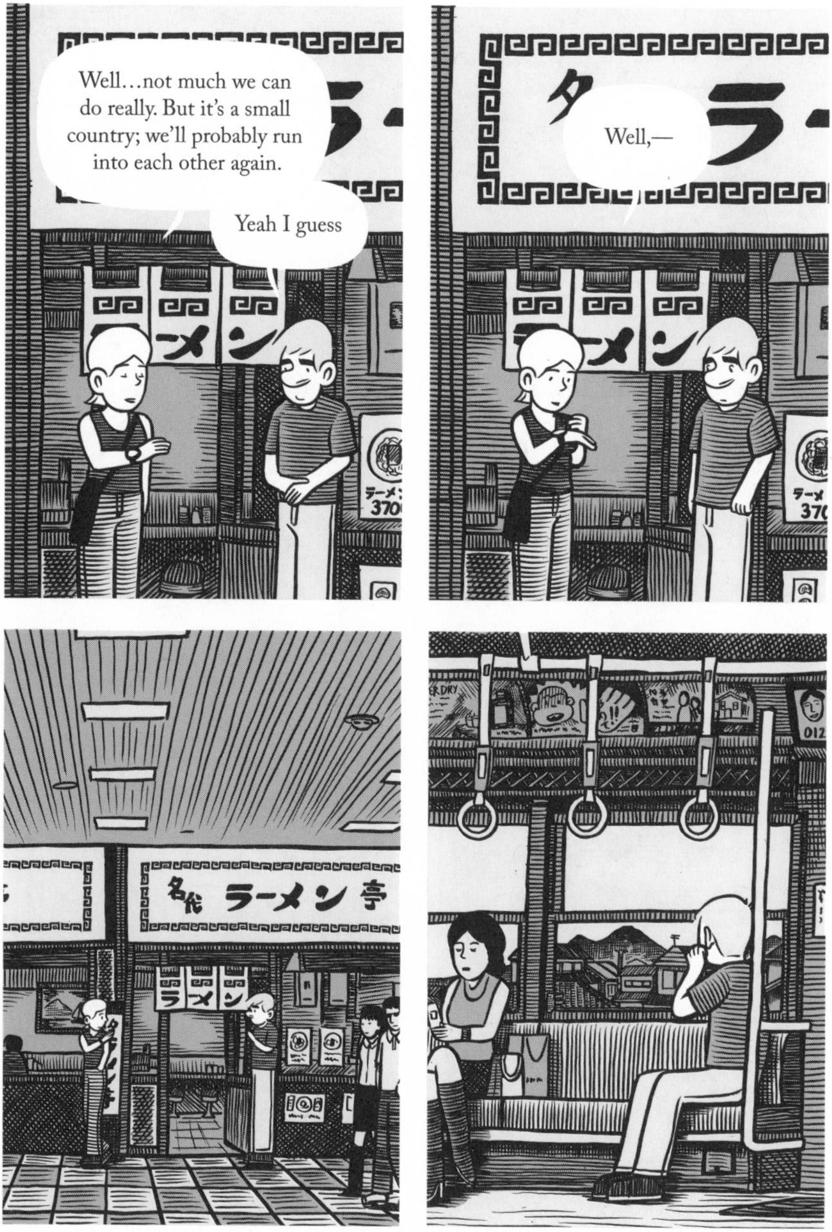
Well…not much we can do really. But it's a small country; we'll probably run into each other again.
Yeah I guess
ラーメン
Well,—
名代 ラーメン 亭

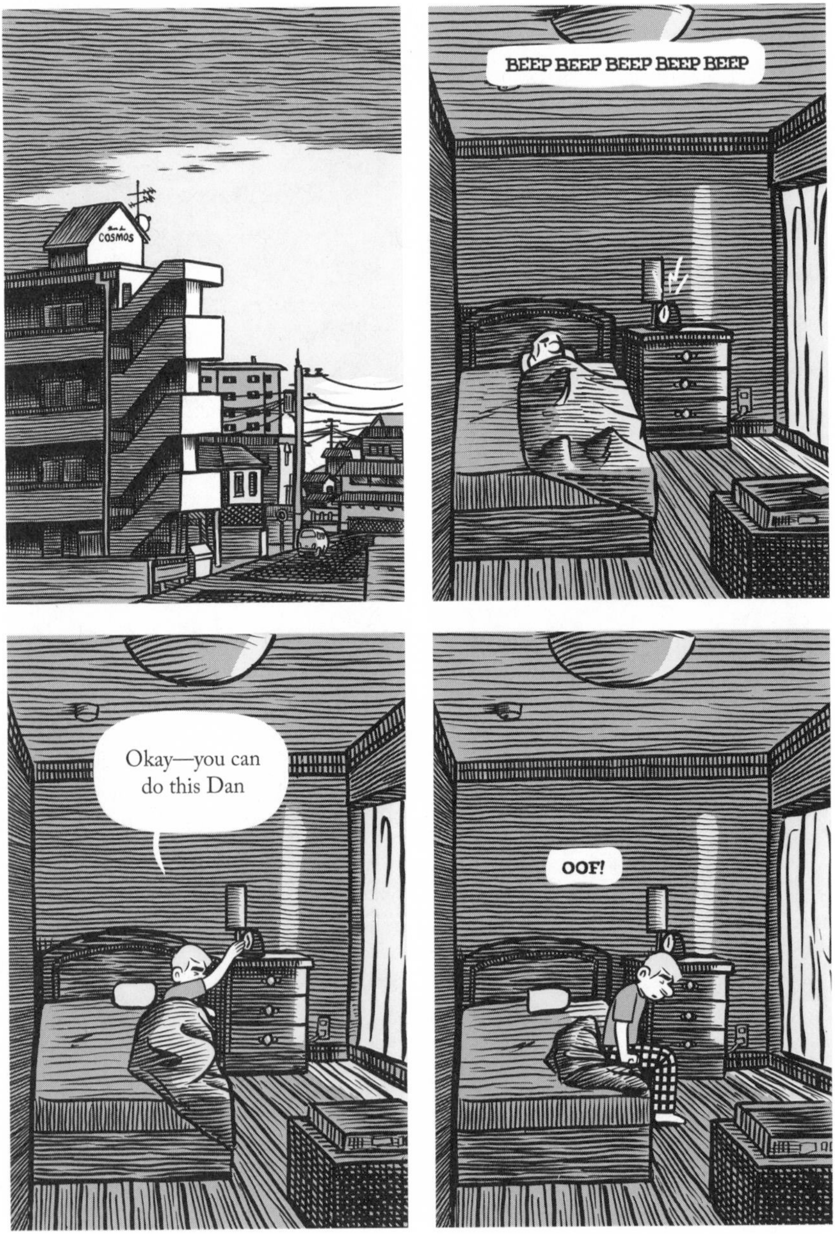
COSMOS
BEEP BEEP BEEP BEEP BEEP
Okay—you can do this Dan
OOF!

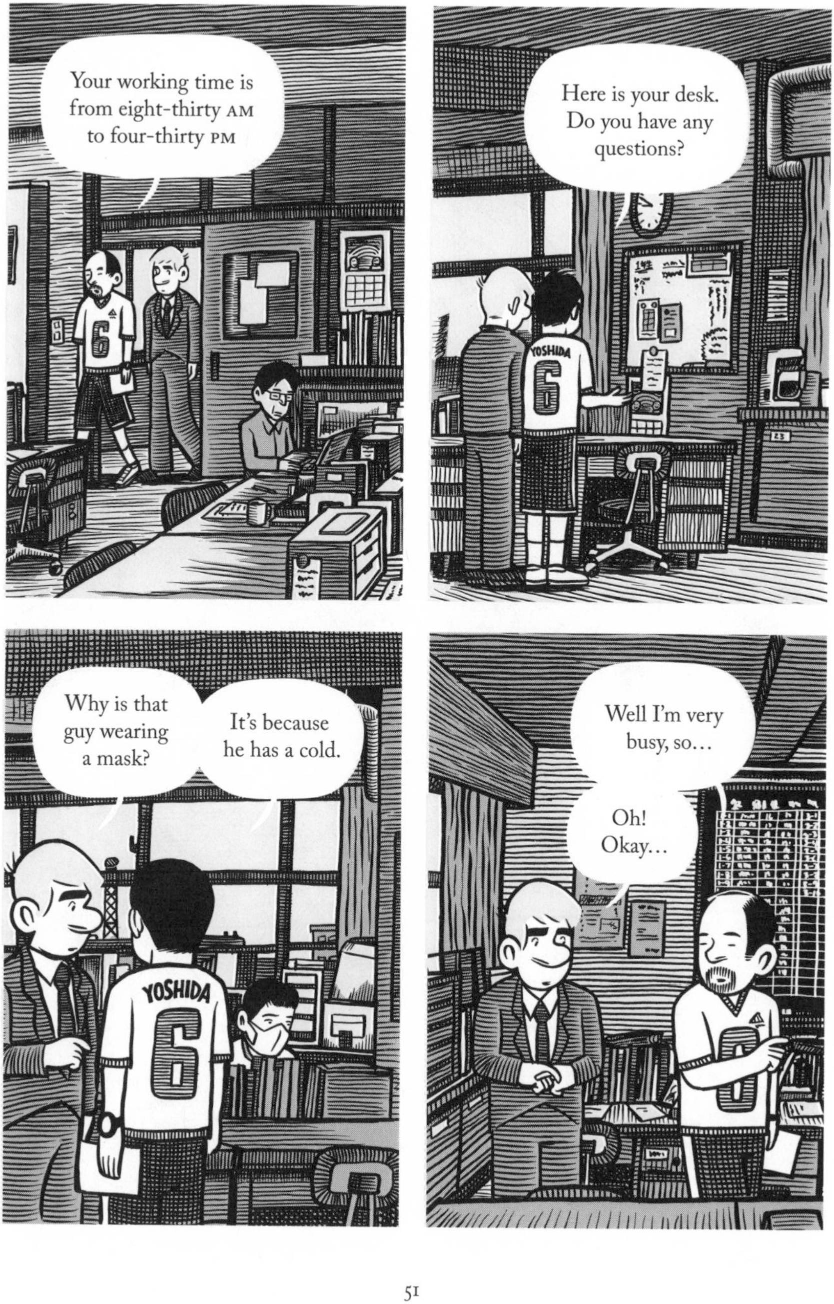
Your working time is from eight-thirty AM to four-thirty PM
Here is your desk. Do you have any questions?
YOSHIDA
Why is that guy wearing a mask?
It's because he has a cold.
YOSHIDA
Well I'm very busy, so...
Oh! Okay...

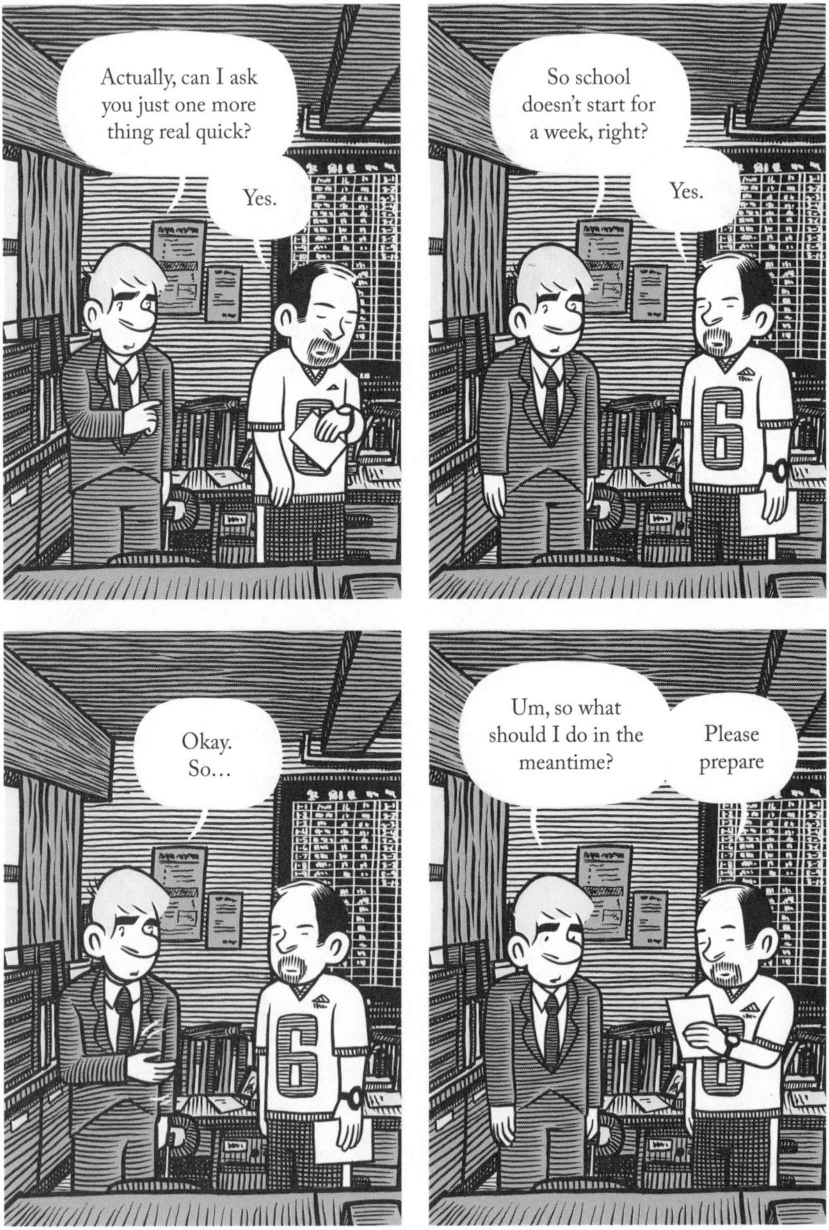
Actually, can I ask you just one more thing real quick?
Yes.
So school doesn't start for a week, right?
Yes.
Okay. So…
Um, so what should I do in the meantime?
Please prepare

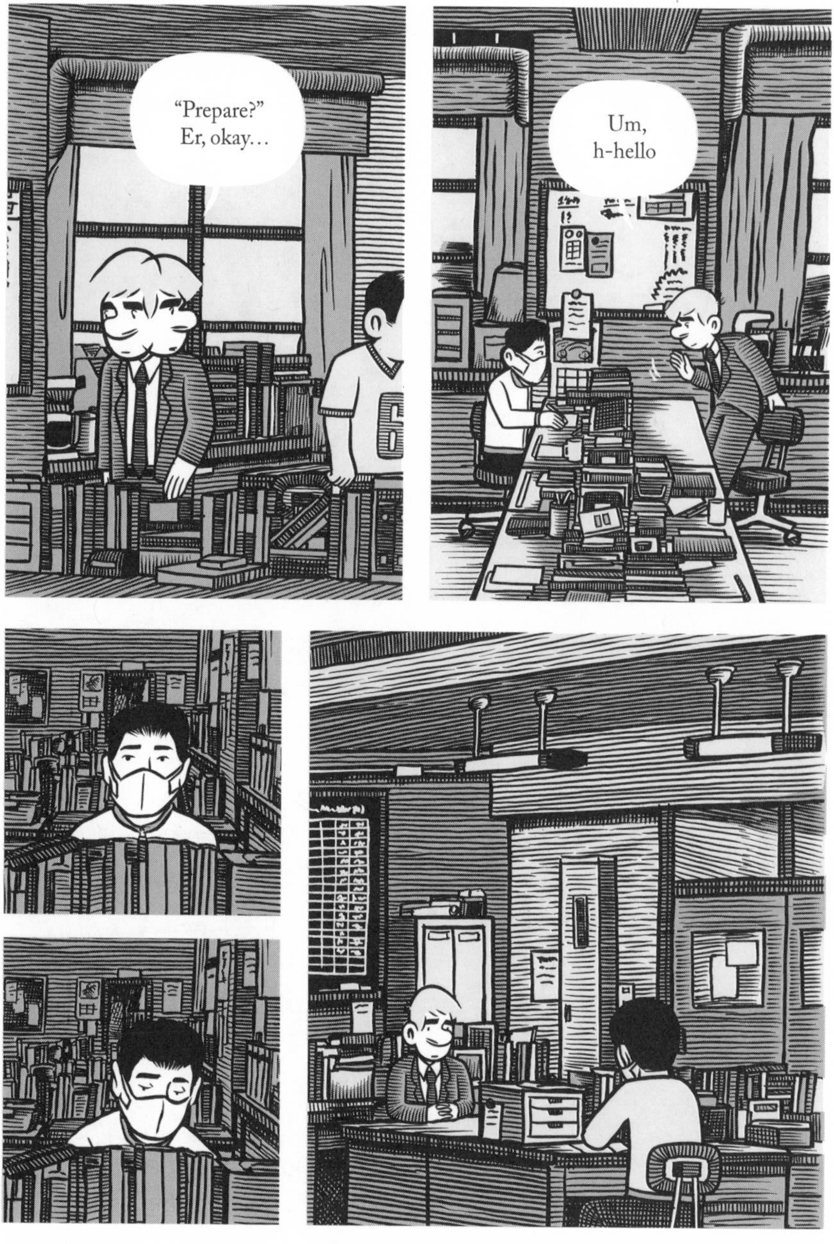
"Prepare?"
Er, okay…
Um,
h-hello

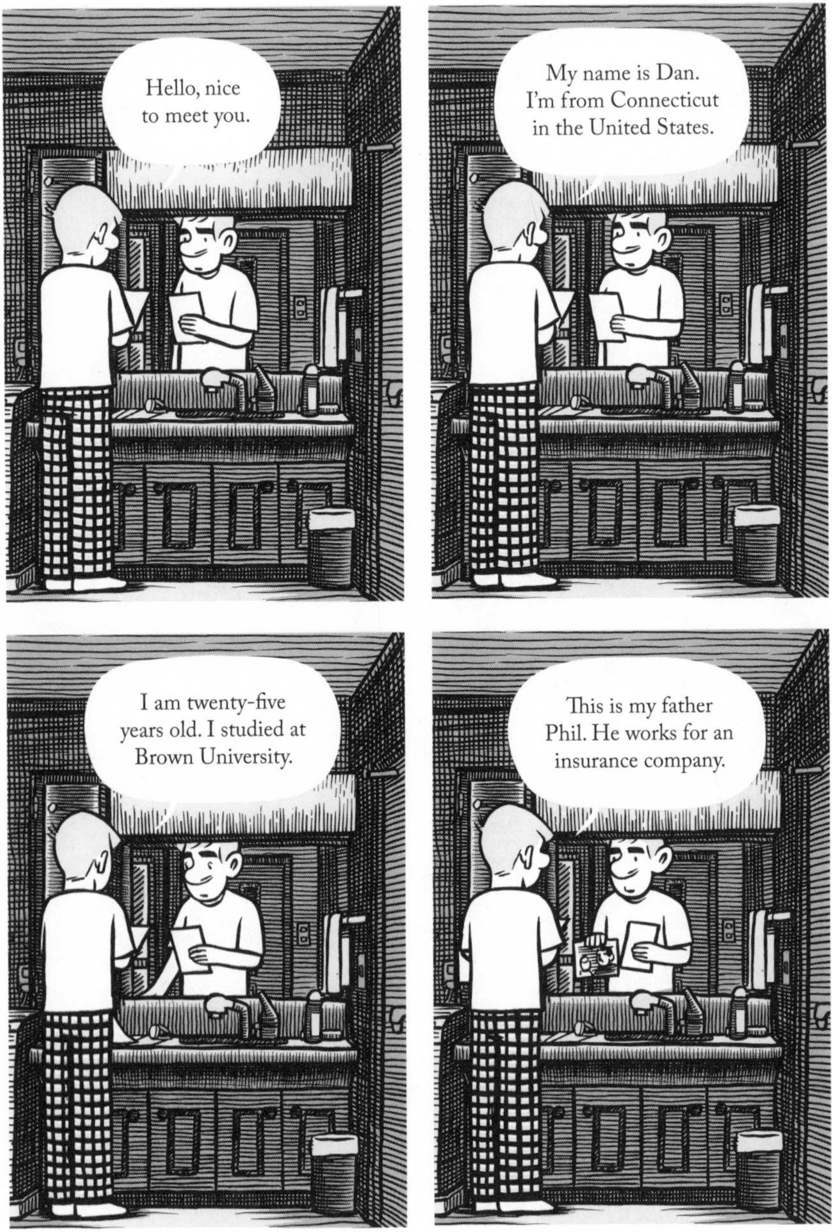
Hello, nice to meet you.
My name is Dan. I'm from Connecticut in the United States.
I am twenty-five years old. I studied at Brown University.
This is my father Phil. He works for an insurance company.

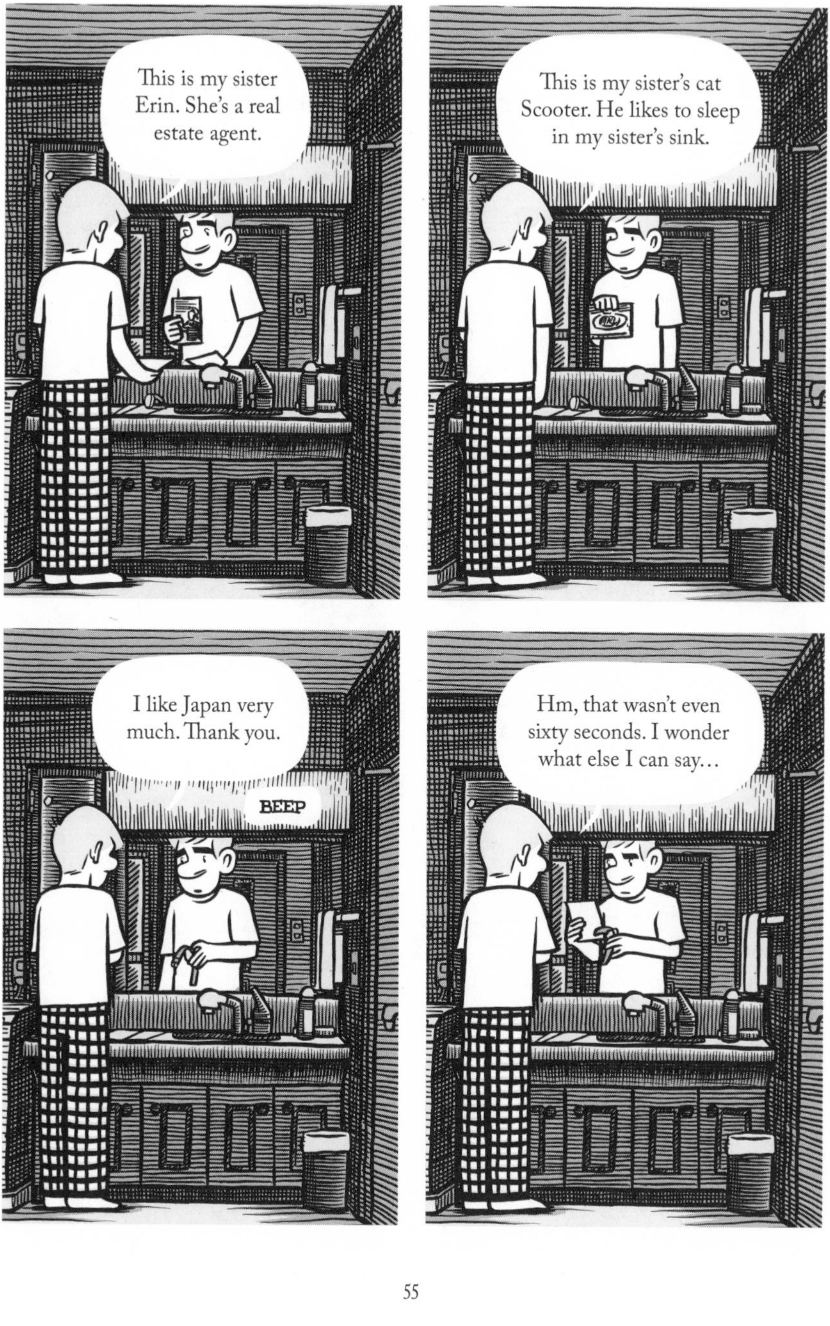
This is my sister Erin. She's a real estate agent.
This is my sister's cat Scooter. He likes to sleep in my sister's sink.
I like Japan very much. Thank you.
BEEP
Hm, that wasn't even sixty seconds. I wonder what else I can say...

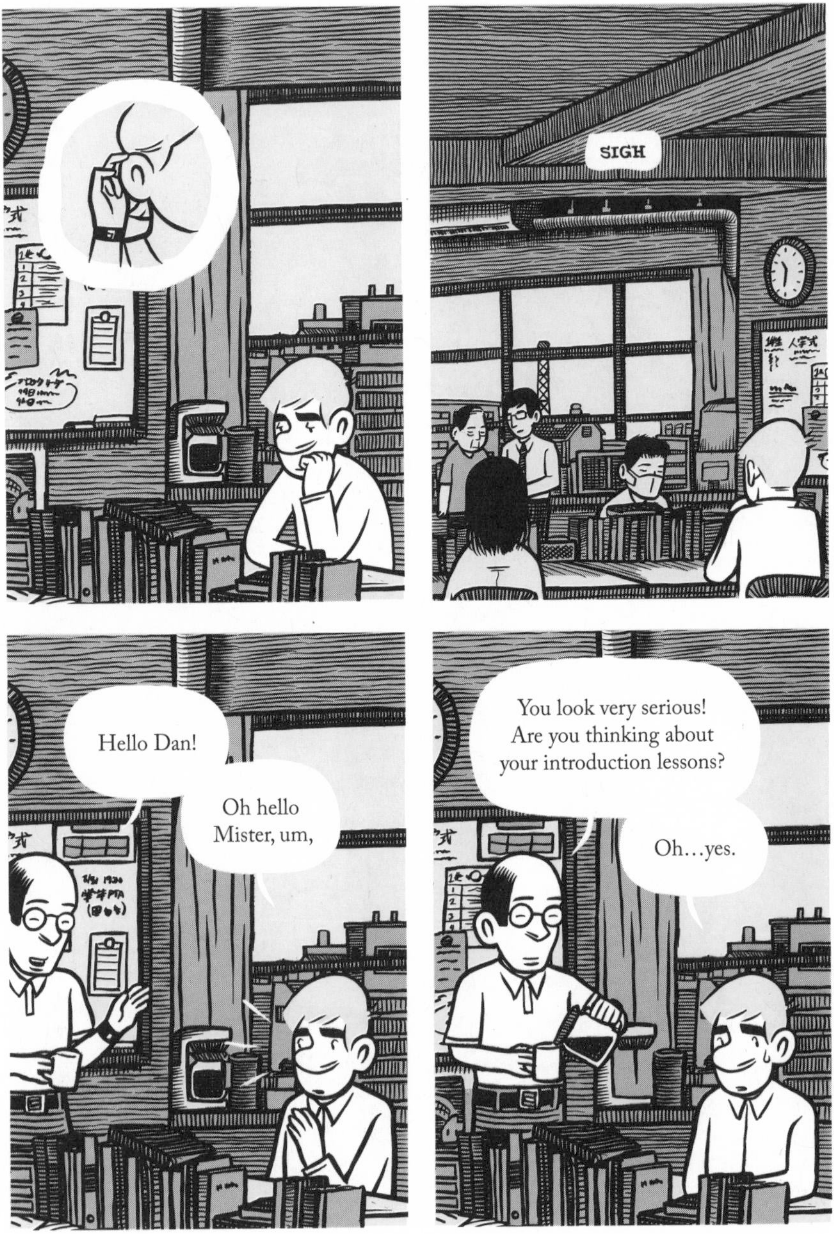
SIGH
Hello Dan!
Oh hello Mister, um,
You look very serious! Are you thinking about your introduction lessons?
Oh…yes.

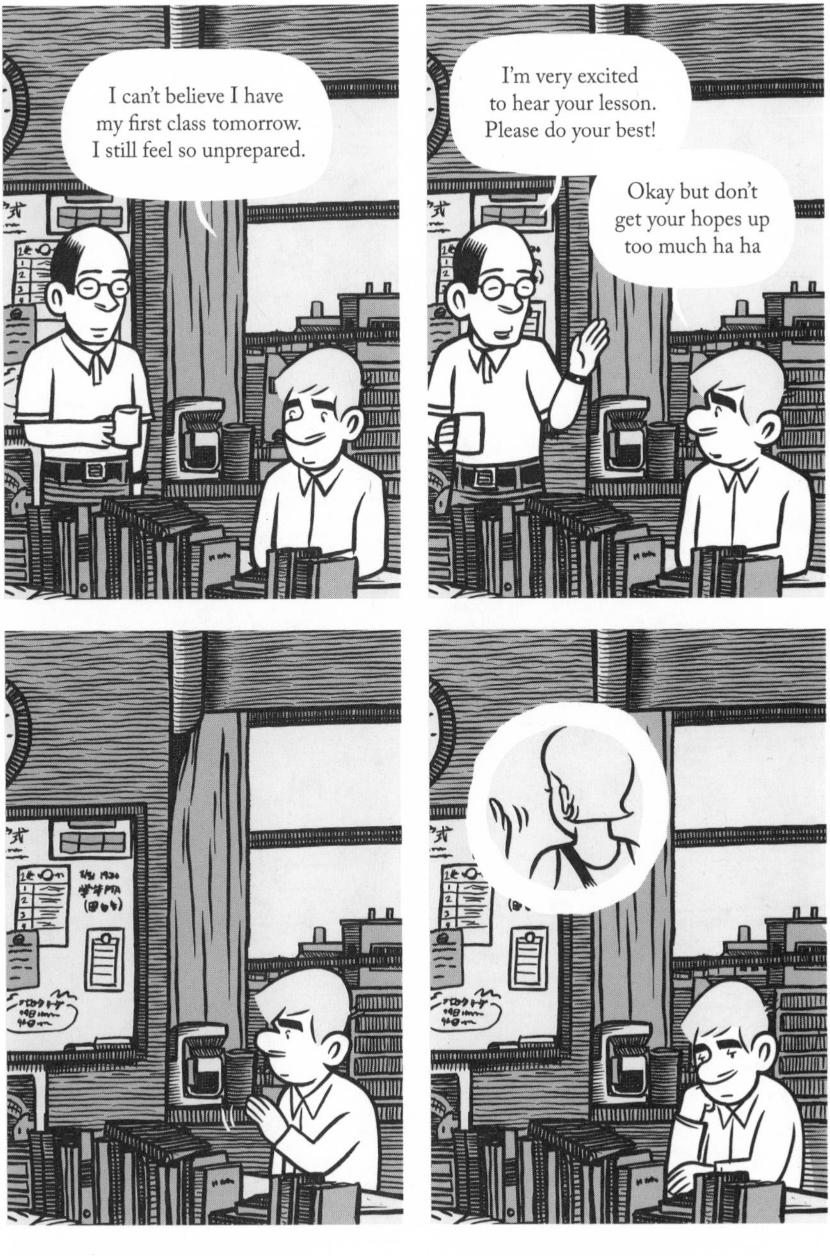
I can't believe I have my first class tomorrow. I still feel so unprepared.
I'm very excited to hear your lesson. Please do your best!
Okay but don't get your hopes up too much ha ha

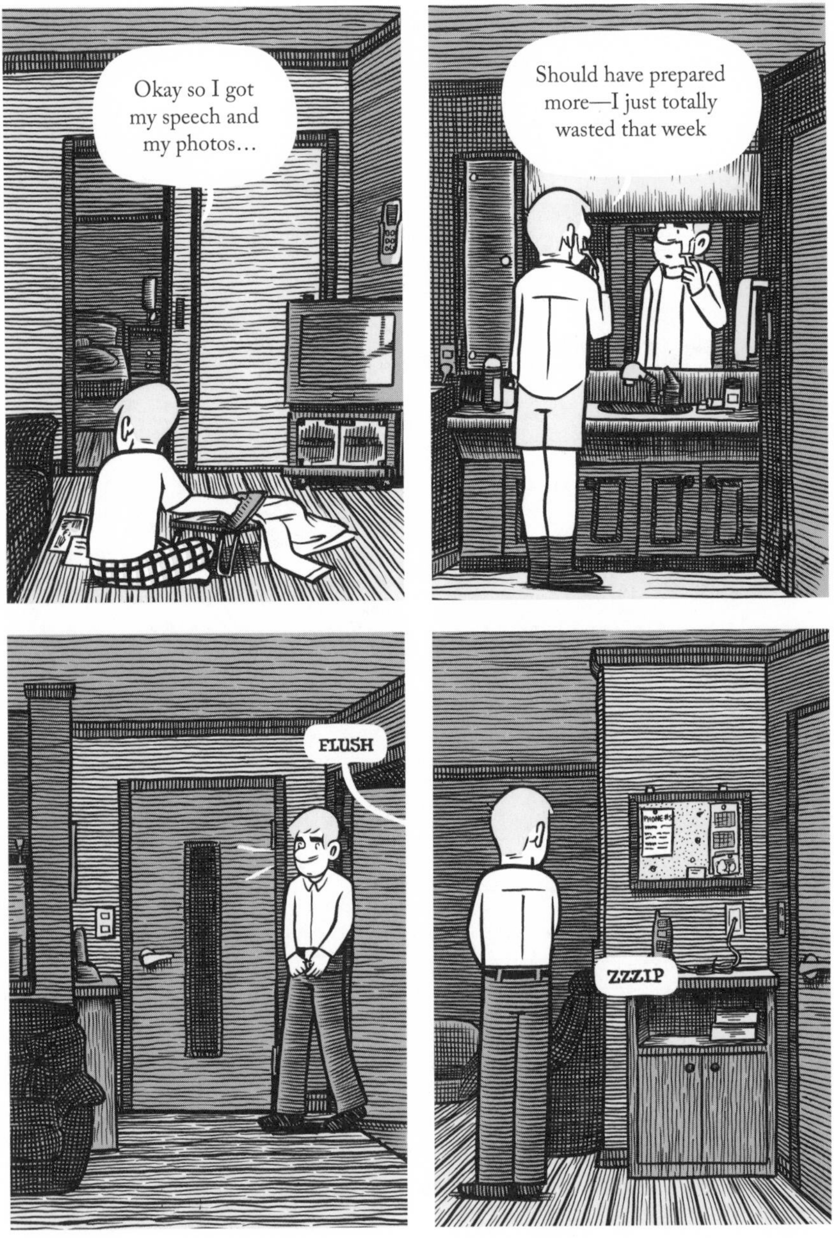
Okay so I got my speech and my photos...
Should have prepared more—I just totally wasted that week
FLUSH
ZZZIP

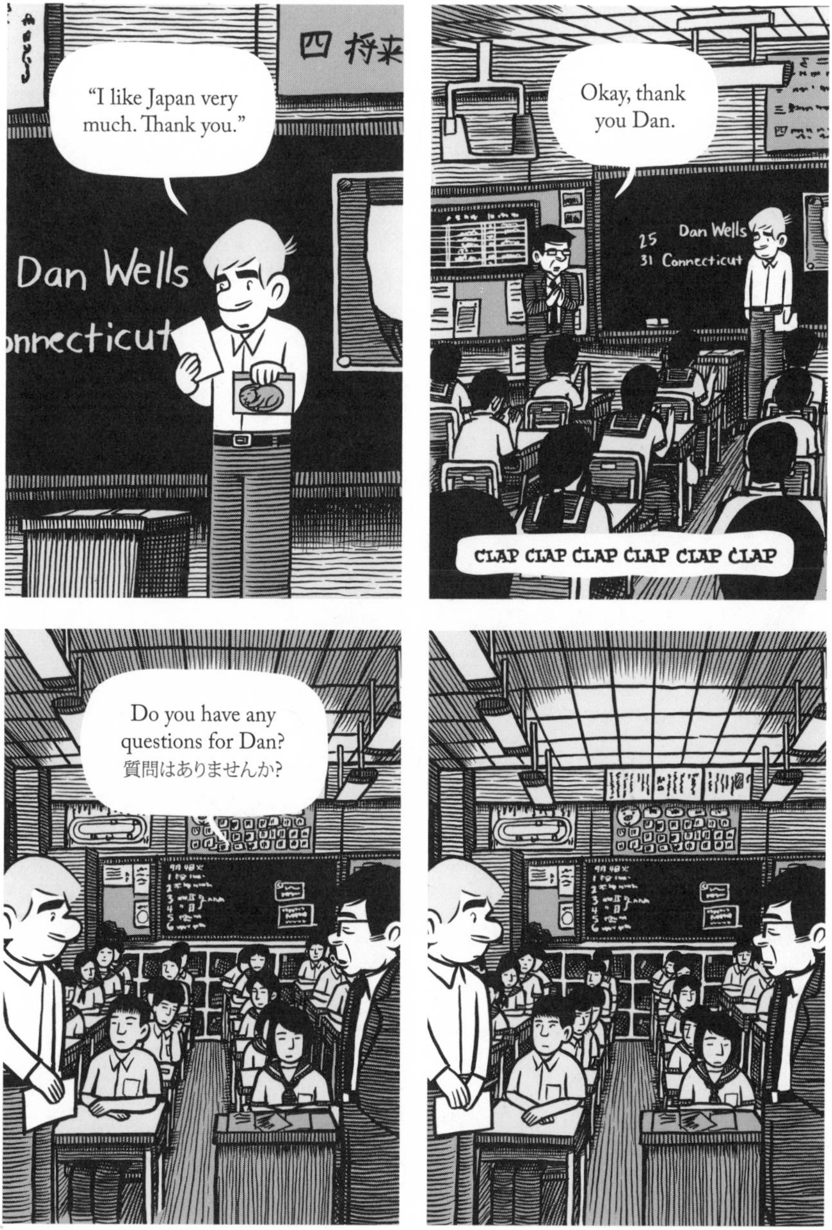
"I like Japan very much. Thank you."
Dan Wells
nnecticut
Okay, thank you Dan.
25 Dan Wells
31 Connecticut
CLAP CLAP CLAP CLAP CLAP CLAP
Do you have any questions for Dan?
質問はありませんか?

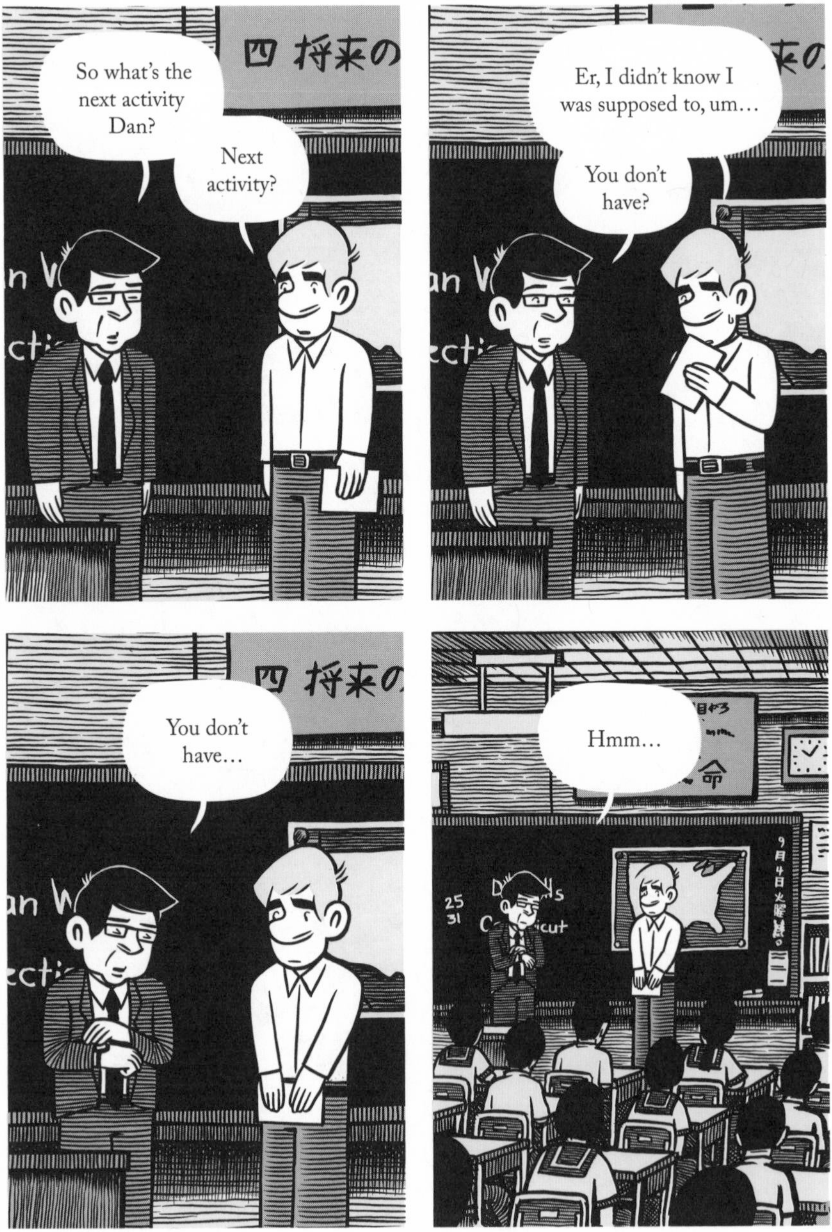
So what's the next activity Dan?
Next activity?
Er, I didn't know I was supposed to, um…
You don't have?
You don't have…
Hmm…

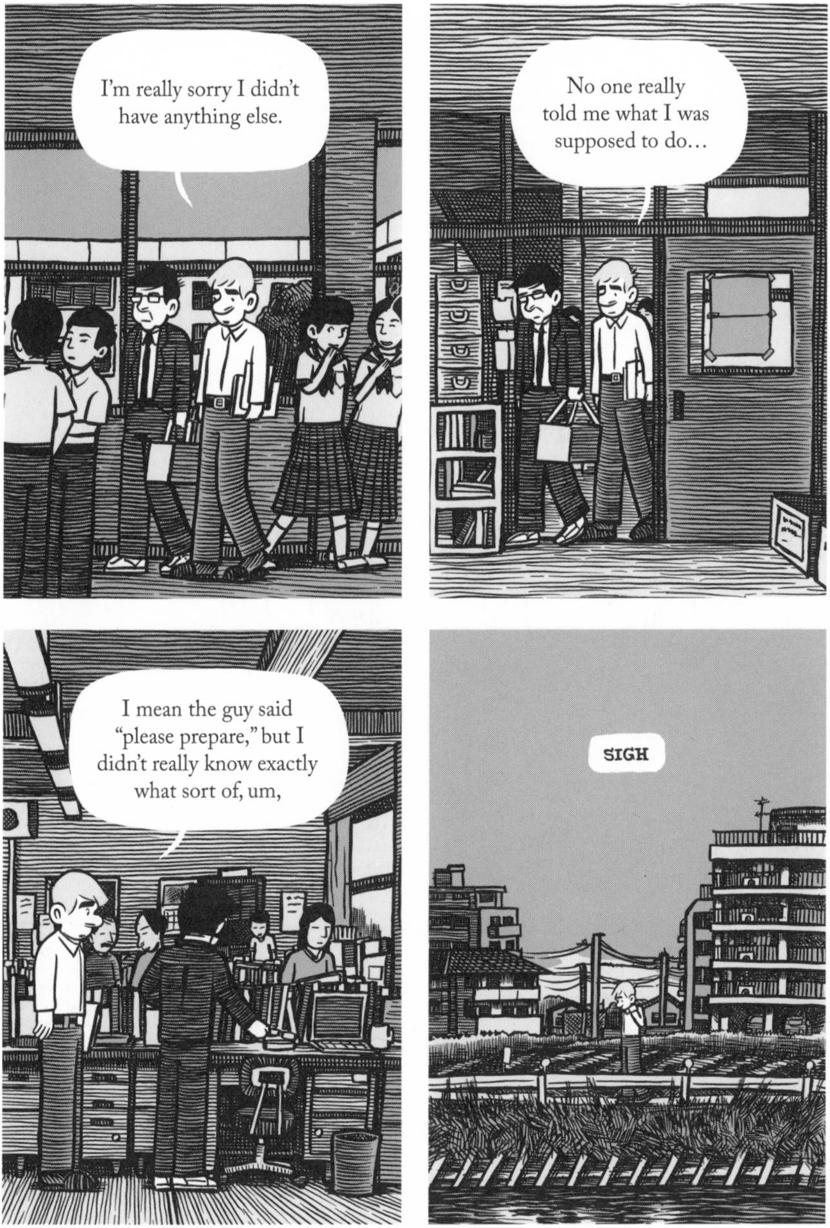
I'm really sorry I didn't have anything else.
No one really told me what I was supposed to do…
I mean the guy said "please prepare," but I didn't really know exactly what sort of, um,
SIGH

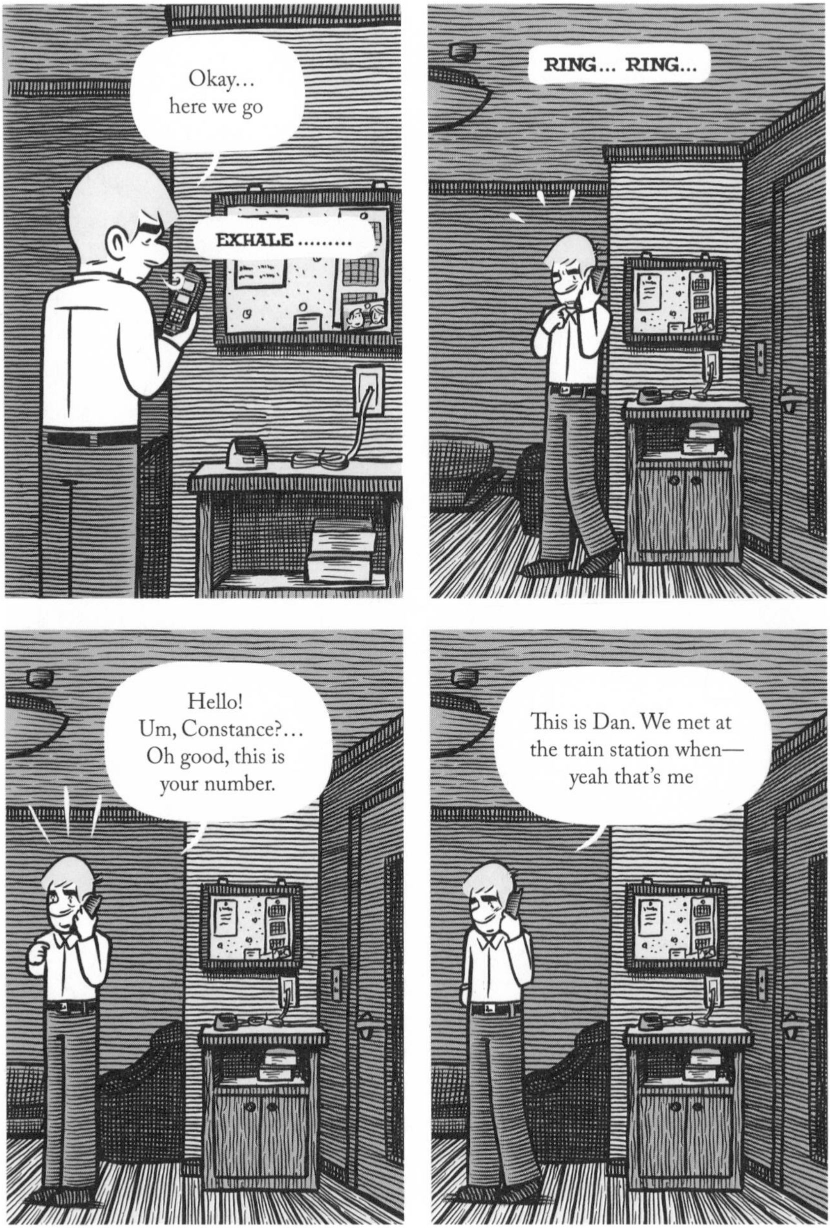
Okay...
here we go
EXHALE.........
RING... RING...
Hello!
Um, Constance?...
Oh good, this is
your number.
This is Dan. We met at
the train station when—
yeah that's me

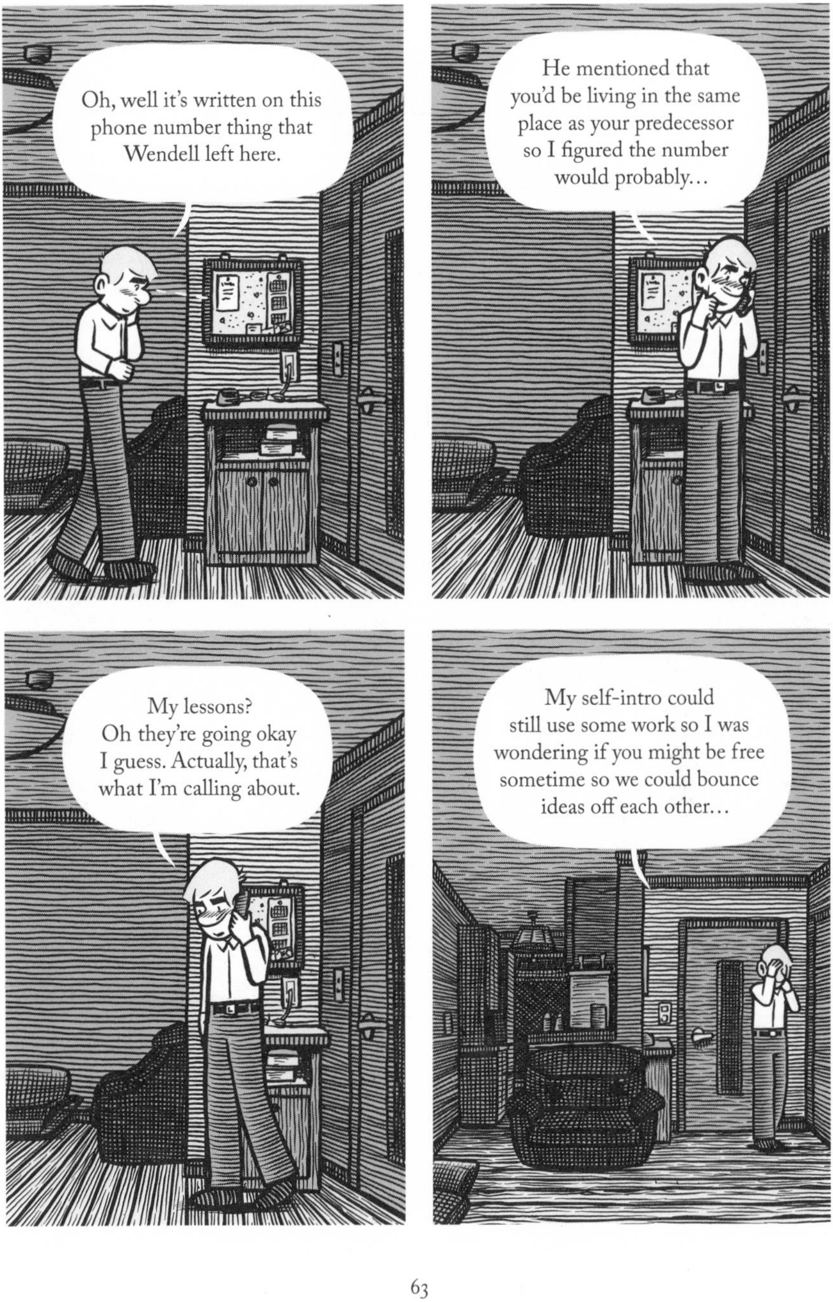
Oh, well it's written on this phone number thing that Wendell left here.
He mentioned that you'd be living in the same place as your predecessor so I figured the number would probably...
My lessons? Oh they're going okay I guess. Actually, that's what I'm calling about.
My self-intro could still use some work so I was wondering if you might be free sometime so we could bounce ideas off each other...

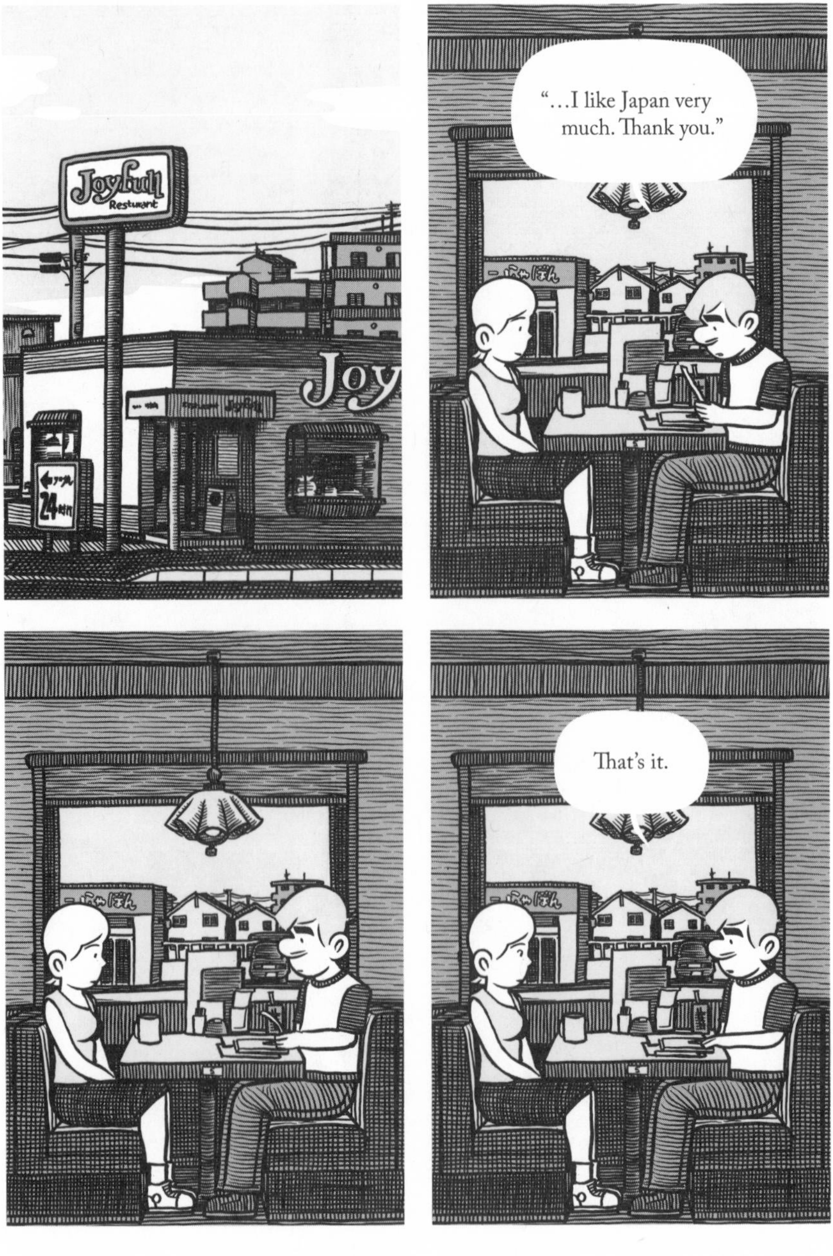
Joyfull
Resturant
24
Joy
"...I like Japan very much. Thank you."
That's it.

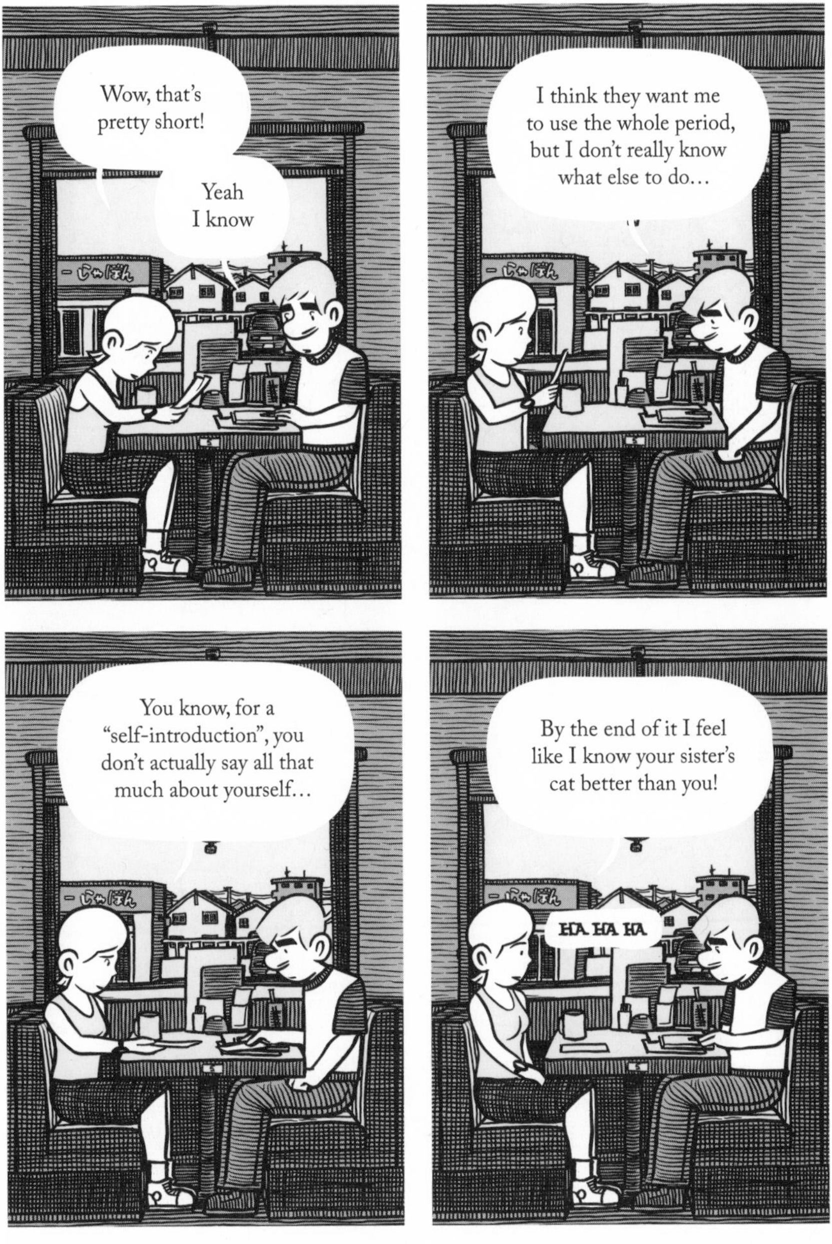
Wow, that's pretty short!
Yeah I know
I think they want me to use the whole period, but I don't really know what else to do…
You know, for a "self-introduction", you don't actually say all that much about yourself…
By the end of it I feel like I know your sister's cat better than you!
HA HA HA

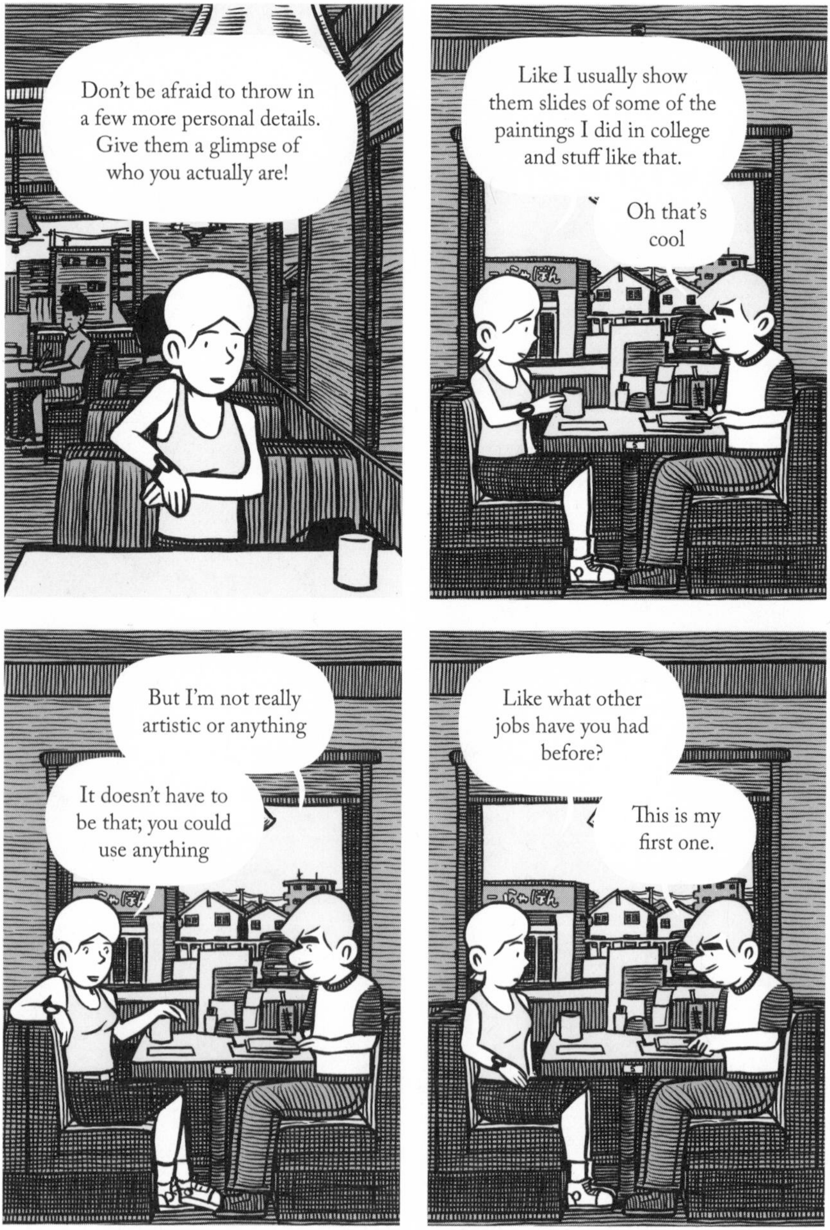
Don't be afraid to throw in a few more personal details. Give them a glimpse of who you actually are!
Like I usually show them slides of some of the paintings I did in college and stuff like that.
Oh that's cool
But I'm not really artistic or anything
It doesn't have to be that; you could use anything
Like what other jobs have you had before?
This is my first one.

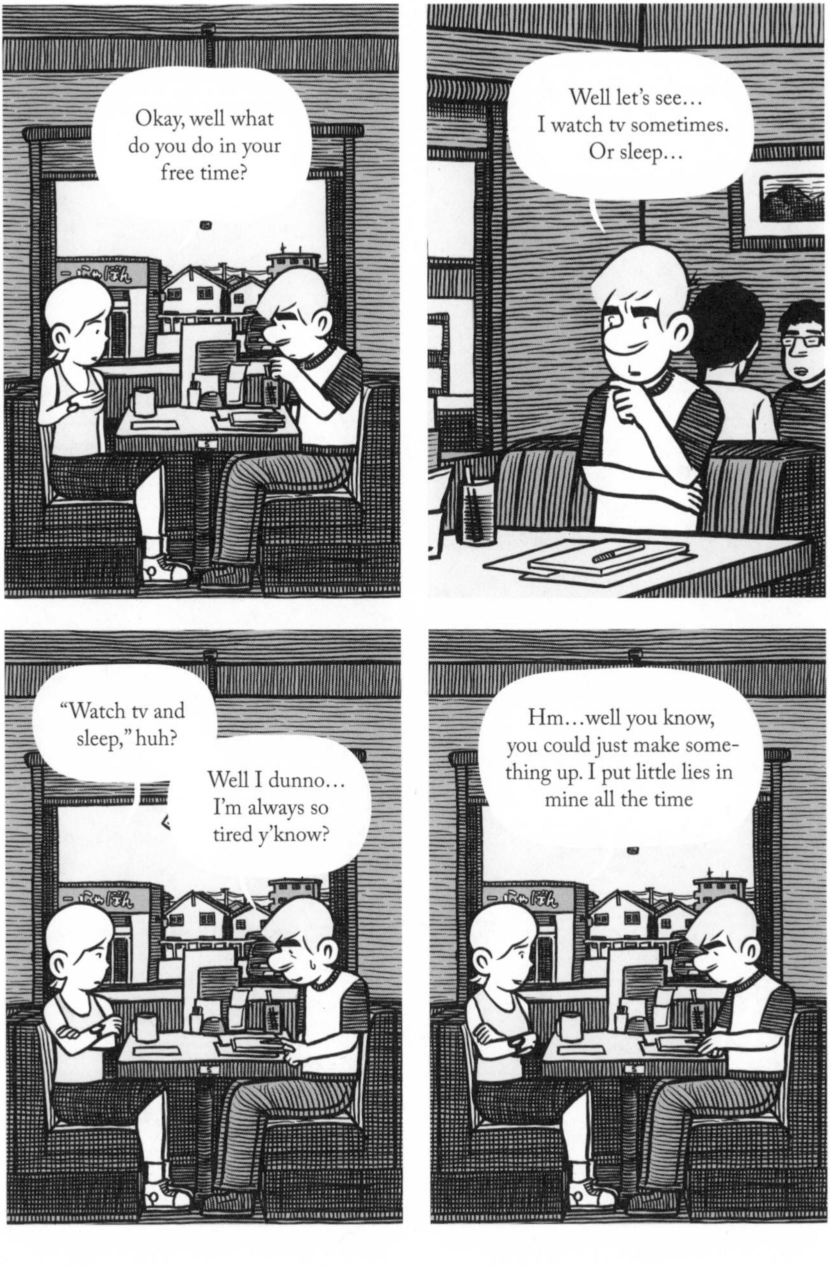
Okay, well what do you do in your free time?
Well let's see... I watch tv sometimes. Or sleep...
"Watch tv and sleep," huh?
Well I dunno... I'm always so tired y'know?
Hm...well you know, you could just make something up. I put little lies in mine all the time

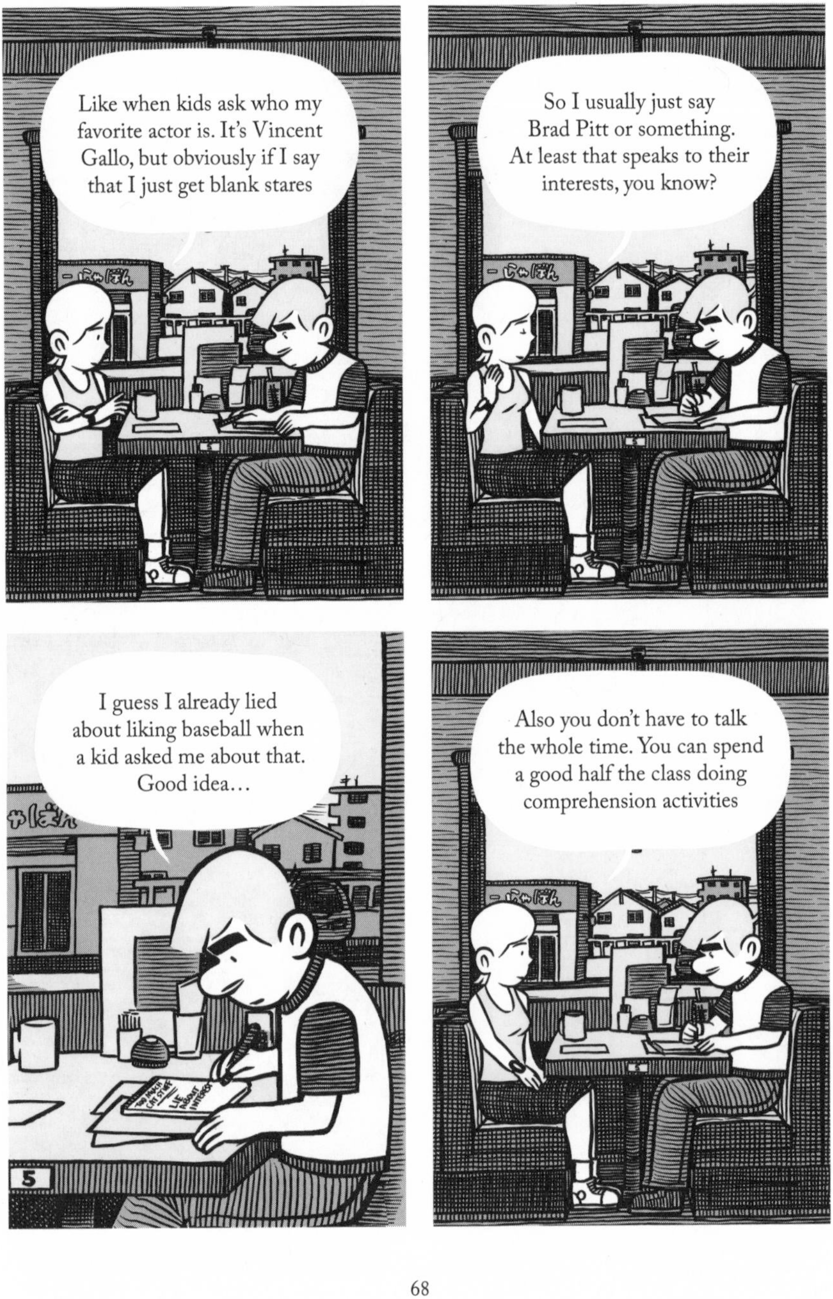
Like when kids ask who my favorite actor is. It's Vincent Gallo, but obviously if I say that I just get blank stares
So I usually just say Brad Pitt or something. At least that speaks to their interests, you know?
I guess I already lied about liking baseball when a kid asked me about that. Good idea…
Also you don't have to talk the whole time. You can spend a good half the class doing comprehension activities

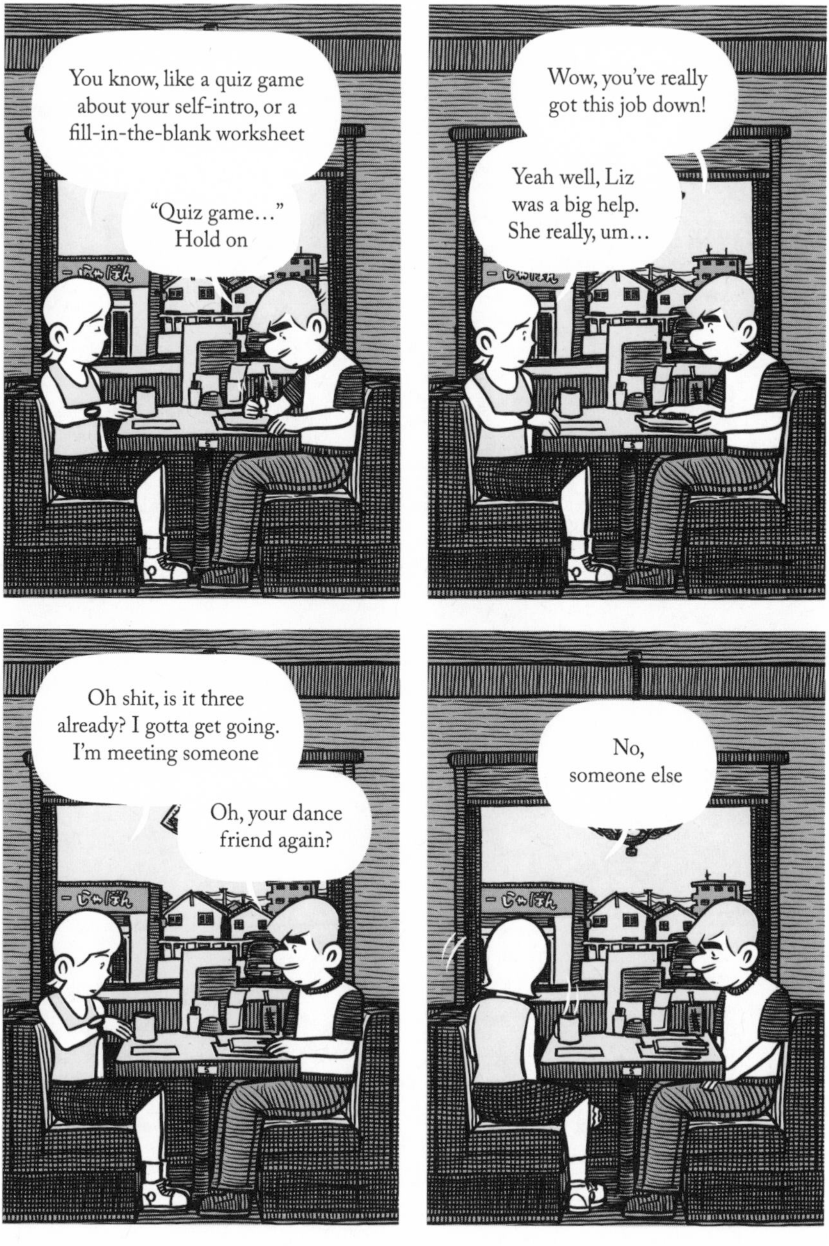
You know, like a quiz game about your self-intro, or a fill-in-the-blank worksheet
"Quiz game…" Hold on
Wow, you've really got this job down!
Yeah well, Liz was a big help. She really, um…
Oh shit, is it three already? I gotta get going. I'm meeting someone
Oh, your dance friend again?
No, someone else

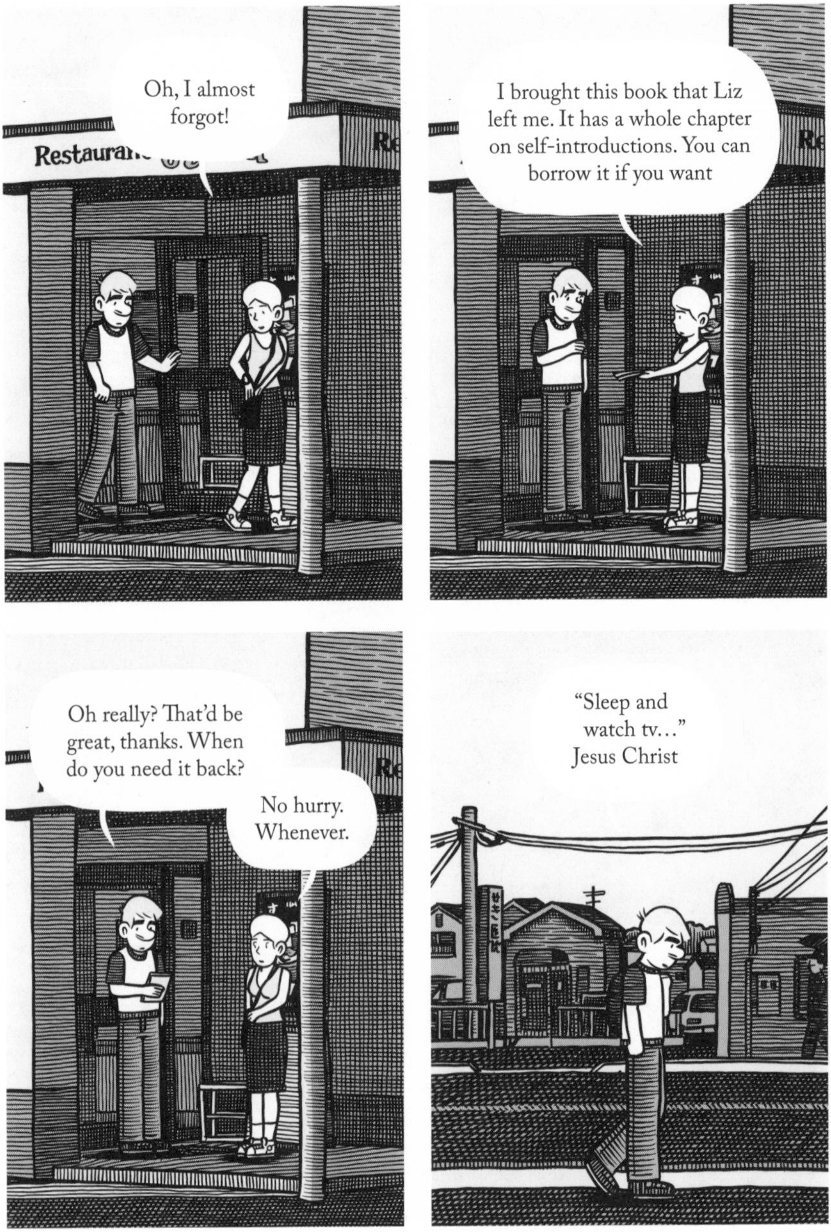
Oh, I almost forgot!
I brought this book that Liz left me. It has a whole chapter on self-introductions. You can borrow it if you want
Oh really? That'd be great, thanks. When do you need it back?
No hurry. Whenever.
"Sleep and watch tv…" Jesus Christ

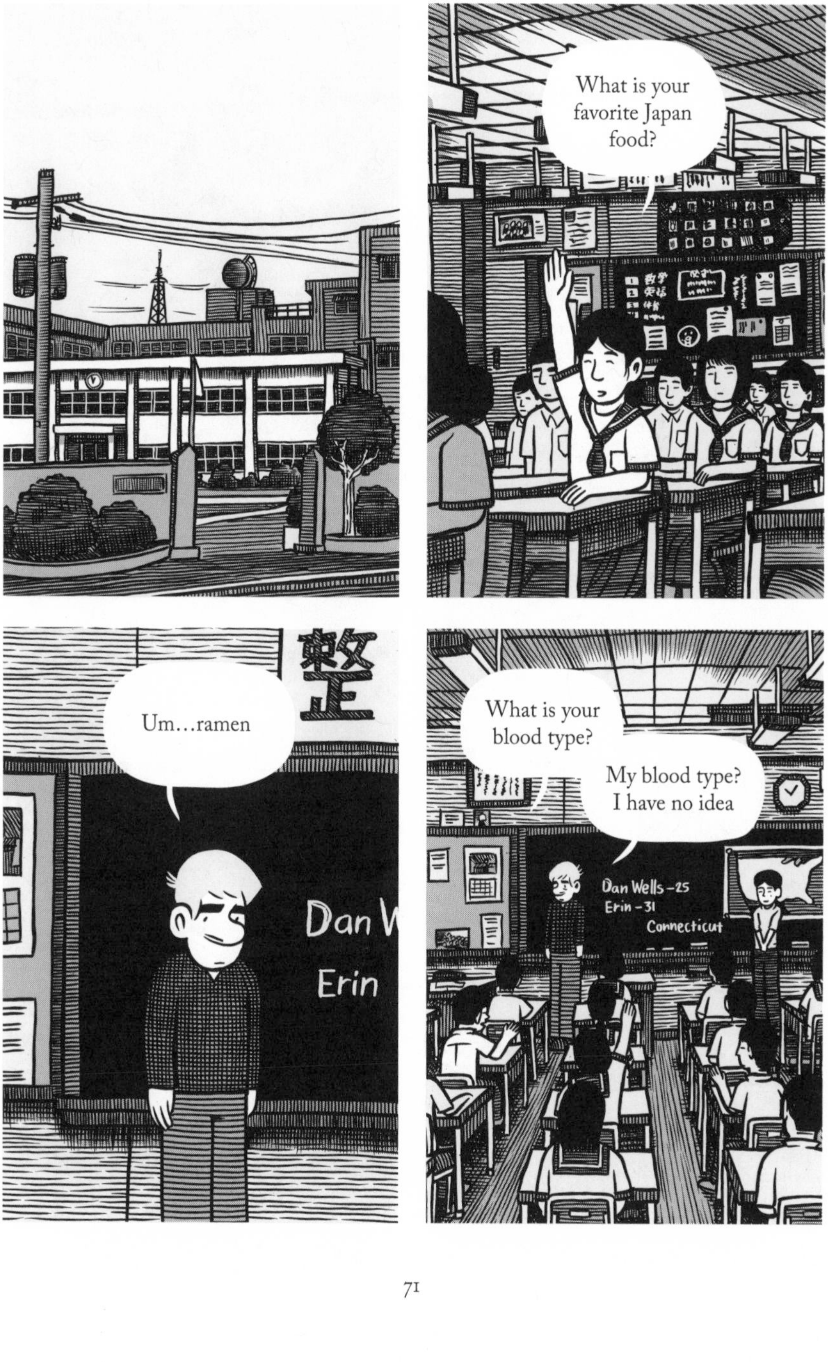

What is your favorite Japan food?
整
Um…ramen
Dan W
Erin
What is your blood type?
My blood type? I have no idea
Dan Wells -25
Erin -31
Connecticut

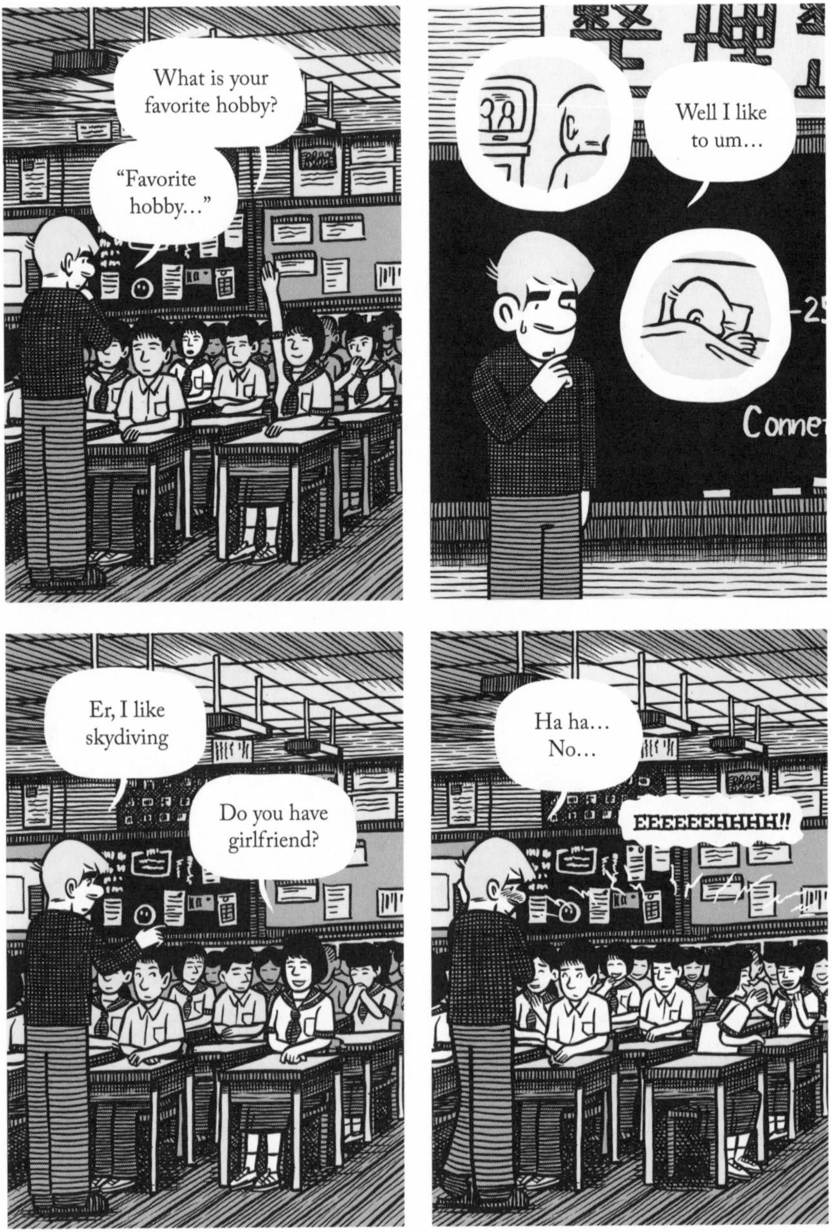
What is your favorite hobby?
"Favorite hobby..."
Well I like to um...
Er, I like skydiving
Do you have girlfriend?
Ha ha... No...
EEEEEEHHHH!!

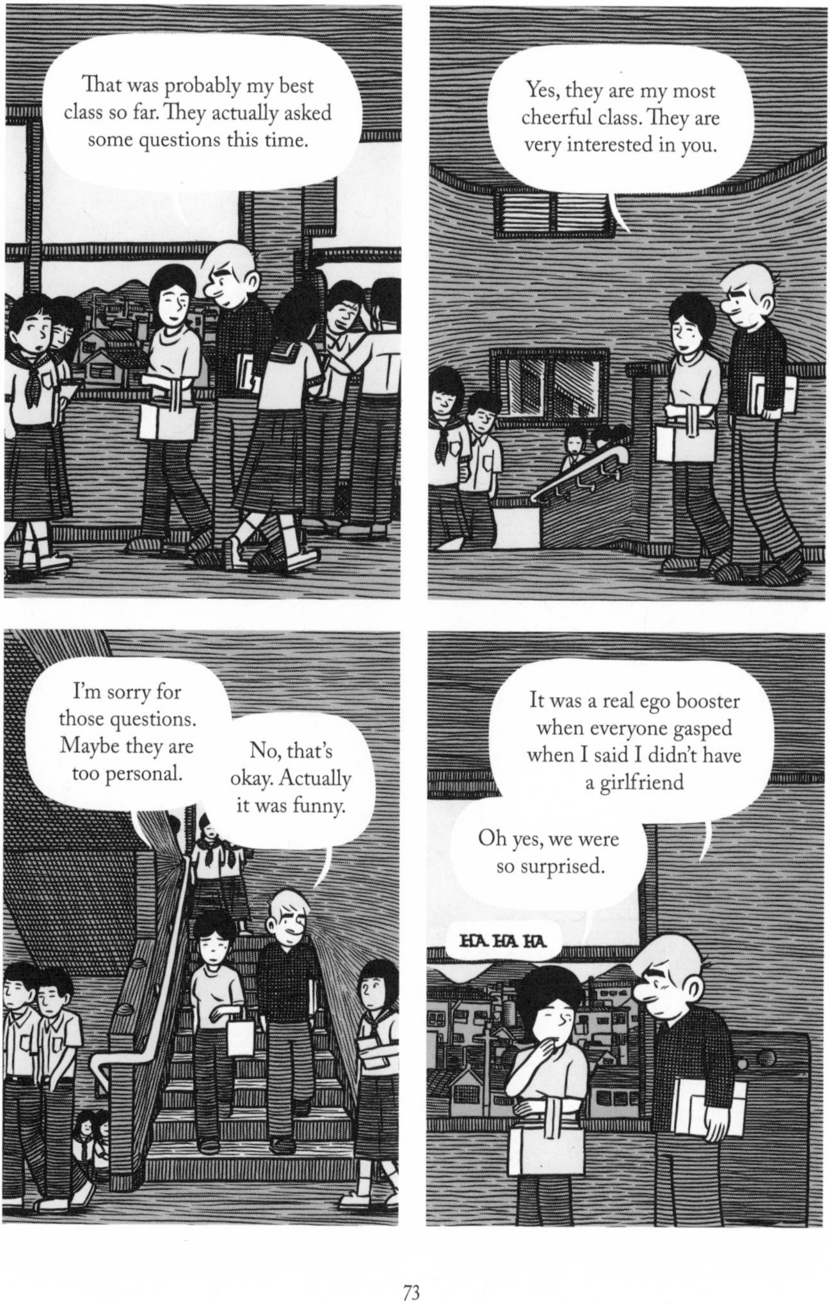
That was probably my best class so far. They actually asked some questions this time.
Yes, they are my most cheerful class. They are very interested in you.
I'm sorry for those questions. Maybe they are too personal.
No, that's okay. Actually it was funny.
It was a real ego booster when everyone gasped when I said I didn't have a girlfriend
Oh yes, we were so surprised.
HA HA HA

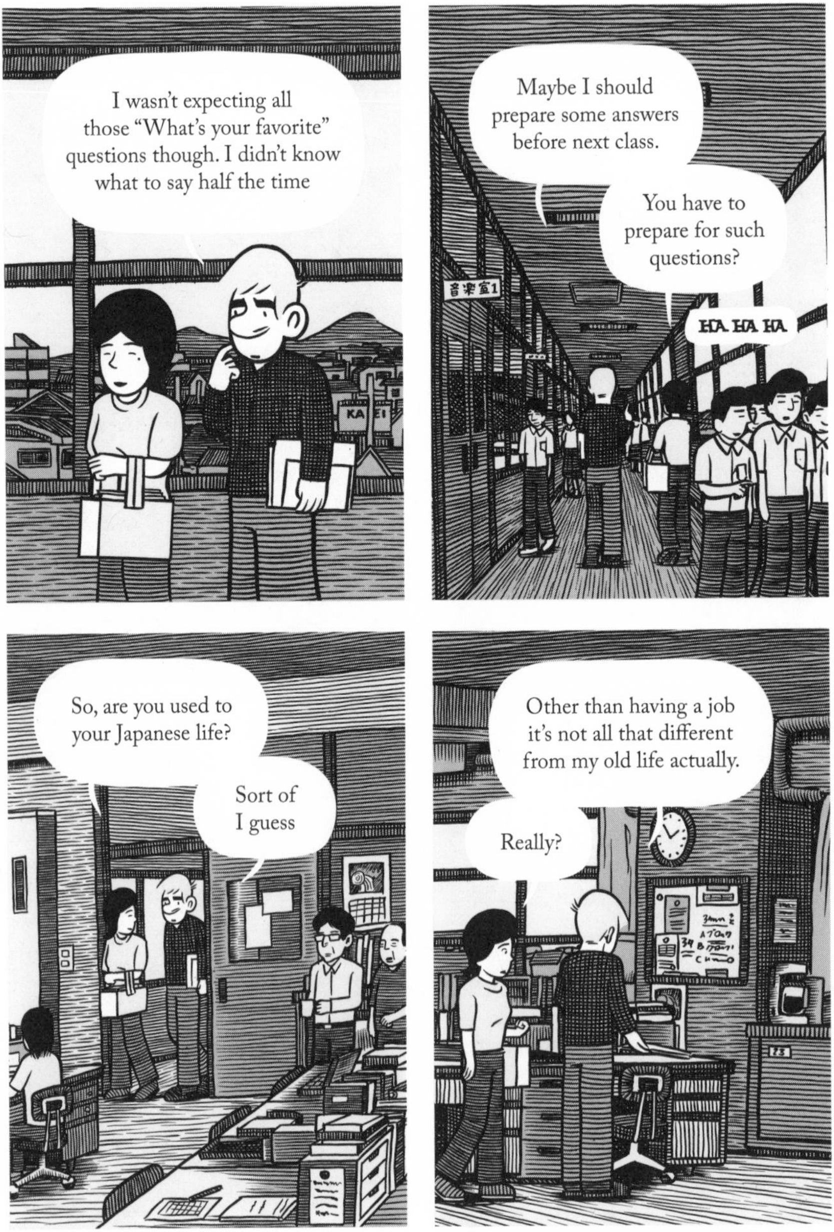
I wasn't expecting all those "What's your favorite" questions though. I didn't know what to say half the time
Maybe I should prepare some answers before next class.
You have to prepare for such questions?
音楽室1
HA HA HA
So, are you used to your Japanese life?
Sort of I guess
Other than having a job it's not all that different from my old life actually.
Really?

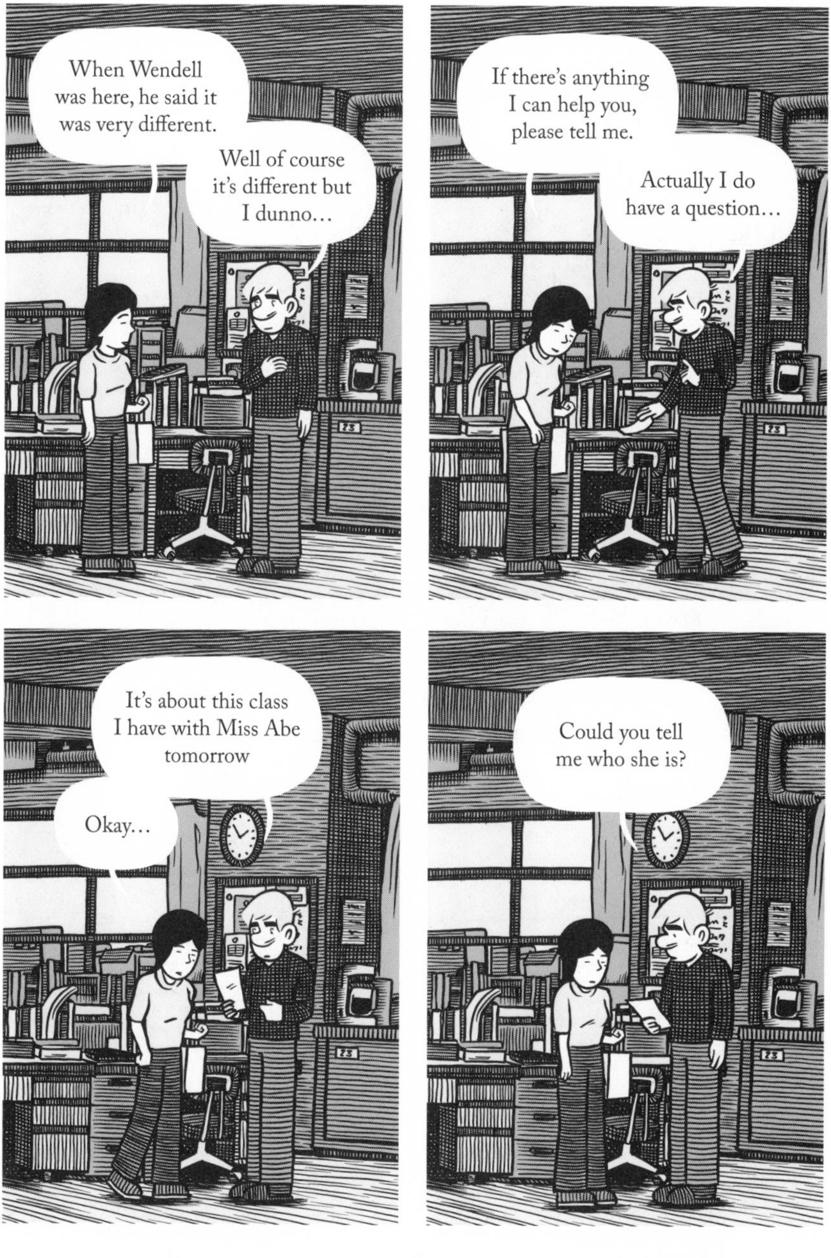
When Wendell was here, he said it was very different.
Well of course it's different but I dunno...
If there's anything I can help you, please tell me.
Actually I do have a question...
It's about this class I have with Miss Abe tomorrow
Okay...
Could you tell me who she is?

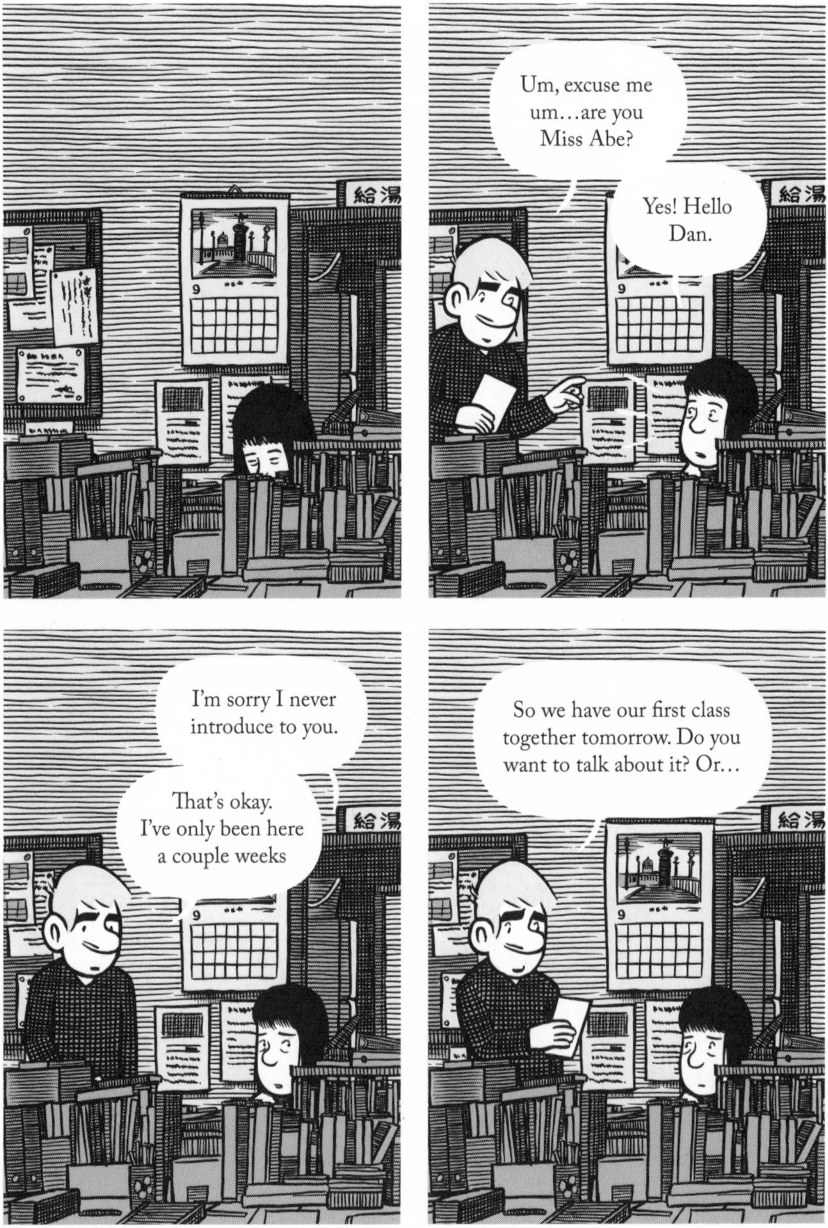
給湯
Um, excuse me um…are you Miss Abe?
Yes! Hello Dan.
給湯
I'm sorry I never introduce to you.
That's okay. I've only been here a couple weeks
給湯
So we have our first class together tomorrow. Do you want to talk about it? Or…
給湯

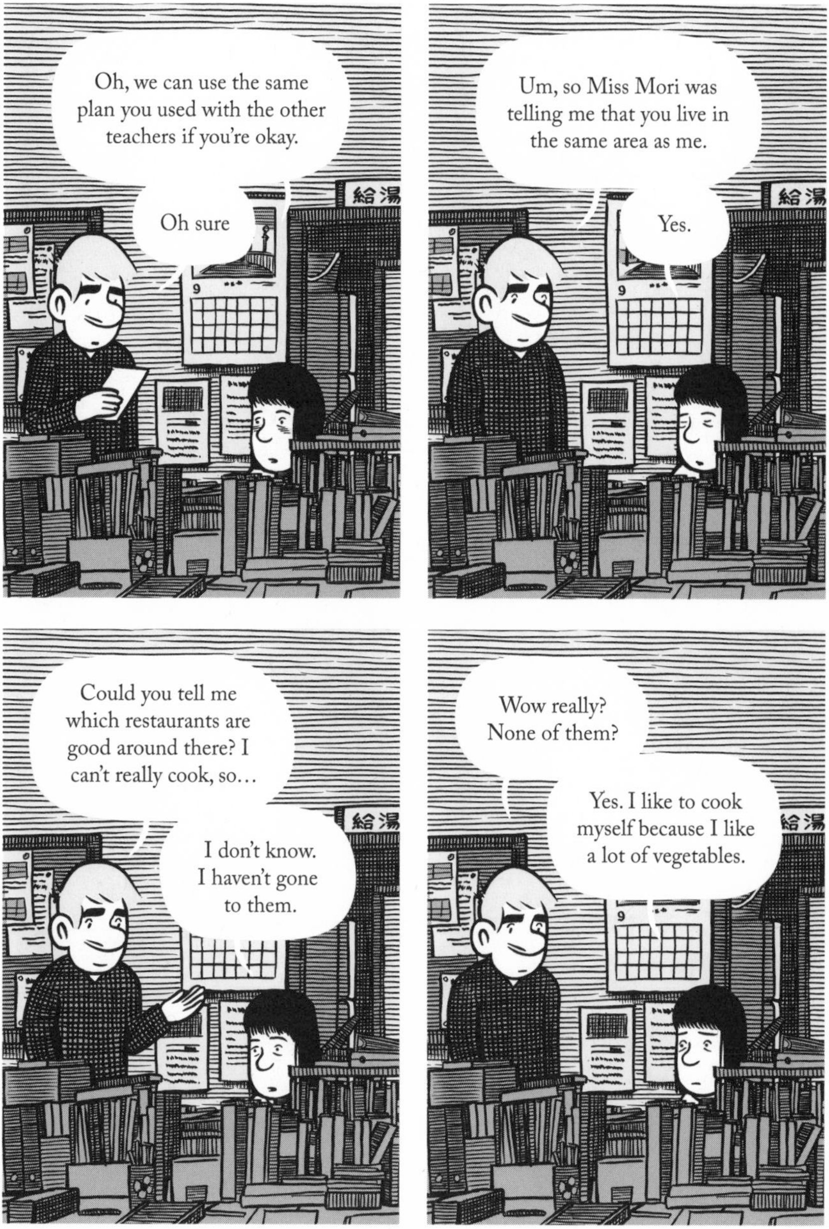
Oh, we can use the same plan you used with the other teachers if you're okay.
Oh sure
給湯
9
Um, so Miss Mori was telling me that you live in the same area as me.
Yes.
給湯
9
Could you tell me which restaurants are good around there? I can't really cook, so...
I don't know. I haven't gone to them.
給湯
Wow really? None of them?
Yes. I like to cook myself because I like a lot of vegetables.
給湯
9

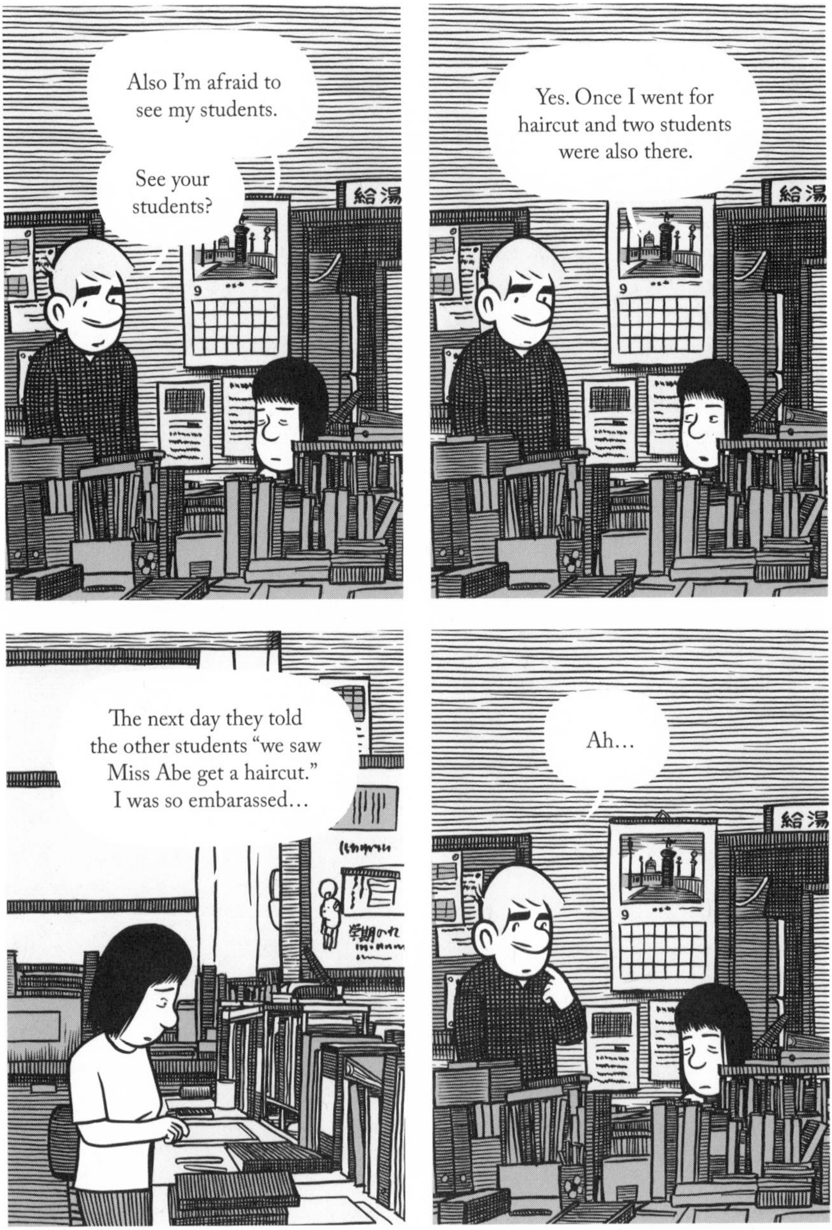
Also I'm afraid to see my students.
See your students?
Yes. Once I went for haircut and two students were also there.
The next day they told the other students "we saw Miss Abe get a haircut." I was so embarassed…
Ah…

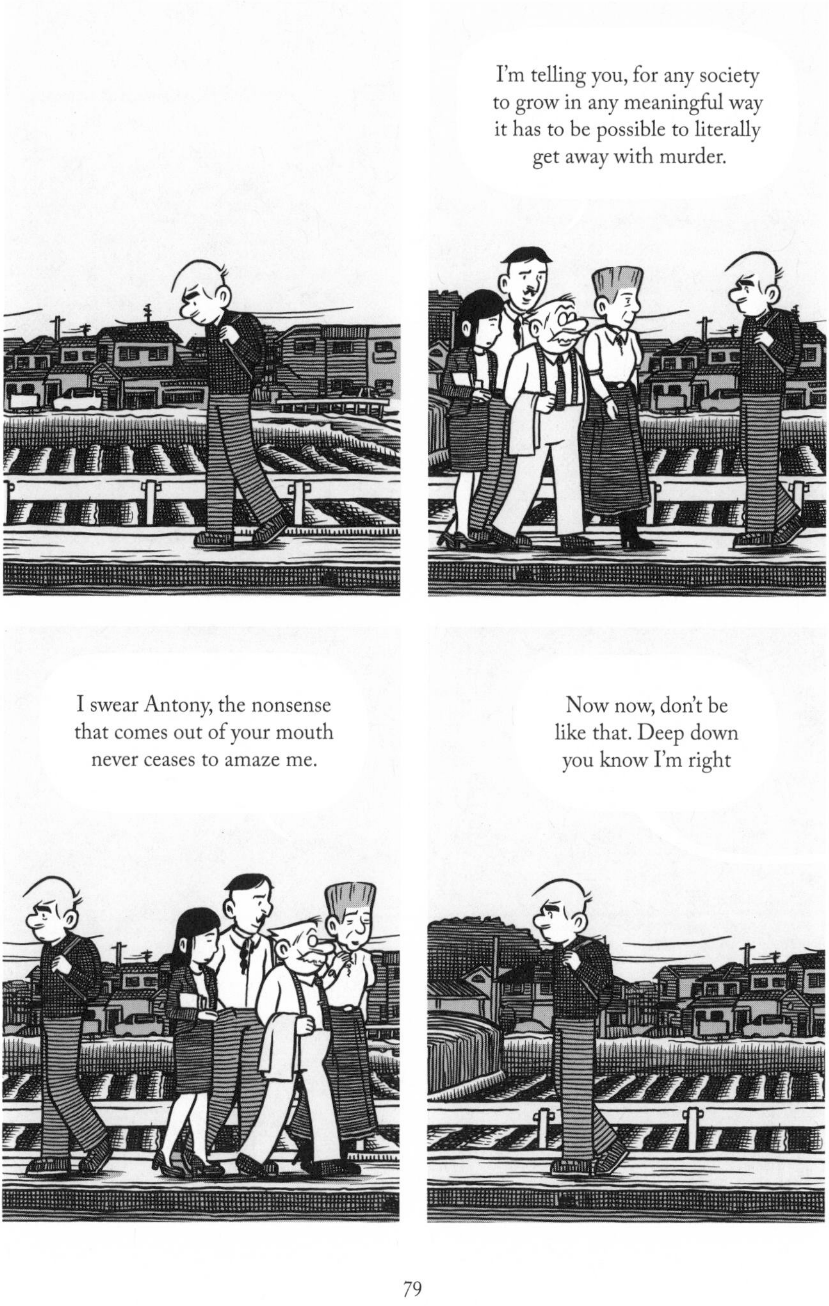
I'm telling you, for any society to grow in any meaningful way it has to be possible to literally get away with murder.
I swear Antony, the nonsense that comes out of your mouth never ceases to amaze me.
Now now, don't be like that. Deep down you know I'm right

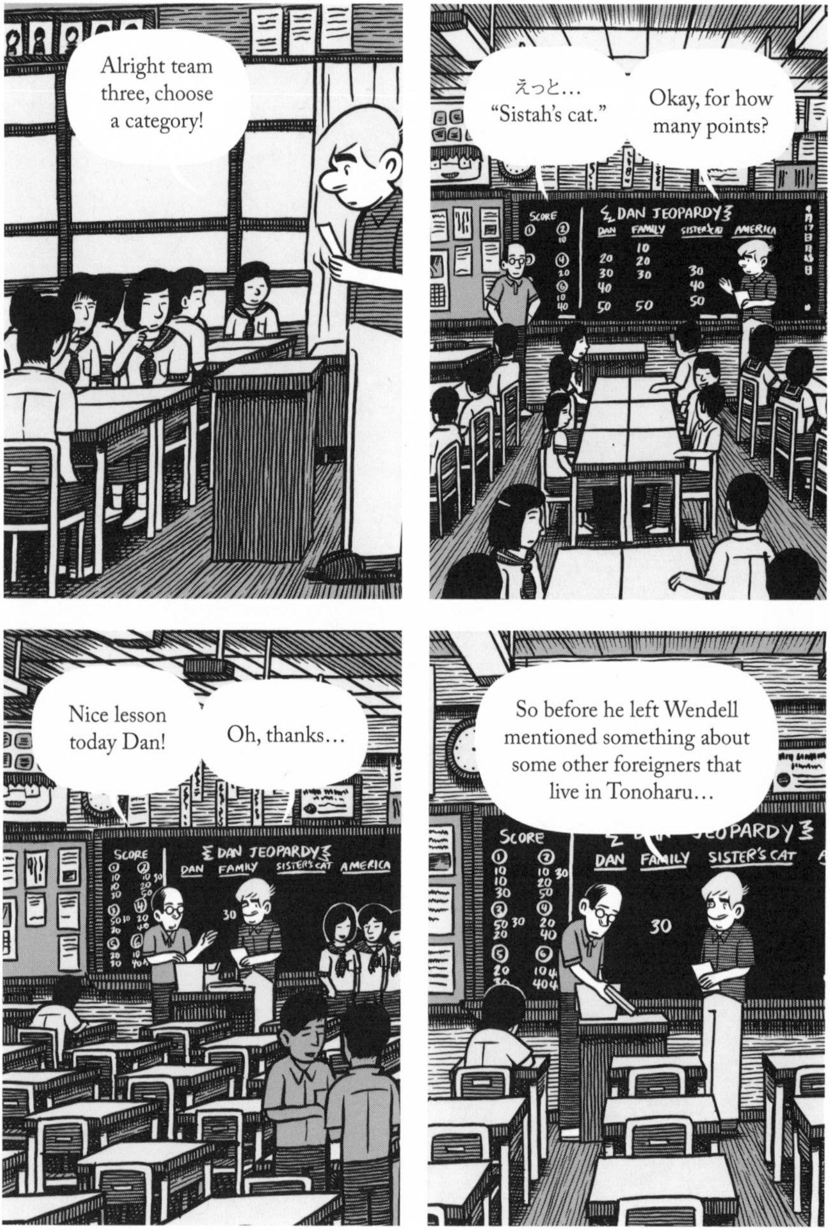
Alright team three, choose a category!
えっと…
"Sistah's cat."
Okay, for how many points?
DAN JEOPARDY
SCORE
DAN FAMILY SISTER'S CAT AMERICA
Nice lesson today Dan!
Oh, thanks…
So before he left Wendell mentioned something about some other foreigners that live in Tonoharu…

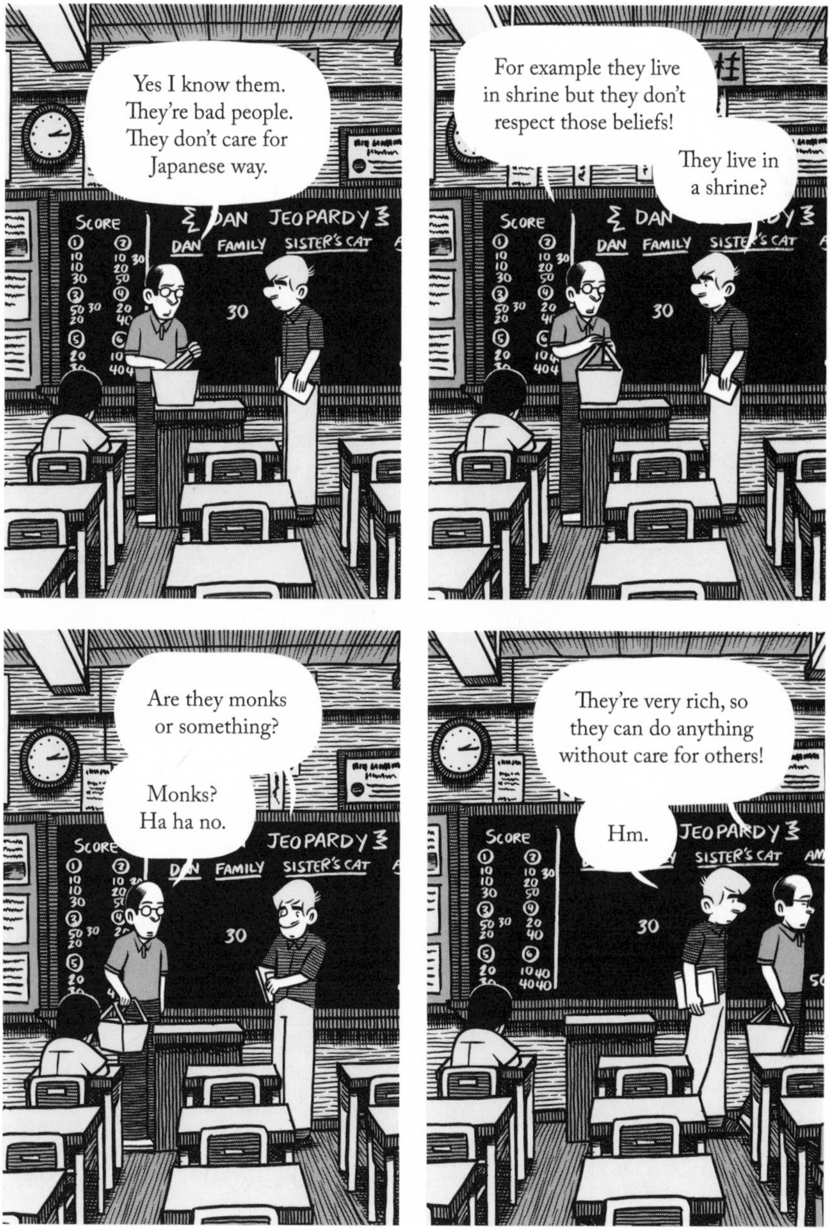
Yes I know them. They're bad people. They don't care for Japanese way.
SCORE
DAN JEOPARDY
DAN FAMILY SISTER'S CAT
For example they live in shrine but they don't respect those beliefs!
They live in a shrine?
Are they monks or something?
Monks? Ha ha no.
They're very rich, so they can do anything without care for others!
Hm.

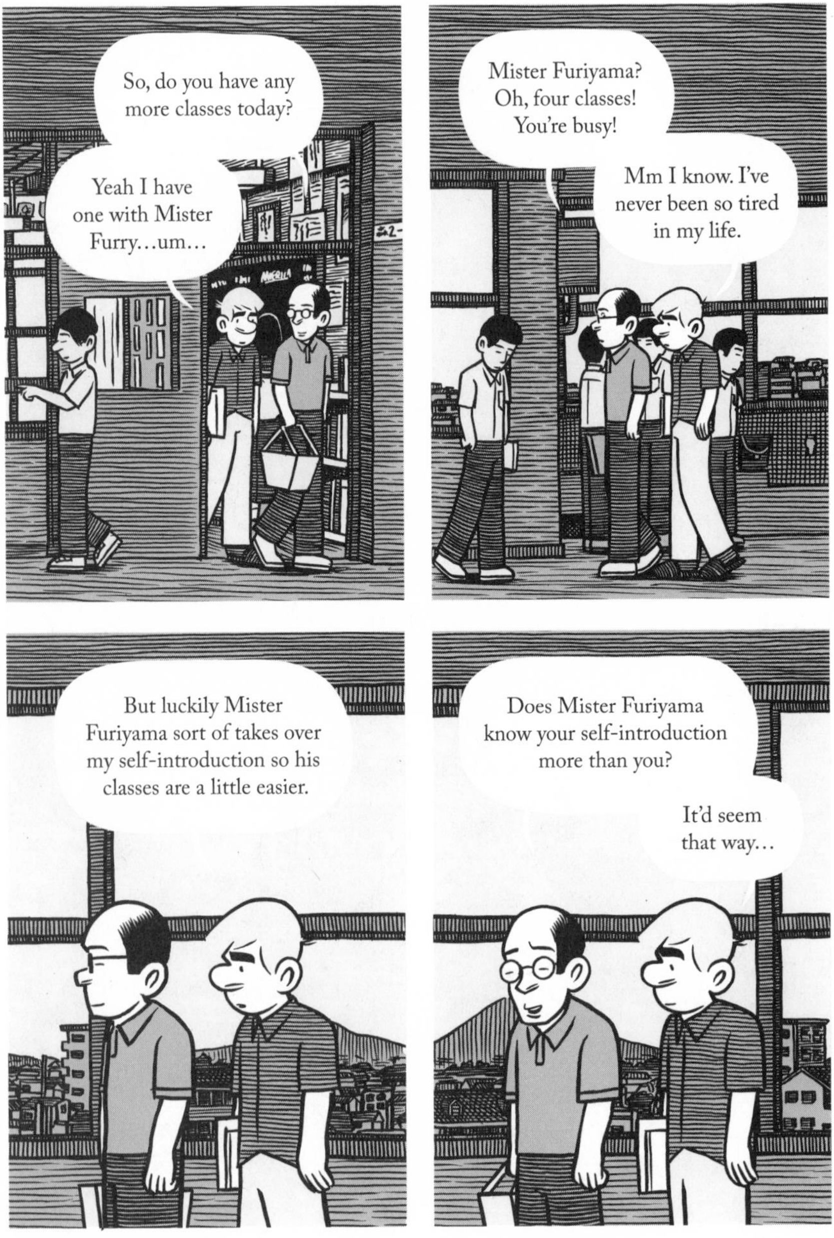
So, do you have any more classes today?
Yeah I have one with Mister Furry...um...
Mister Furiyama? Oh, four classes! You're busy!
Mm I know. I've never been so tired in my life.
But luckily Mister Furiyama sort of takes over my self-introduction so his classes are a little easier.
Does Mister Furiyama know your self-introduction more than you?
It'd seem that way...

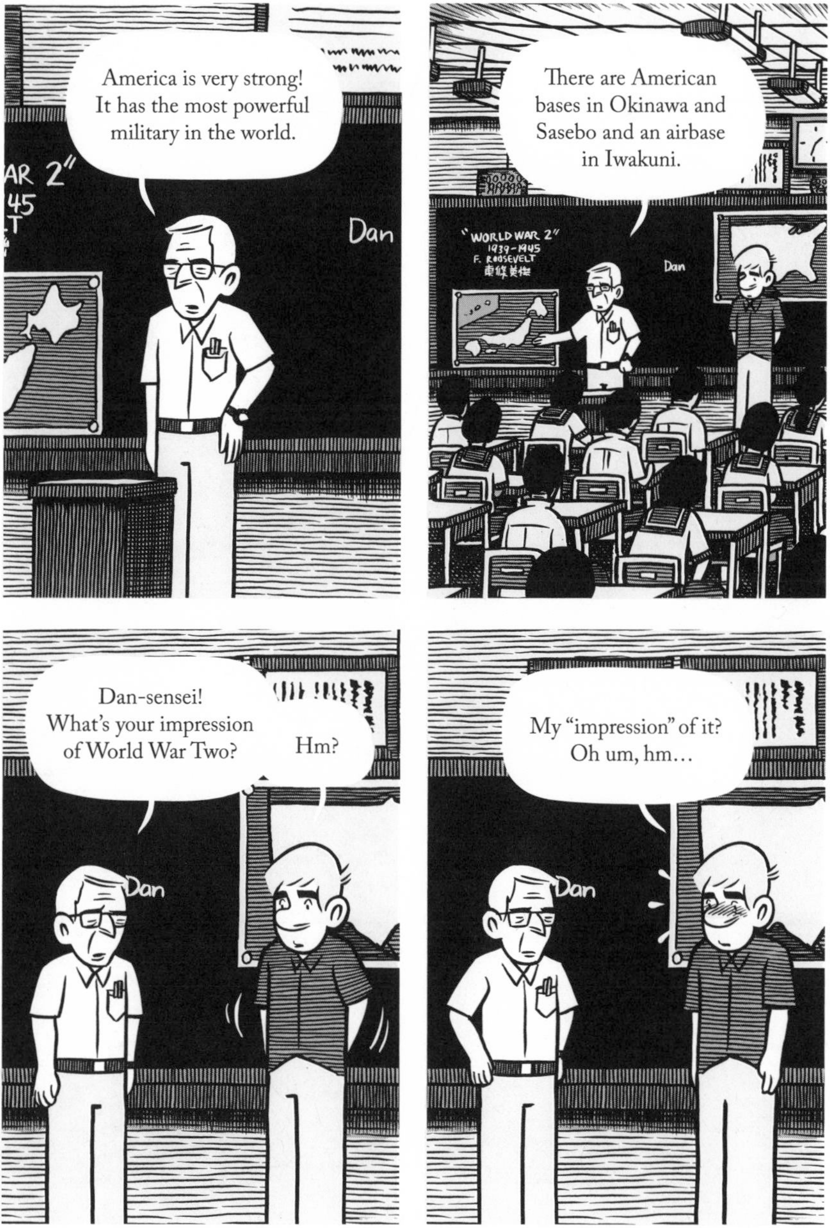
America is very strong! It has the most powerful military in the world.
Dan
There are American bases in Okinawa and Sasebo and an airbase in Iwakuni.
"WORLD WAR 2" 1939–1945 F. ROOSEVELT 東條英機
Dan
Dan-sensei! What's your impression of World War Two?
Hm?
Dan
My "impression" of it? Oh um, hm…
Dan

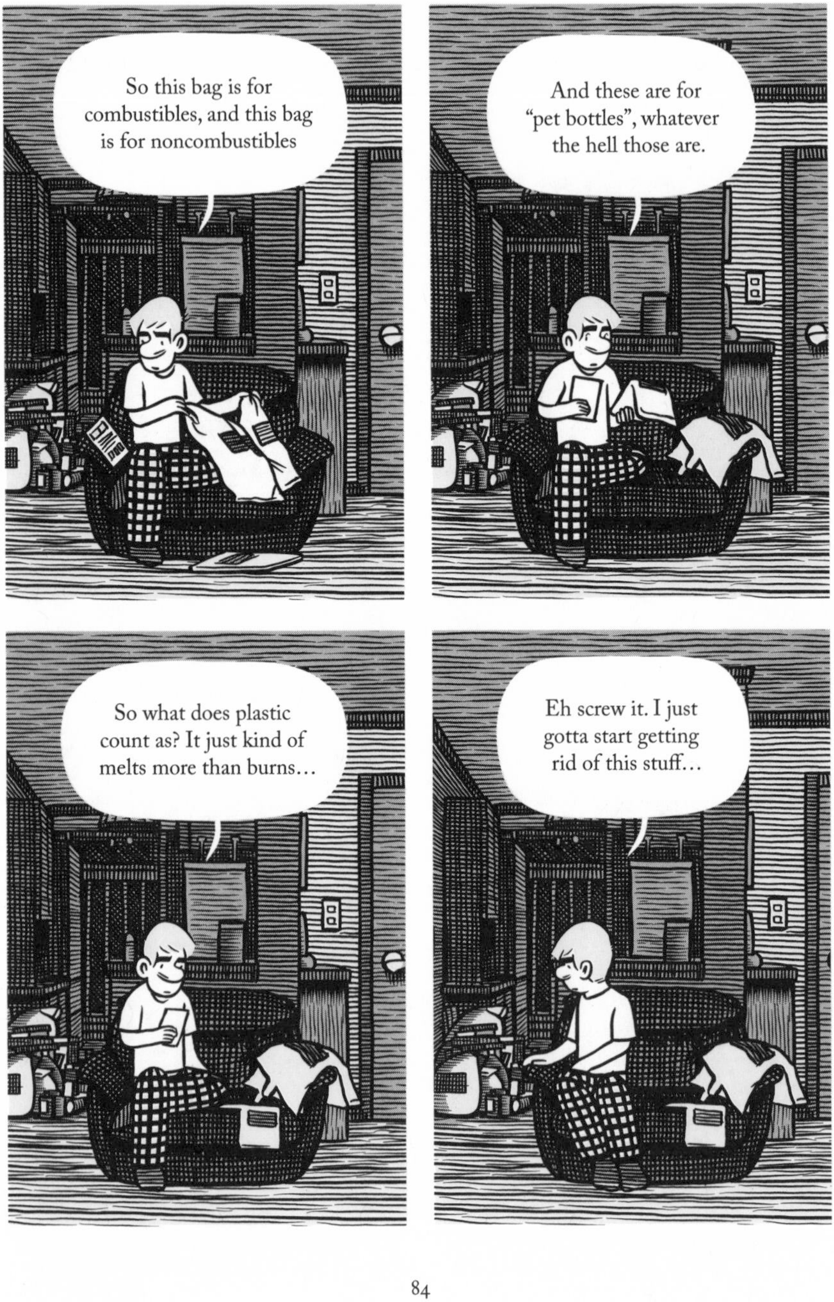
So this bag is for combustibles, and this bag is for noncombustibles
And these are for "pet bottles", whatever the hell those are.
So what does plastic count as? It just kind of melts more than burns...
Eh screw it. I just gotta start getting rid of this stuff...

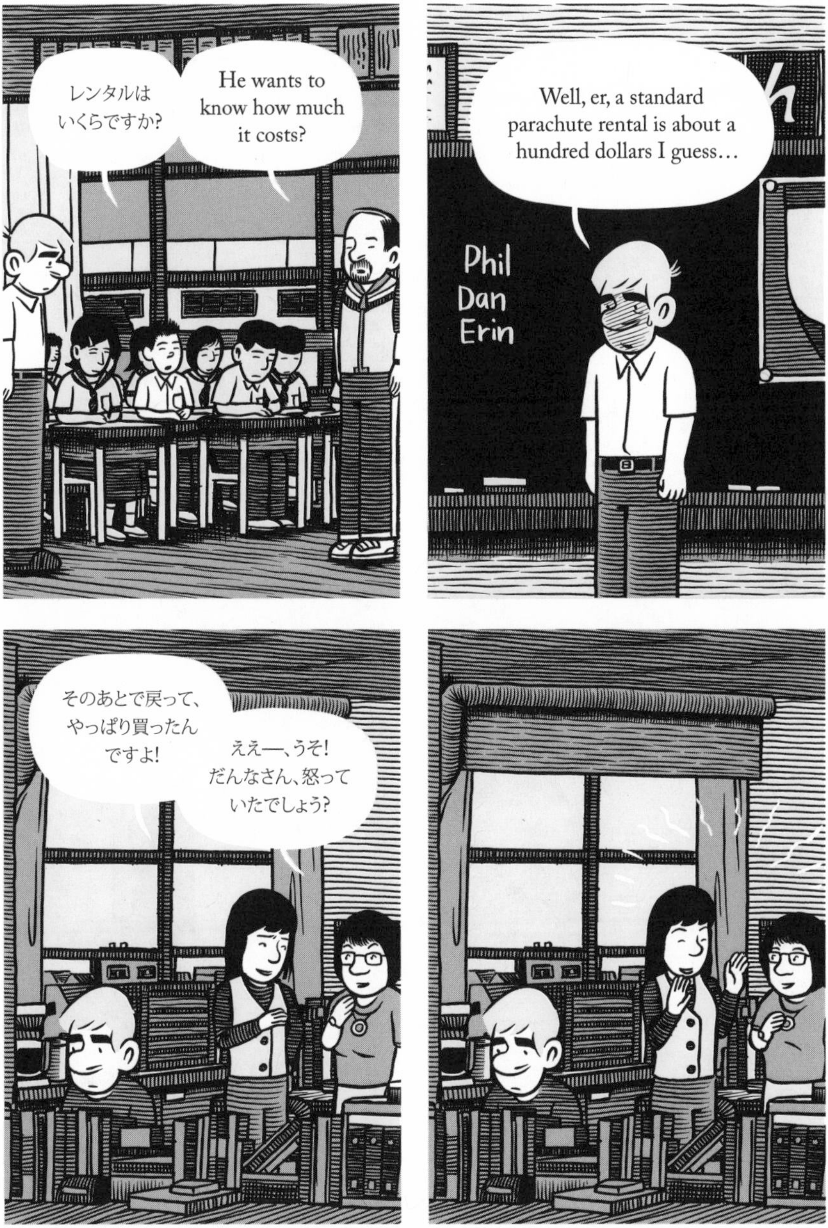
レンタルは
いくらですか?
He wants to know how much it costs?
Well, er, a standard parachute rental is about a hundred dollars I guess…
Phil
Dan
Erin
そのあとで戻って、やっぱり買ったんですよ!
ええー、うそ!だんなさん、怒っていたでしょう?

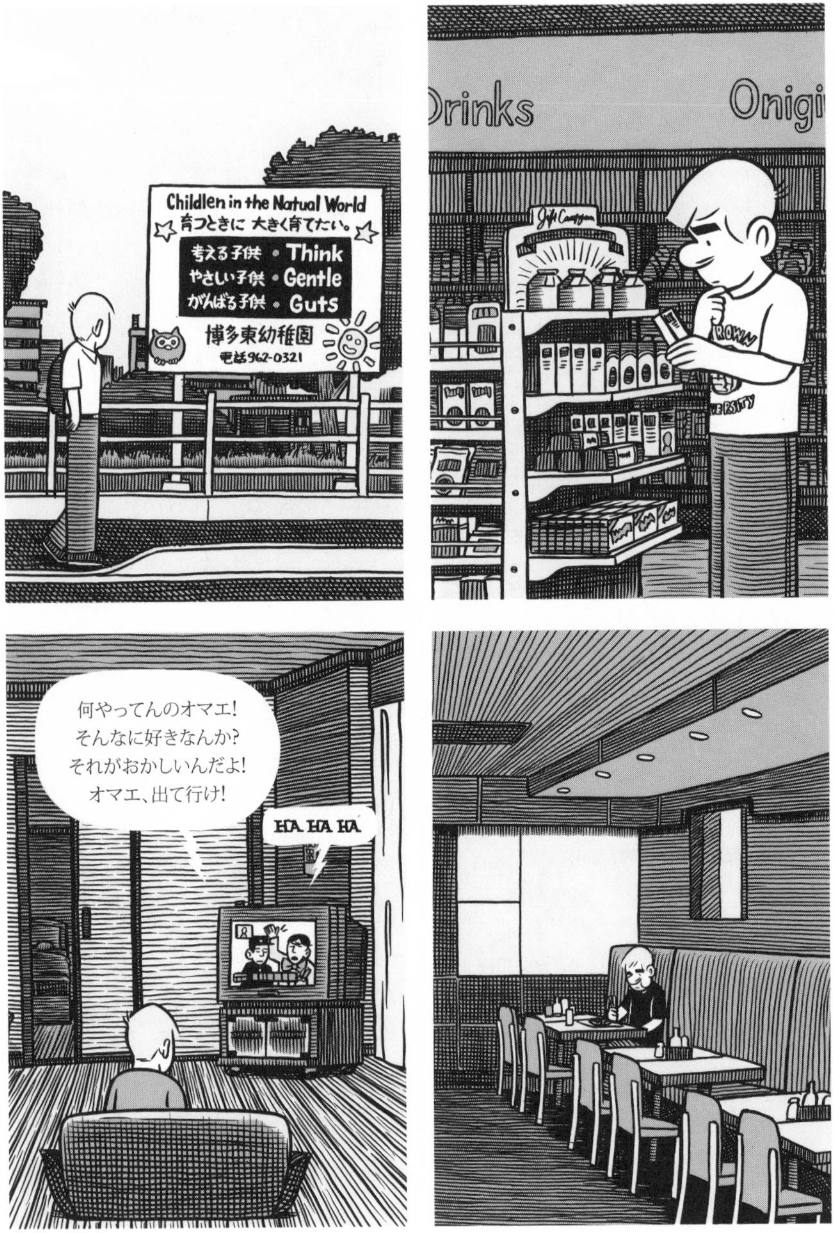
Childlen in the Natual World
育つときに 大きく育てたい。
考える子供 • Think
やさしい子供 • Gentle
がんばる子供 • Guts
博多東幼稚園
電話 962-0321
rinks
Onigi
何やってんのオマエ!
そんなに好きなんか?
それがおかしいんだよ!
オマエ、出て行け!
HA HA HA

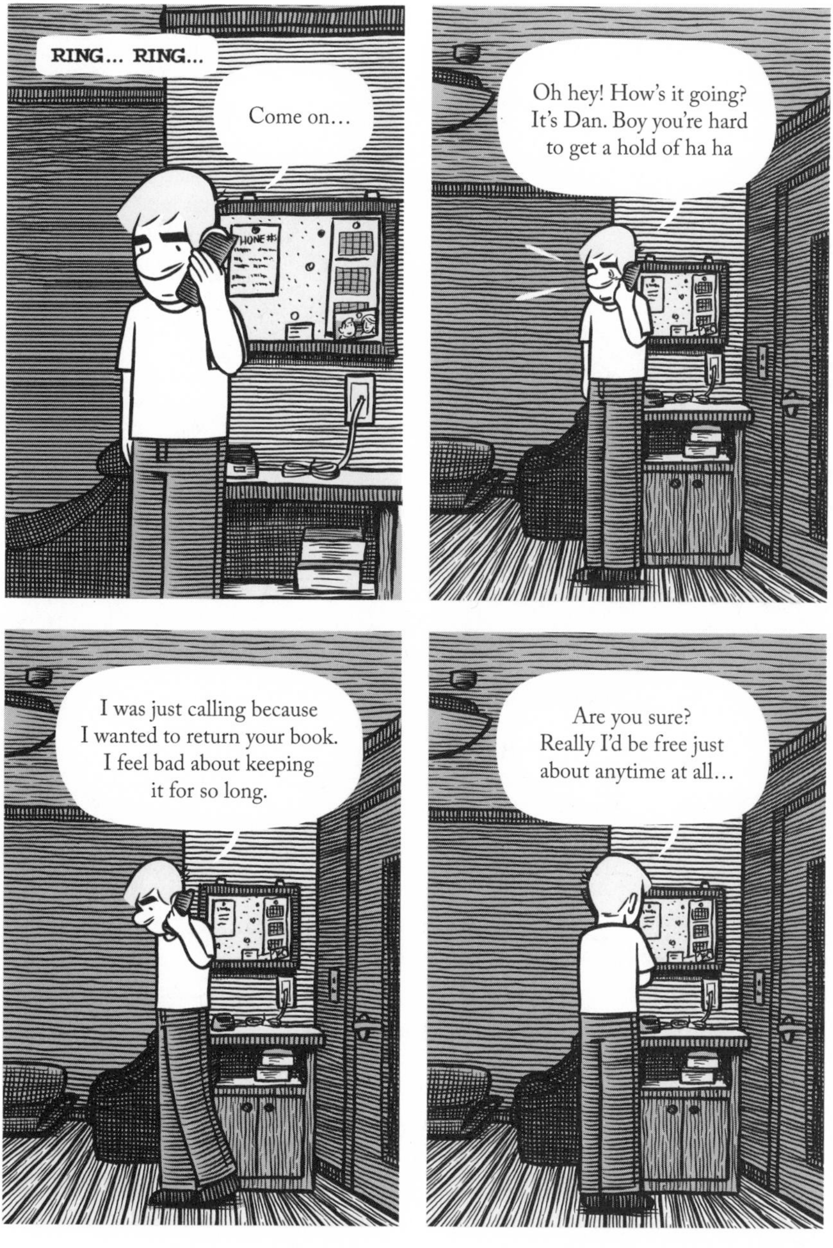
RING... RING...
Come on...
Oh hey! How's it going? It's Dan. Boy you're hard to get a hold of ha ha
I was just calling because I wanted to return your book. I feel bad about keeping it for so long.
Are you sure? Really I'd be free just about anytime at all...

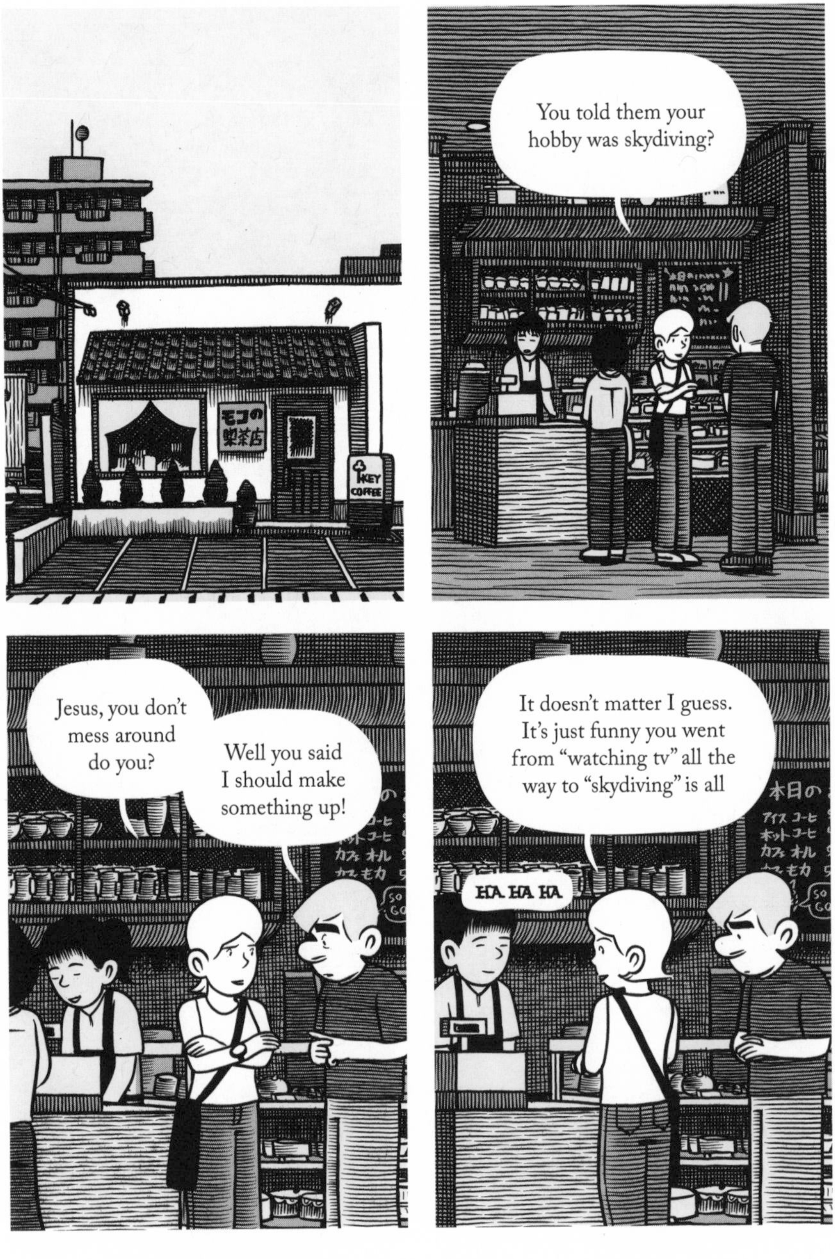
モコの
喫茶店
KEY
COFFEE
You told them your hobby was skydiving?
Jesus, you don't mess around do you?
Well you said I should make something up!
It doesn't matter I guess. It's just funny you went from "watching tv" all the way to "skydiving" is all
HA HA HA
本日の

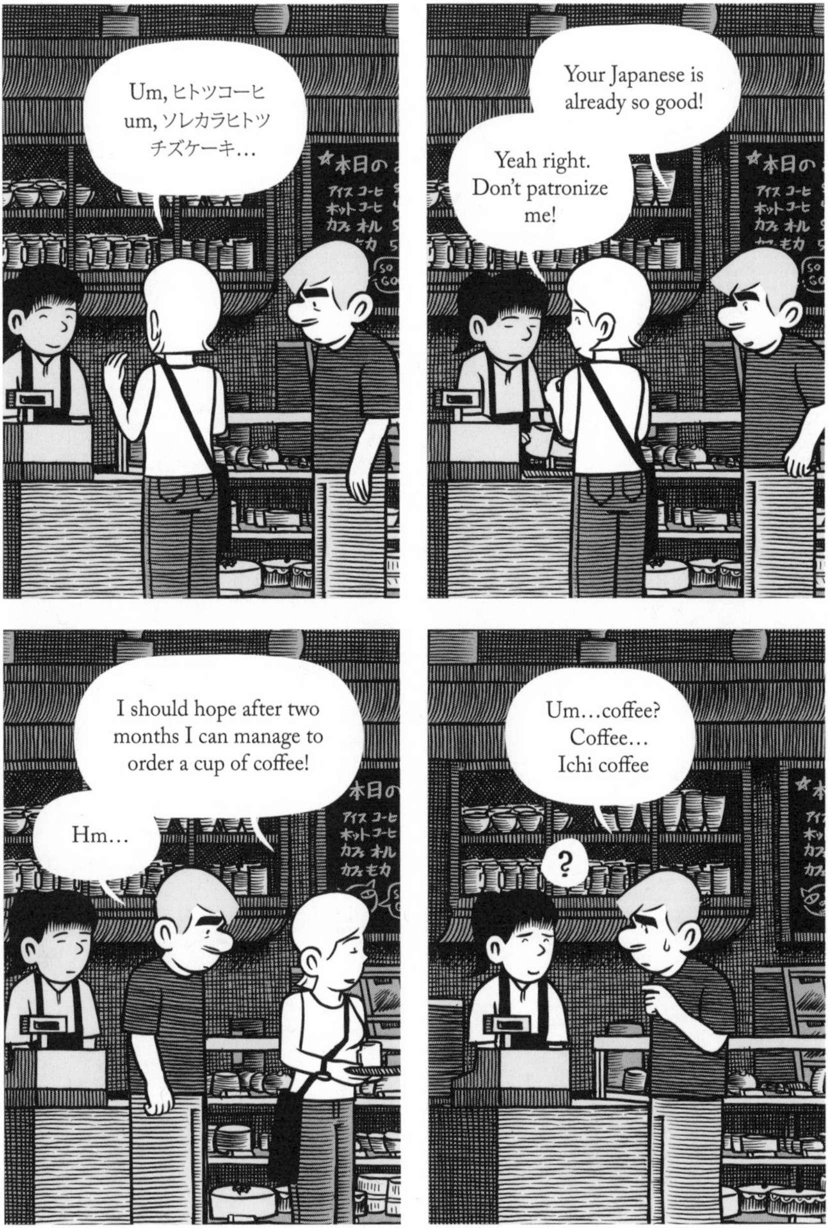
Um, ヒトツコーヒ
um, ソレカラヒトツ
チズケーキ…
Your Japanese is already so good!
Yeah right. Don't patronize me!
I should hope after two months I can manage to order a cup of coffee!
Hm…
Um…coffee? Coffee… Ichi coffee
?

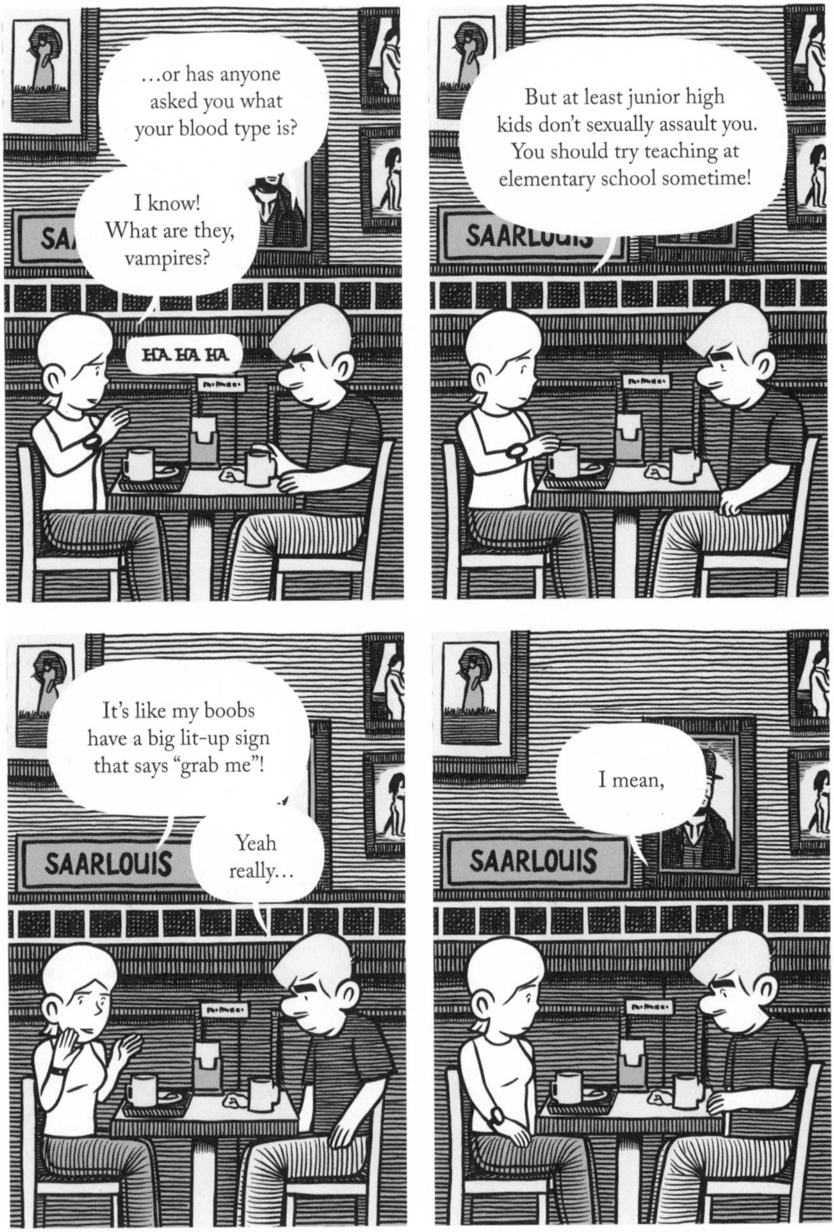
…or has anyone asked you what your blood type is?
I know! What are they, vampires?
HA HA HA
But at least junior high kids don't sexually assault you. You should try teaching at elementary school sometime!
It's like my boobs have a big lit-up sign that says "grab me"!
SAARLOUIS
Yeah really…
SAARLOUIS
I mean,

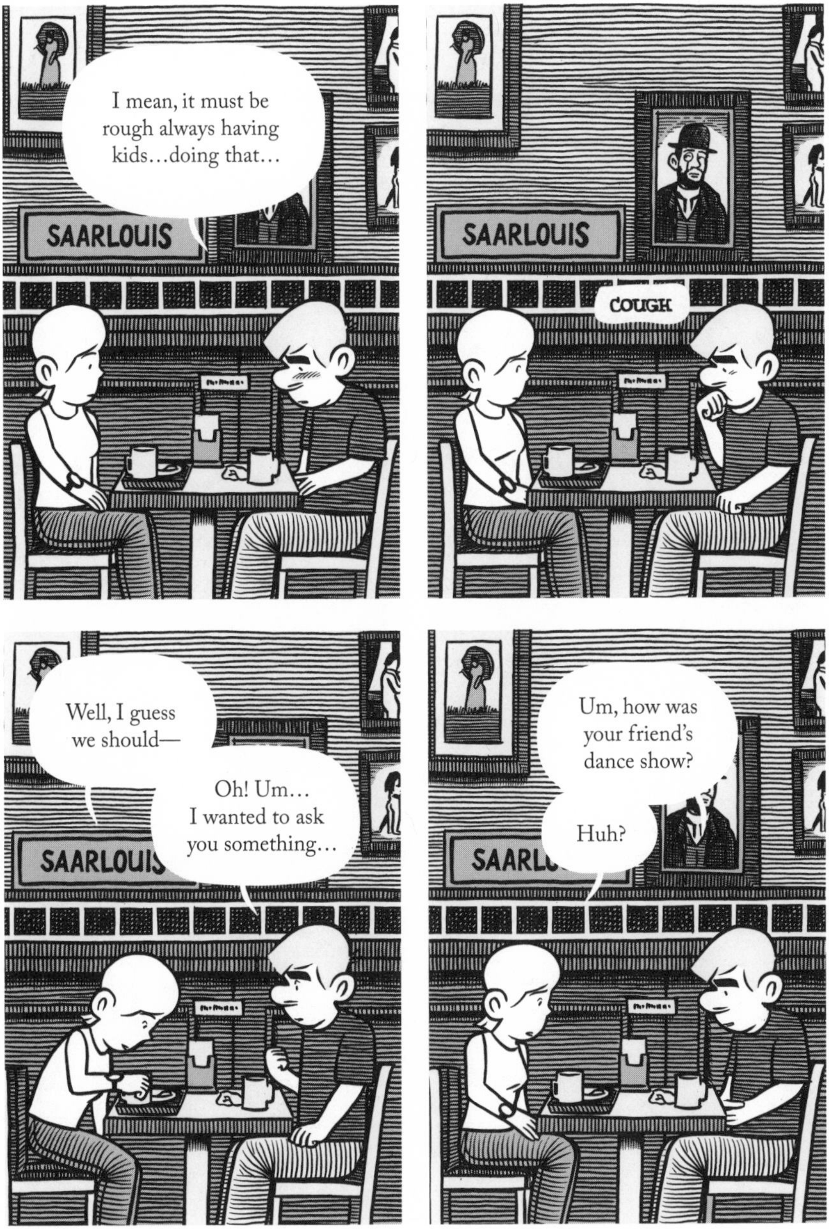

I mean, it must be rough always having kids...doing that...
SAARLOUIS
SAARLOUIS
COUGH
Well, I guess we should—
Oh! Um... I wanted to ask you something...
SAARLOUIS
Um, how was your friend's dance show?
Huh?

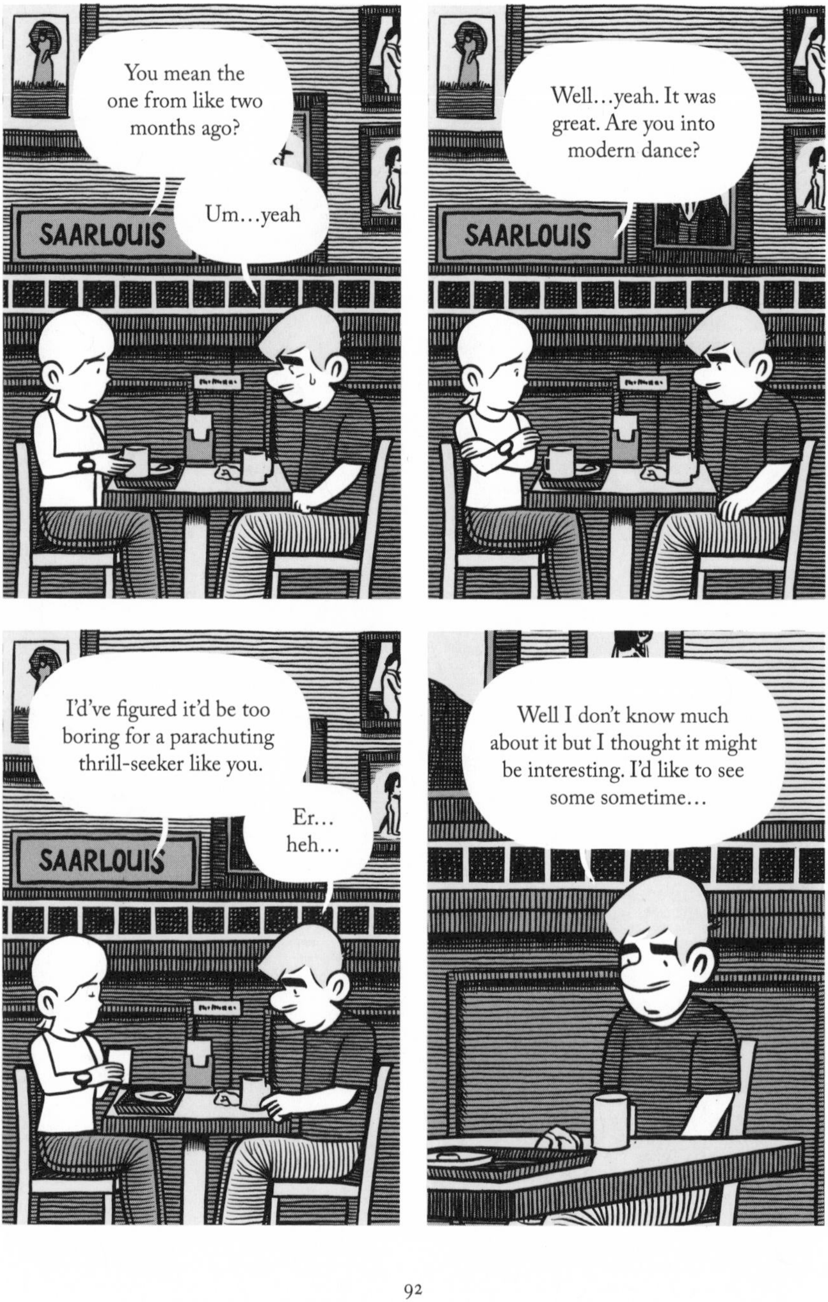
You mean the one from like two months ago?
Um…yeah
SAARLOUIS
Well…yeah. It was great. Are you into modern dance?
SAARLOUIS
I'd've figured it'd be too boring for a parachuting thrill-seeker like you.
Er… heh…
SAARLOUIS
Well I don't know much about it but I thought it might be interesting. I'd like to see some sometime…

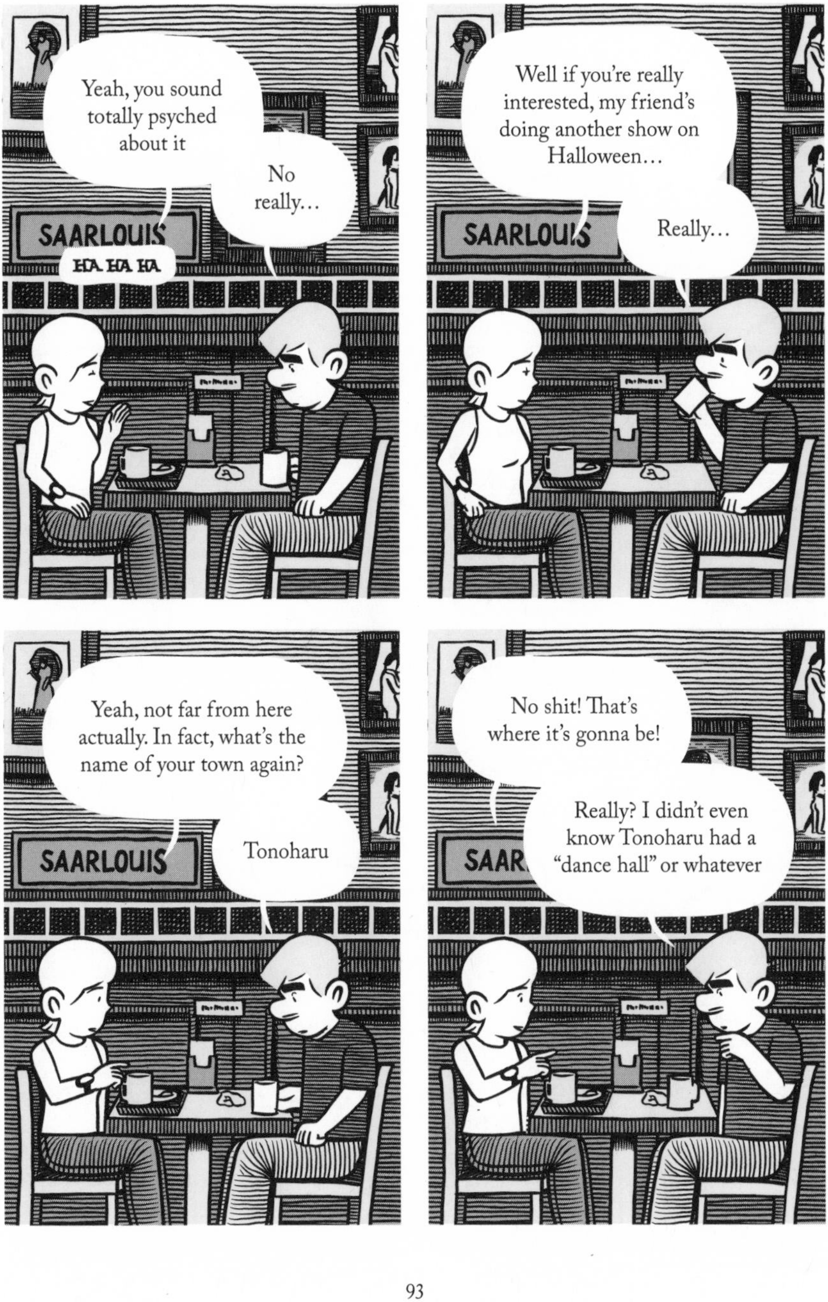

Yeah, you sound totally psyched about it
No really…
SAARLOUIS
HA HA HA
Well if you're really interested, my friend's doing another show on Halloween…
Really…
SAARLOUIS
Yeah, not far from here actually. In fact, what's the name of your town again?
Tonoharu
SAARLOUIS
No shit! That's where it's gonna be!
Really? I didn't even know Tonoharu had a "dance hall" or whatever

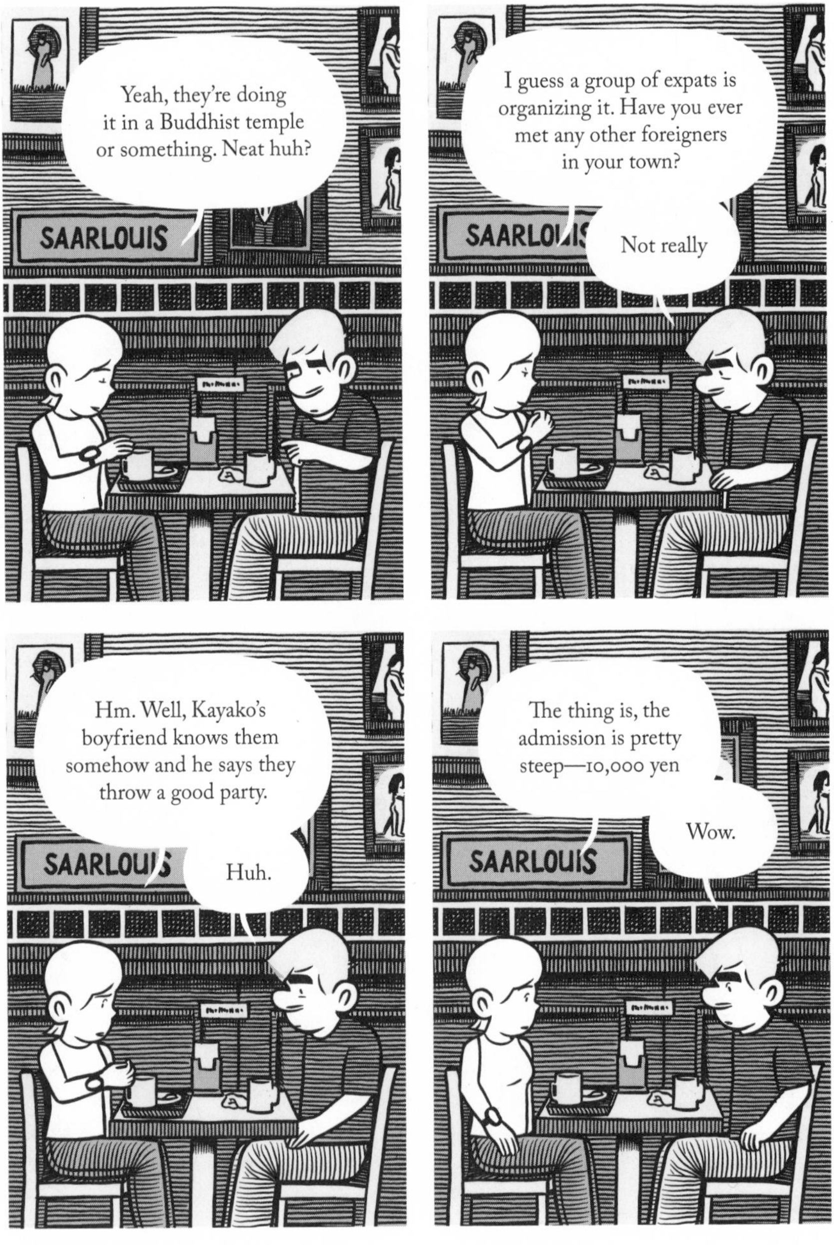
Yeah, they're doing it in a Buddhist temple or something. Neat huh?
SAARLOUIS
I guess a group of expats is organizing it. Have you ever met any other foreigners in your town?
Not really
Hm. Well, Kayako's boyfriend knows them somehow and he says they throw a good party.
Huh.
The thing is, the admission is pretty steep—10,000 yen
Wow.

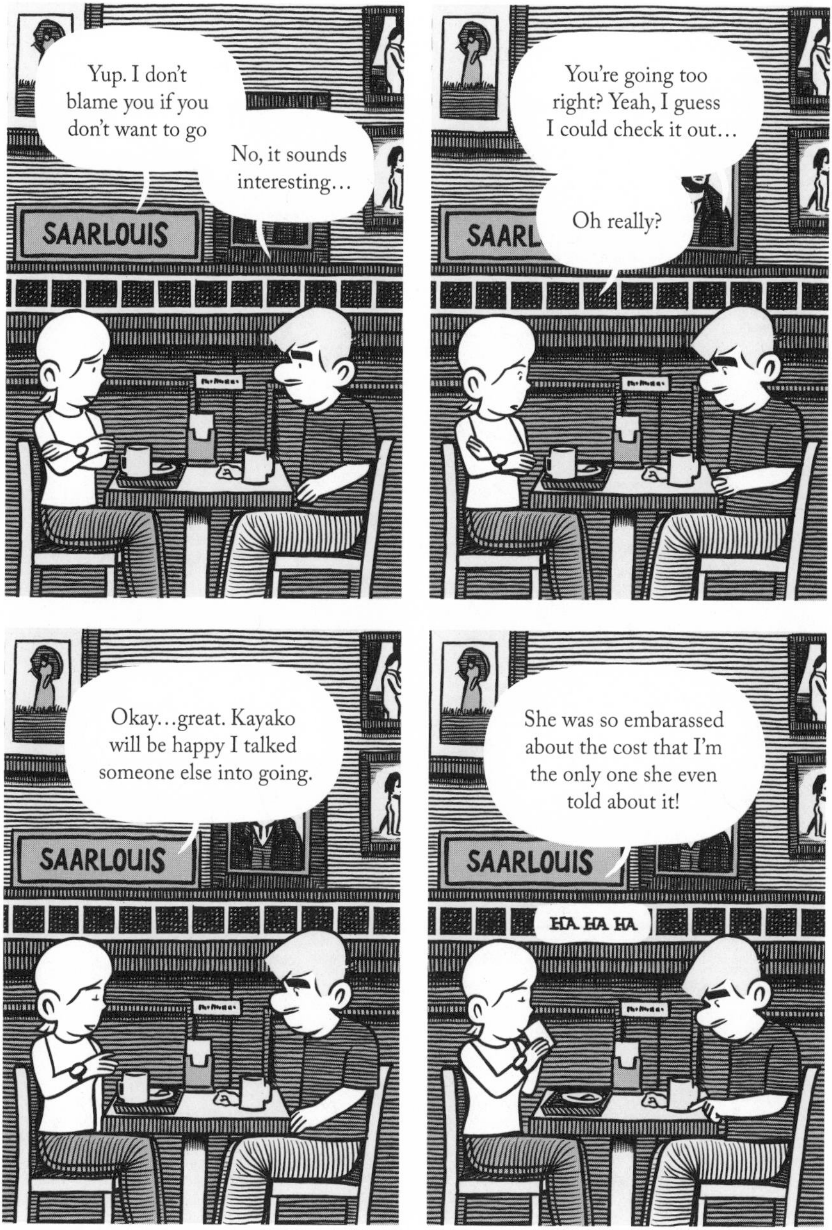
Yup. I don't blame you if you don't want to go
No, it sounds interesting…
SAARLOUIS
You're going too right? Yeah, I guess I could check it out…
Oh really?
Okay…great. Kayako will be happy I talked someone else into going.
SAARLOUIS
She was so embarassed about the cost that I'm the only one she even told about it!
SAARLOUIS
HA HA HA

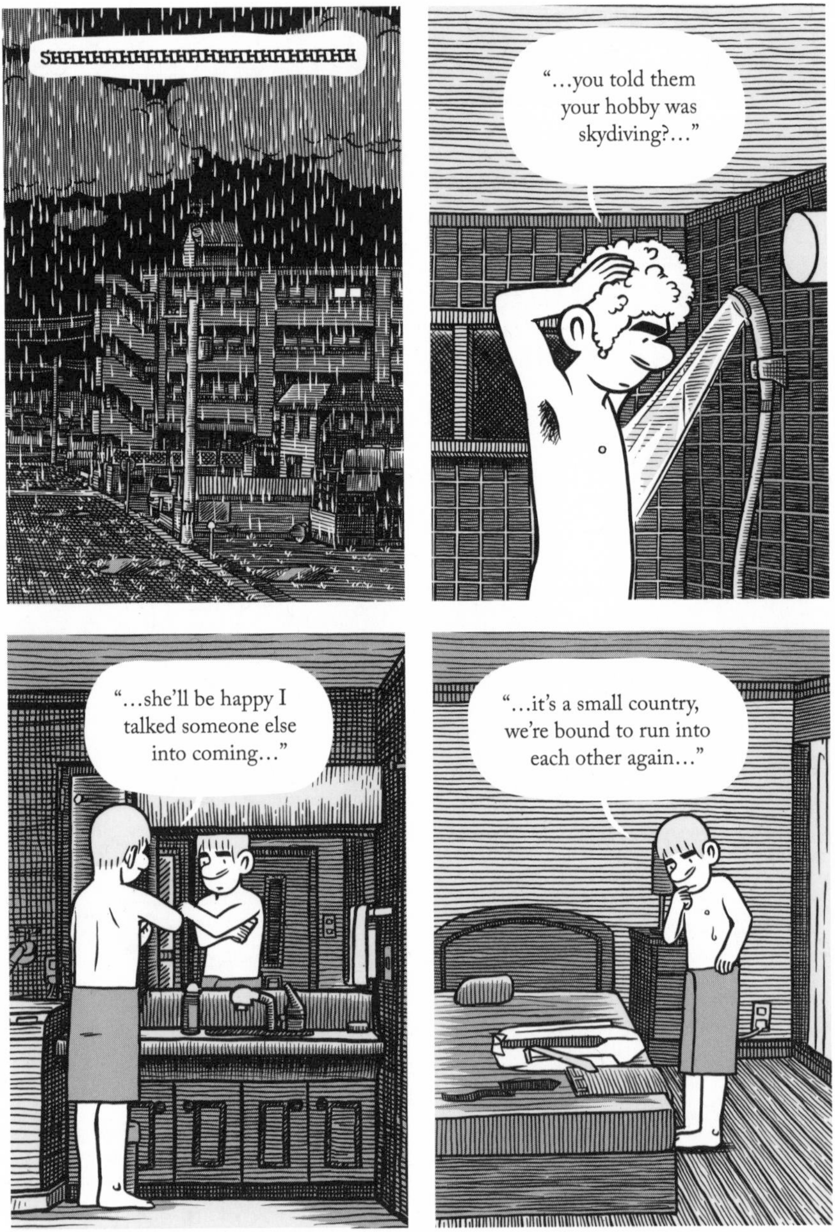
SHHHHHHHHHHHHHHHHHHHHHHHH
"...you told them your hobby was skydiving?..."
"...she'll be happy I talked someone else into coming..."
"...it's a small country, we're bound to run into each other again..."

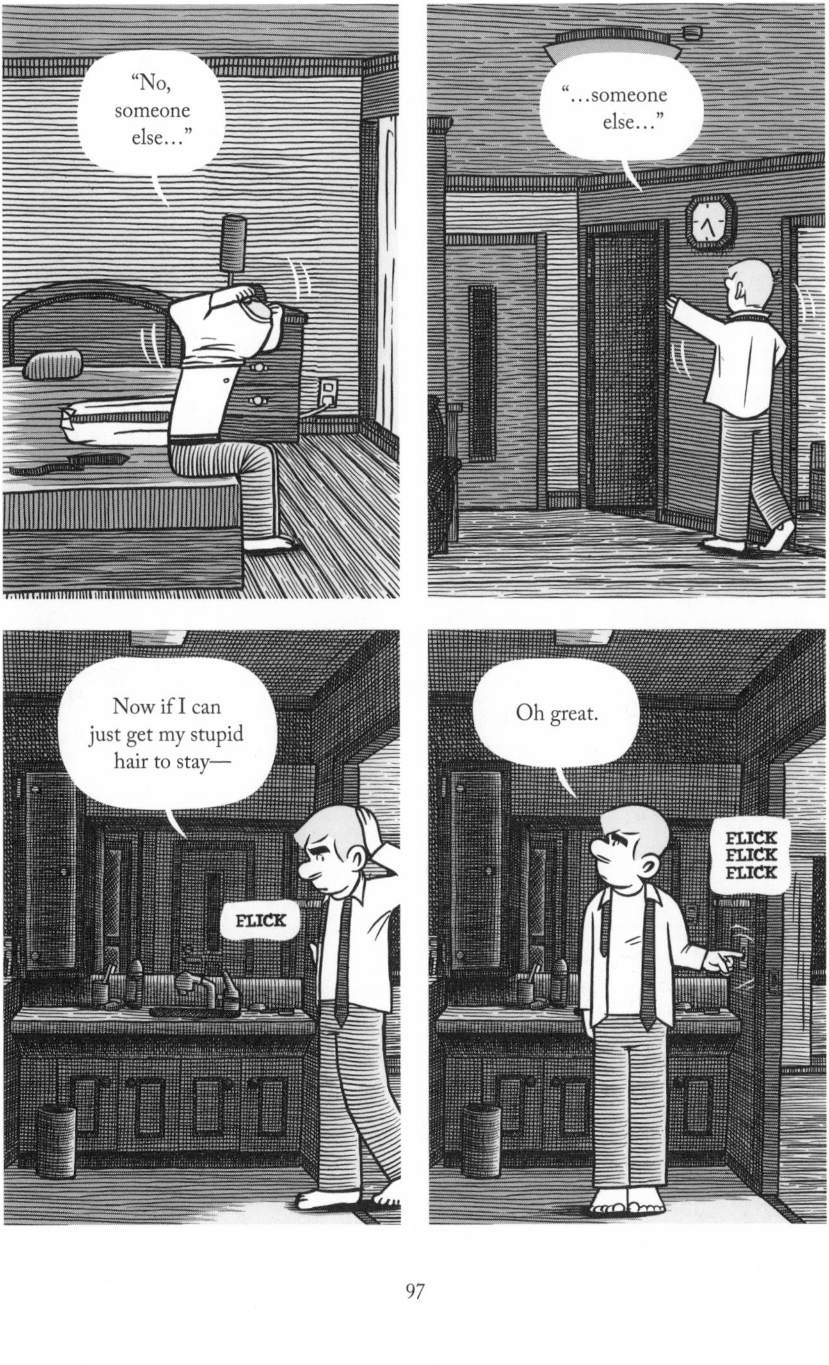
"No, someone else..."
"...someone else..."
Now if I can just get my stupid hair to stay—
FLICK
Oh great.
FLICK FLICK FLICK

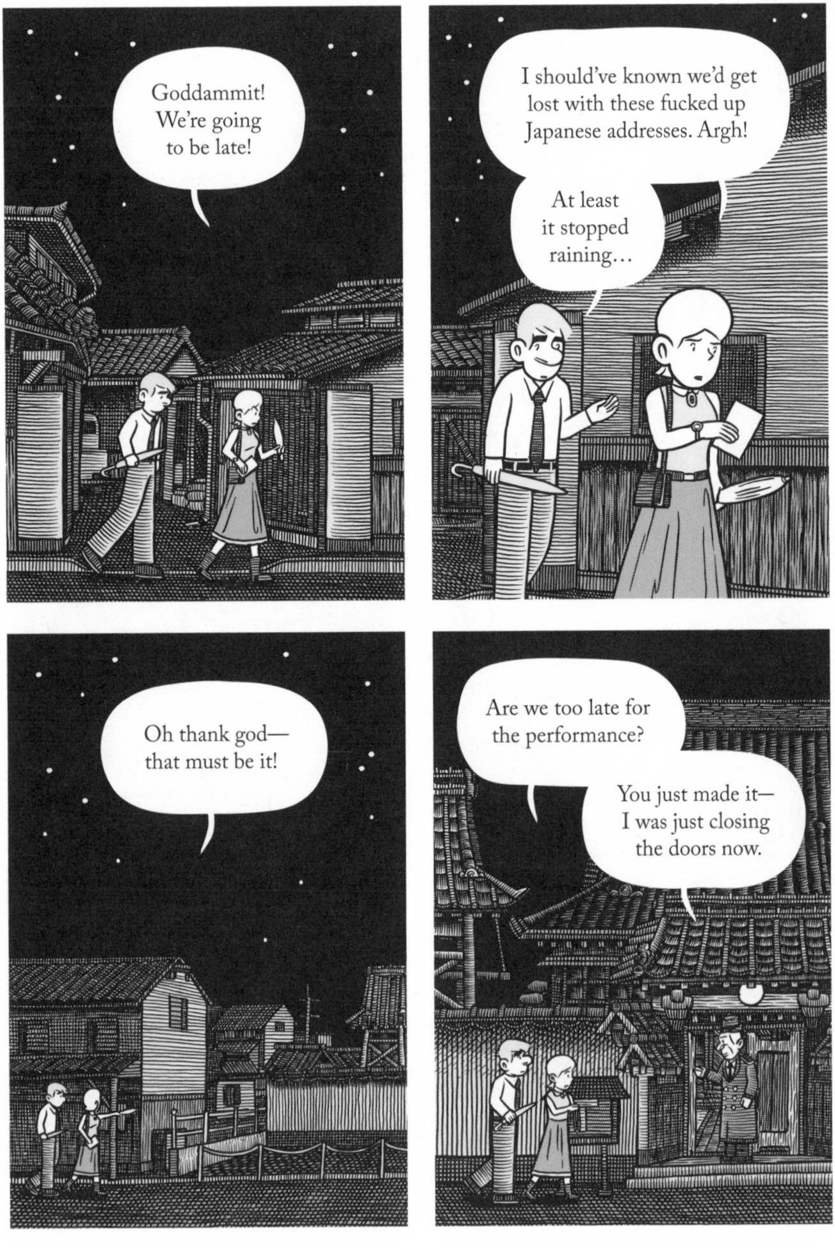
Goddammit! We're going to be late!
I should've known we'd get lost with these fucked up Japanese addresses. Argh!
At least it stopped raining…
Oh thank god—that must be it!
Are we too late for the performance?
You just made it—I was just closing the doors now.

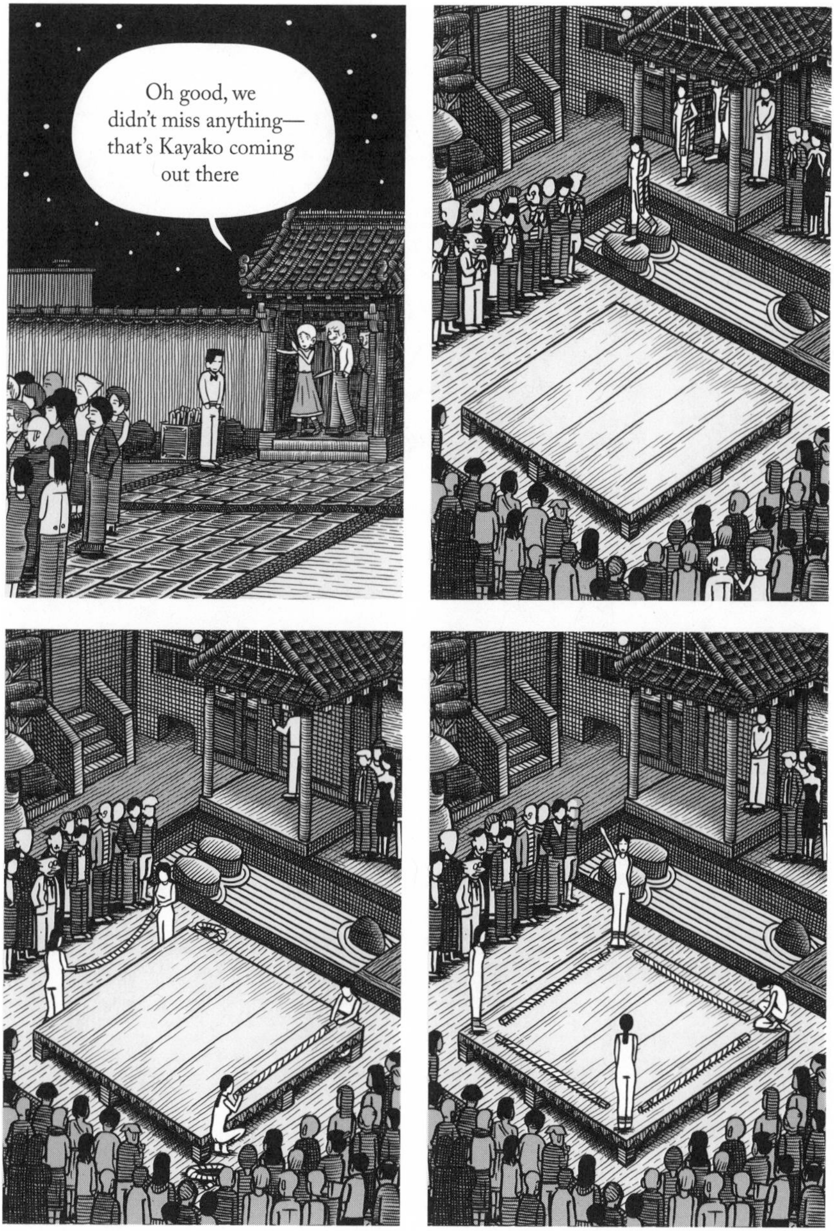
Oh good, we didn't miss anything—that's Kayako coming out there

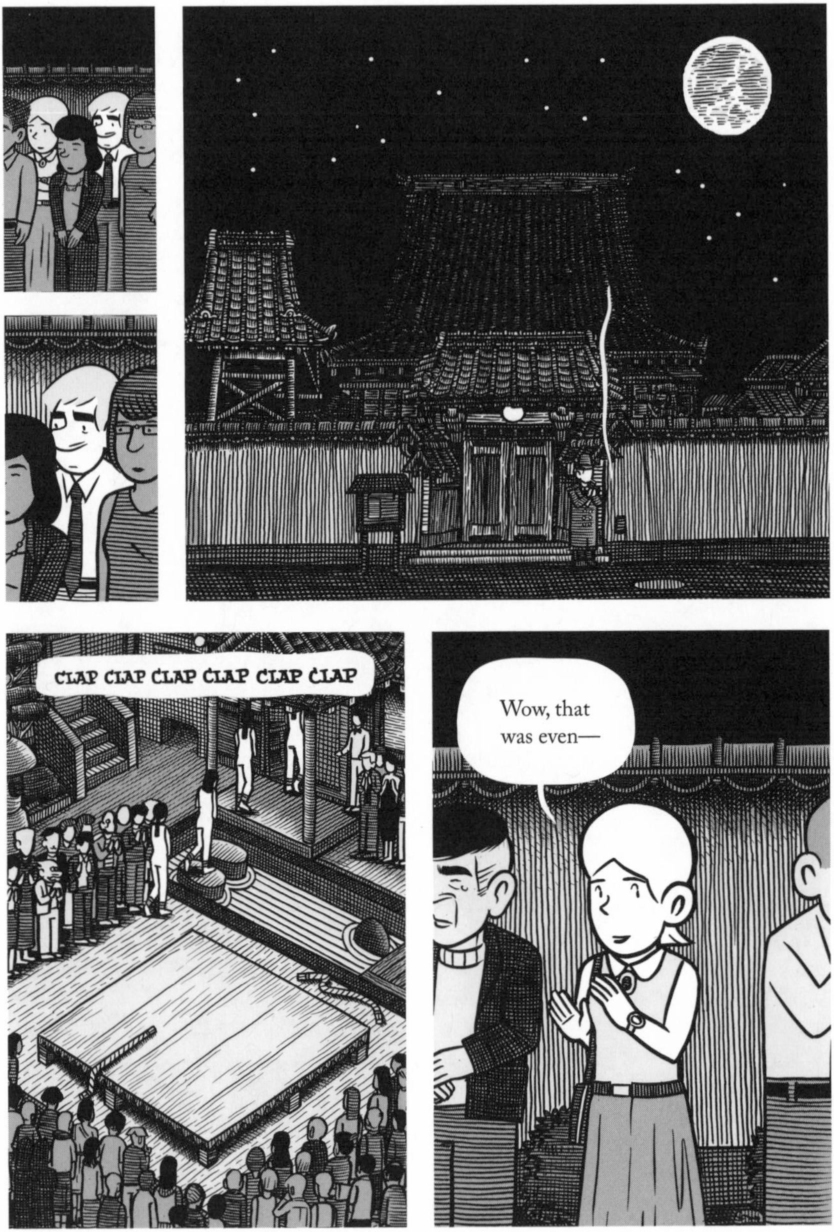
CLAP CLAP CLAP CLAP CLAP CLAP
Wow, that was even—

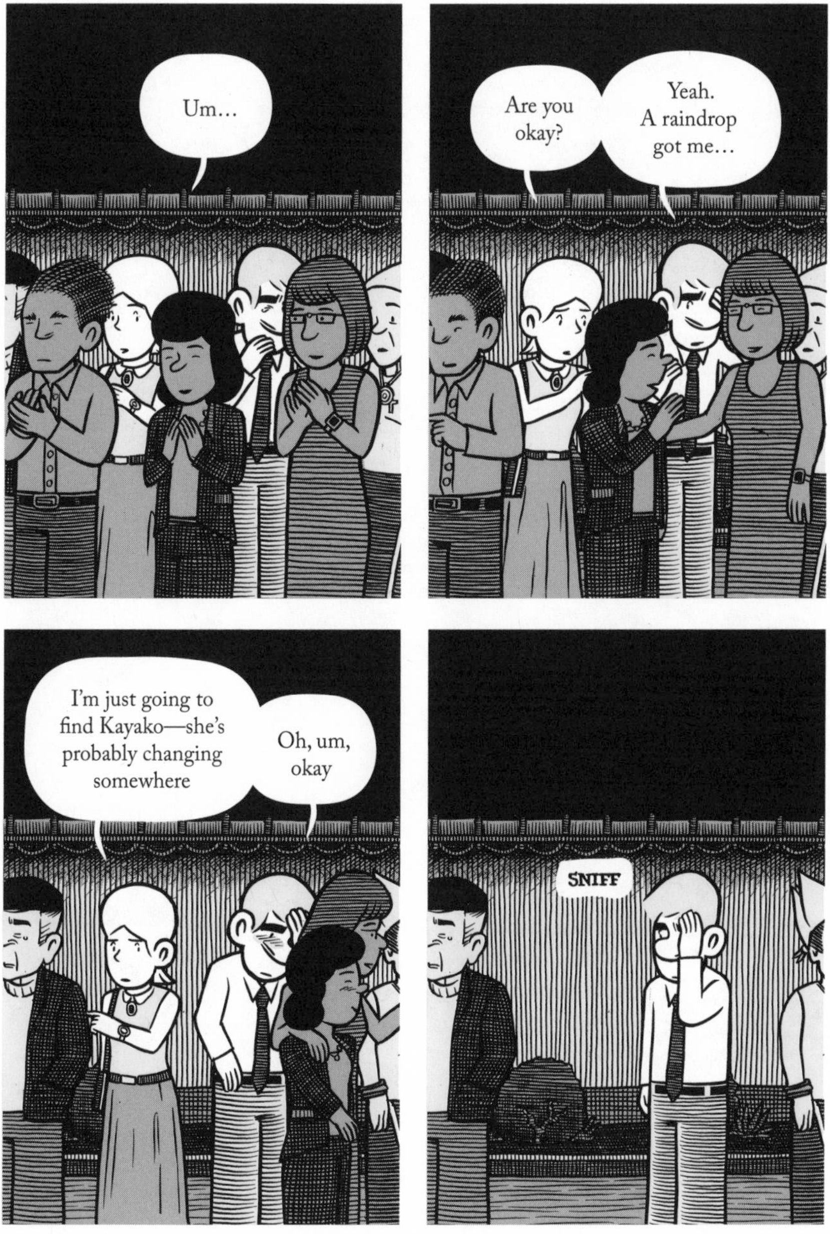
Um…
Are you okay?
Yeah. A raindrop got me…
I'm just going to find Kayako—she's probably changing somewhere
Oh, um, okay
SNIFF

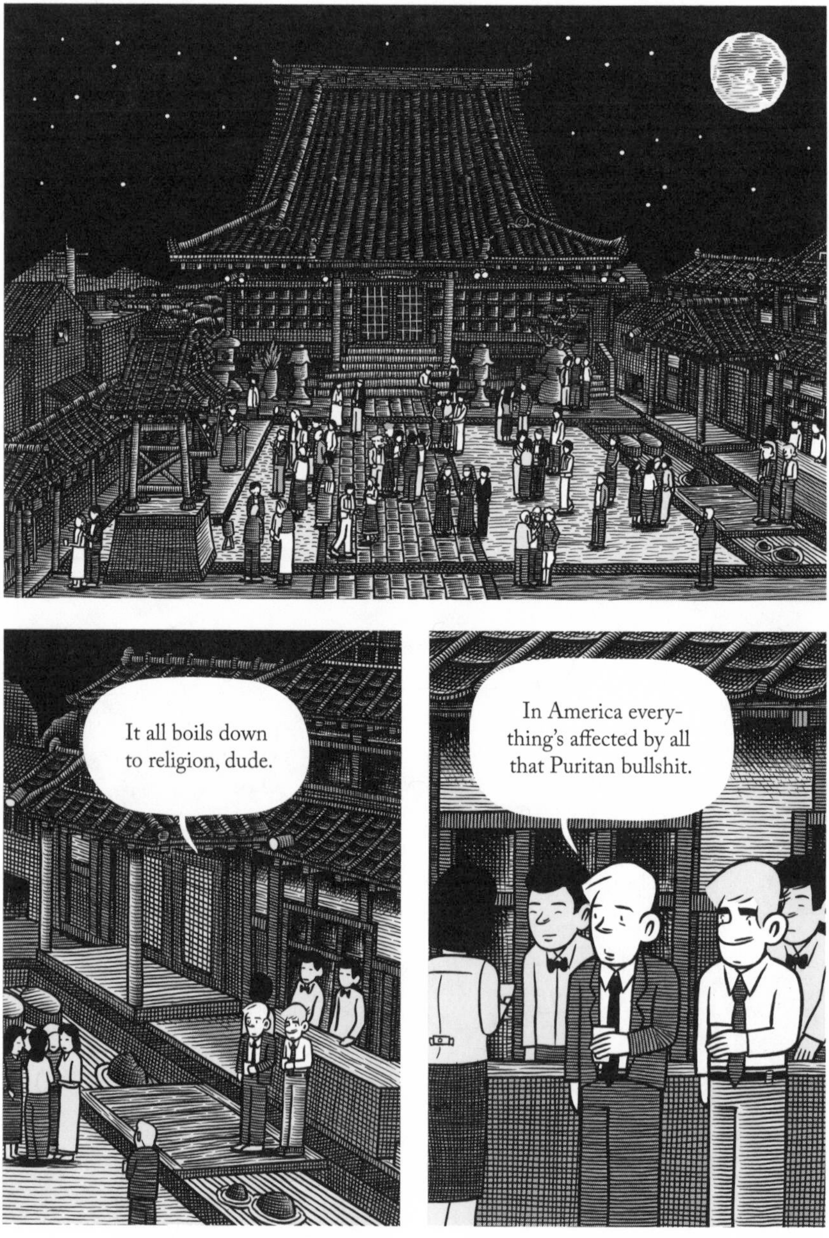
It all boils down to religion, dude.
In America everything's affected by all that Puritan bullshit.

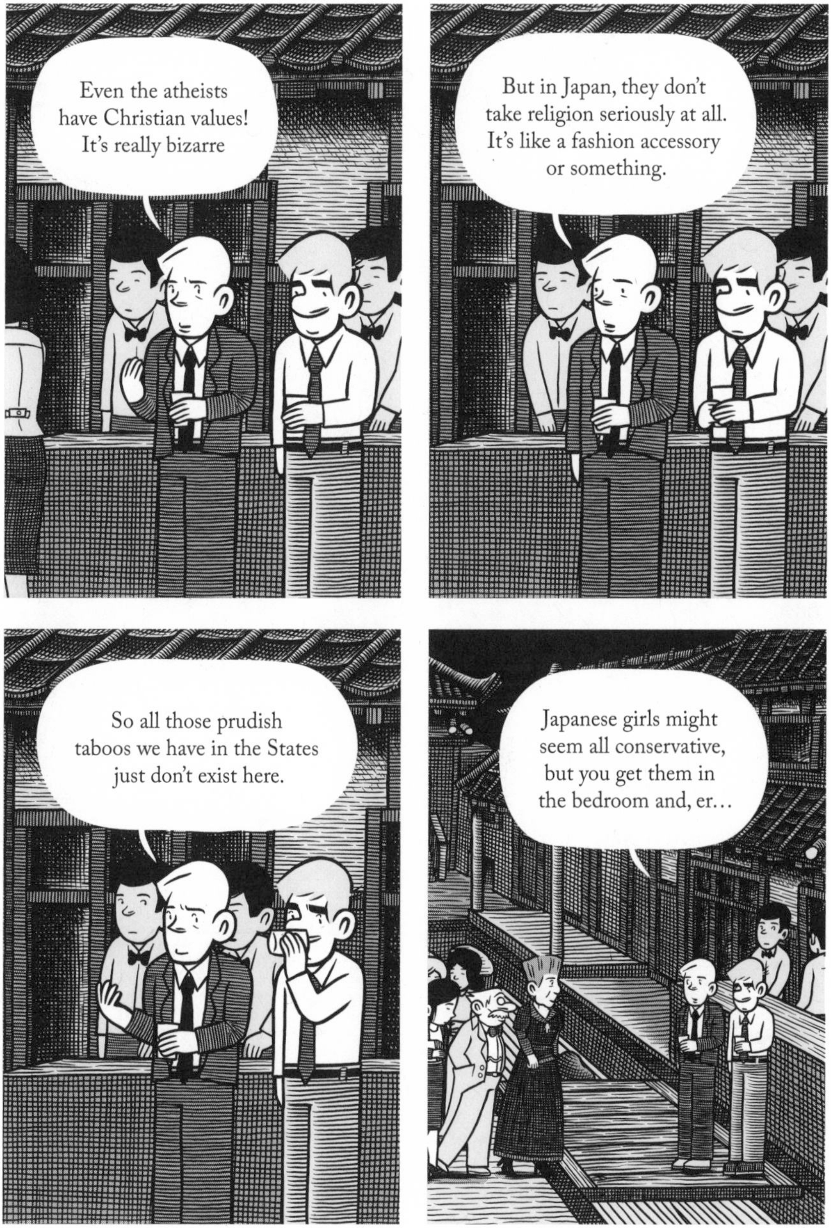
Even the atheists have Christian values! It's really bizarre
But in Japan, they don't take religion seriously at all. It's like a fashion accessory or something.
So all those prudish taboos we have in the States just don't exist here.
Japanese girls might seem all conservative, but you get them in the bedroom and, er…

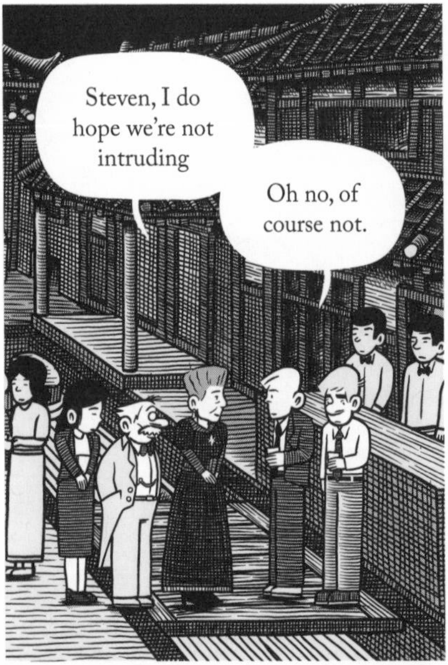
Steven, I do hope we're not intruding
Oh no, of course not.
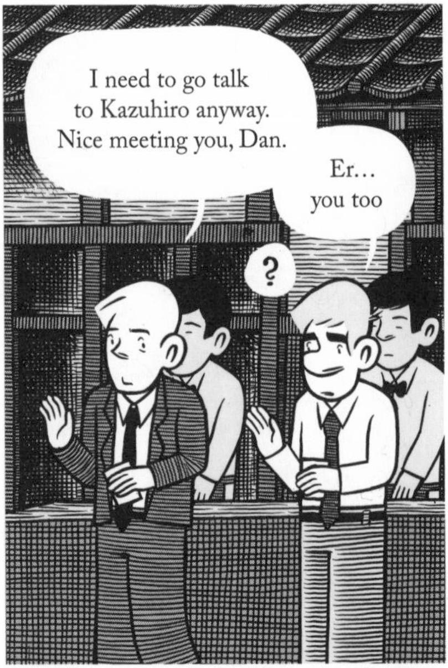
I need to go talk to Kazuhiro anyway. Nice meeting you, Dan.
Er... you too
?
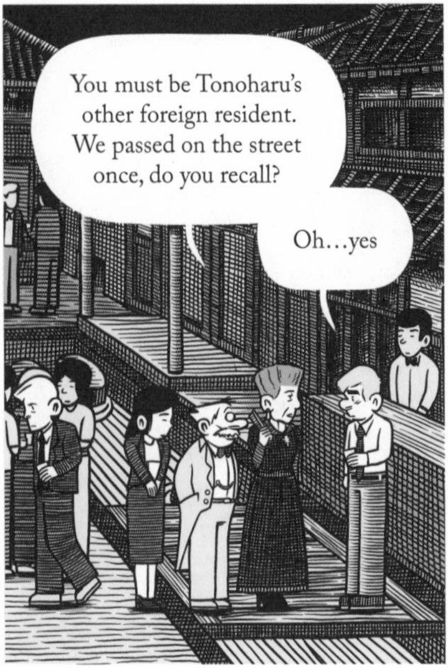
You must be Tonoharu's other foreign resident. We passed on the street once, do you recall?
Oh...yes
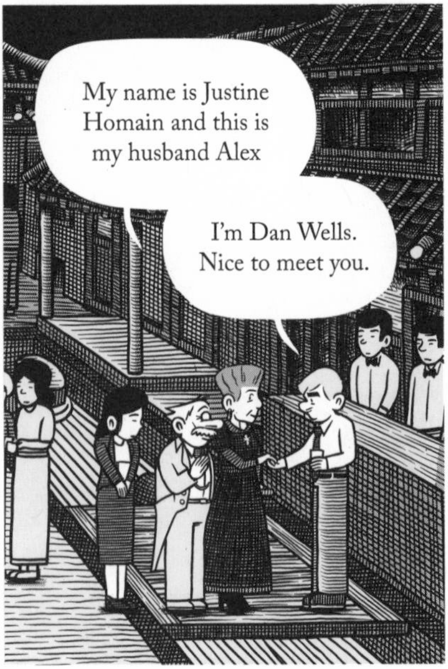
My name is Justine Homain and this is my husband Alex
I'm Dan Wells. Nice to meet you.

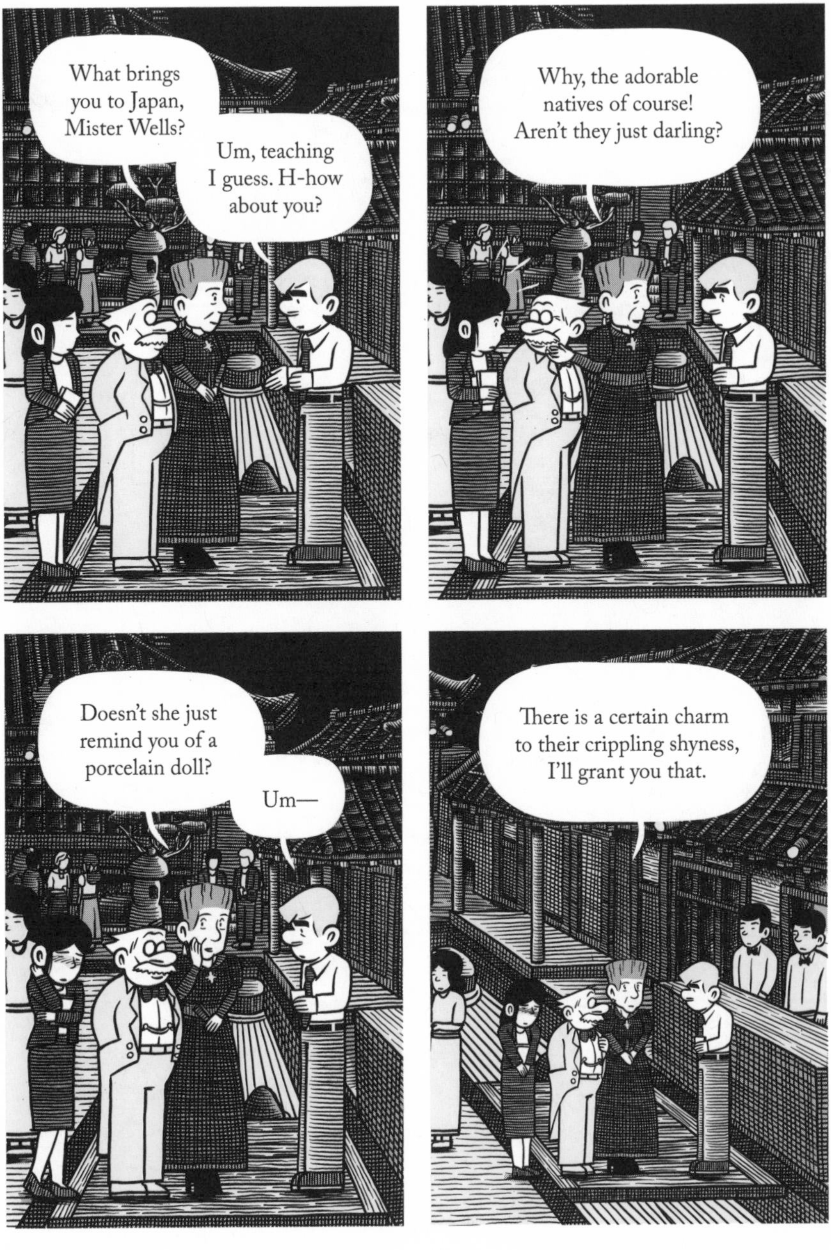
What brings you to Japan, Mister Wells?
Um, teaching I guess. H-how about you?
Why, the adorable natives of course! Aren't they just darling?
Doesn't she just remind you of a porcelain doll?
Um—
There is a certain charm to their crippling shyness, I'll grant you that.

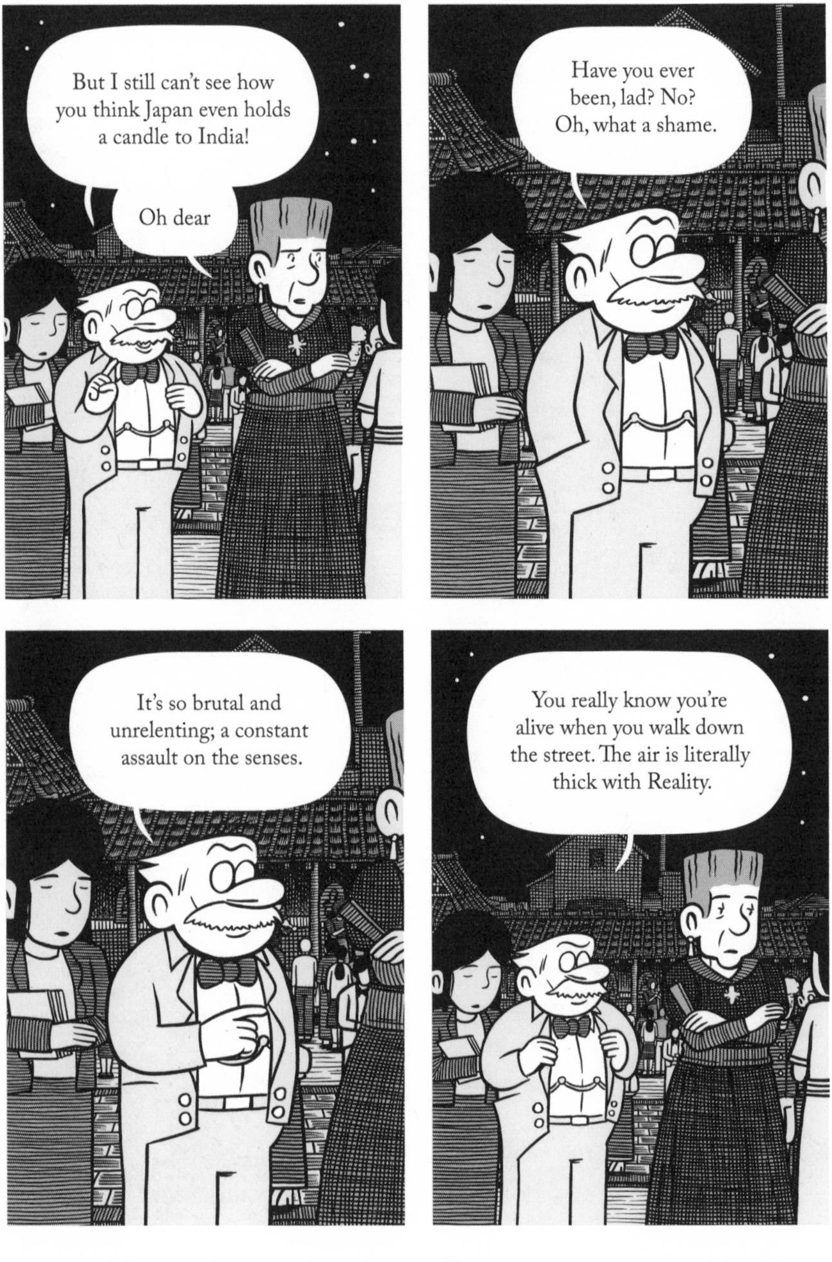
But I still can't see how you think Japan even holds a candle to India!
Oh dear
Have you ever been, lad? No? Oh, what a shame.
It's so brutal and unrelenting; a constant assault on the senses.
You really know you're alive when you walk down the street. The air is literally thick with Reality.

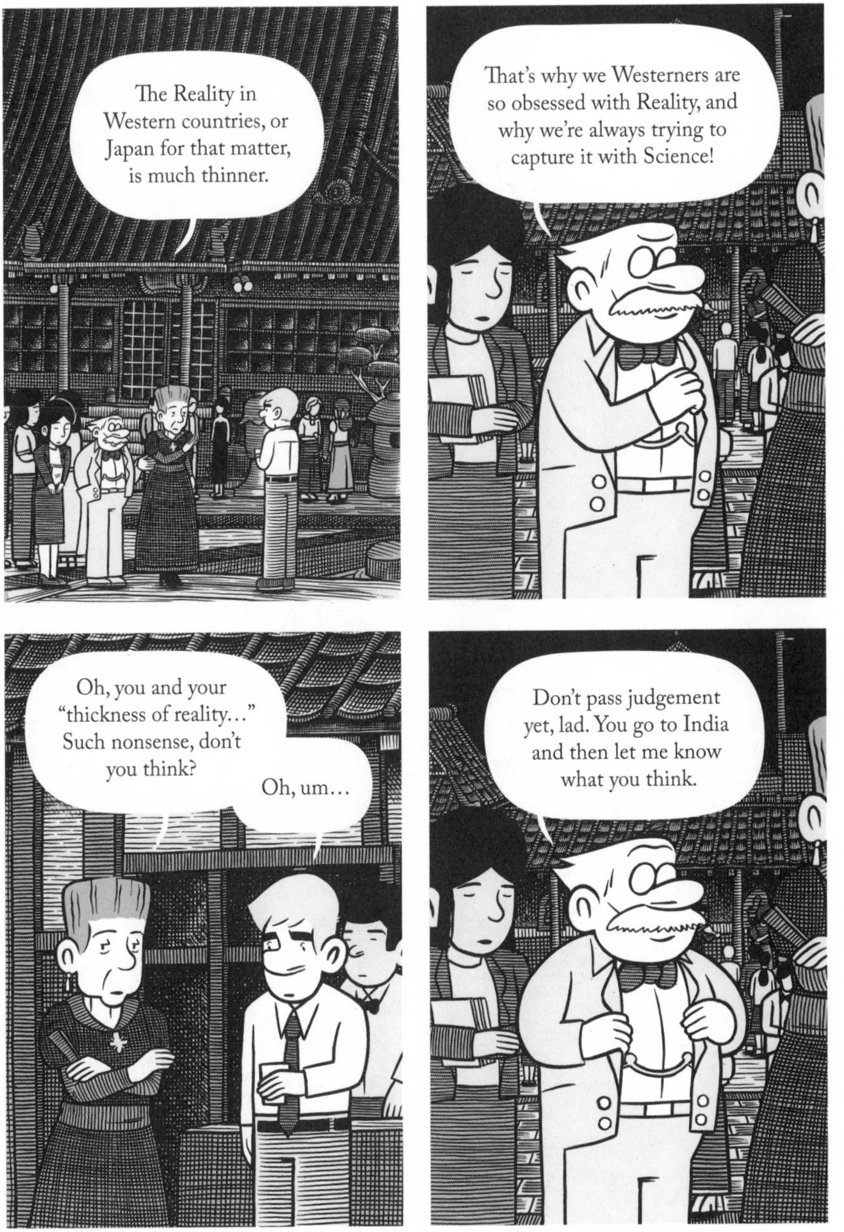
The Reality in Western countries, or Japan for that matter, is much thinner.
That's why we Westerners are so obsessed with Reality, and why we're always trying to capture it with Science!
Oh, you and your "thickness of reality..." Such nonsense, don't you think?
Oh, um...
Don't pass judgement yet, lad. You go to India and then let me know what you think.

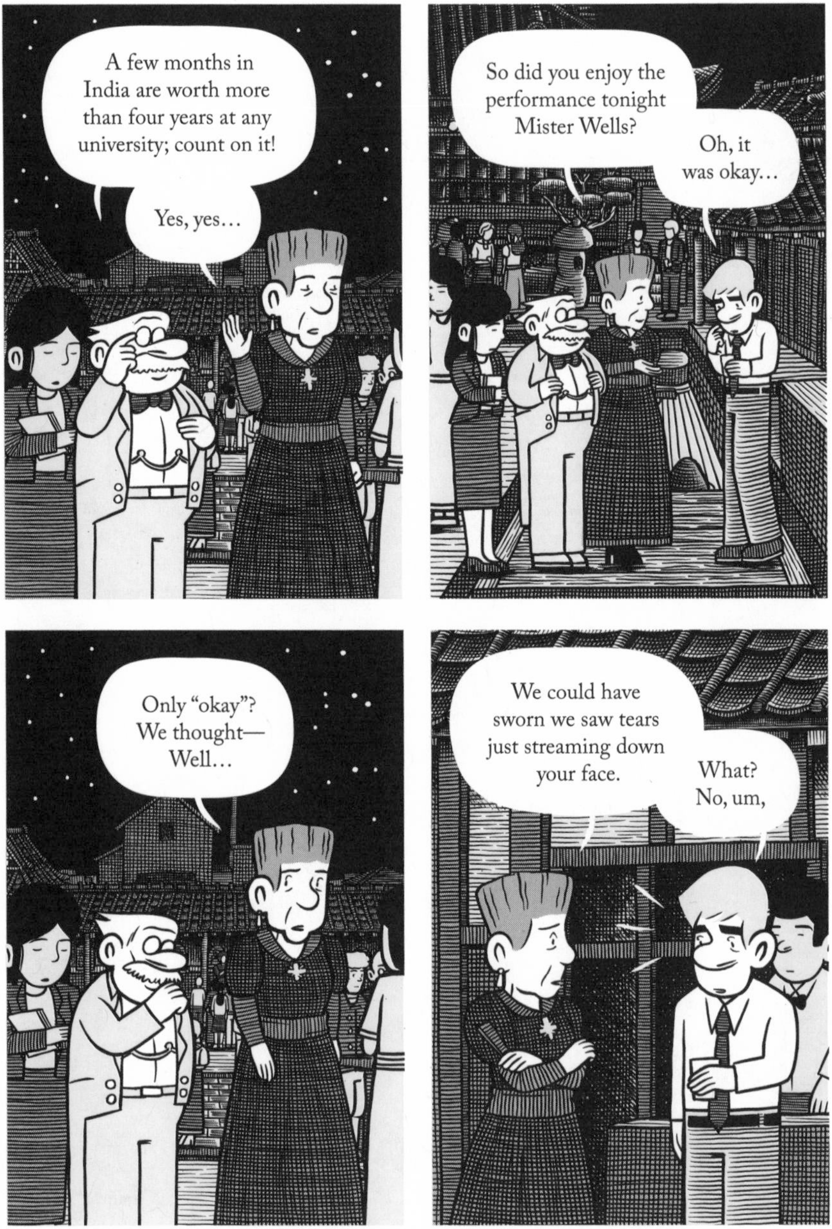
A few months in India are worth more than four years at any university; count on it!
Yes, yes…
So did you enjoy the performance tonight Mister Wells?
Oh, it was okay…
Only "okay"? We thought— Well…
We could have sworn we saw tears just streaming down your face.
What? No, um,

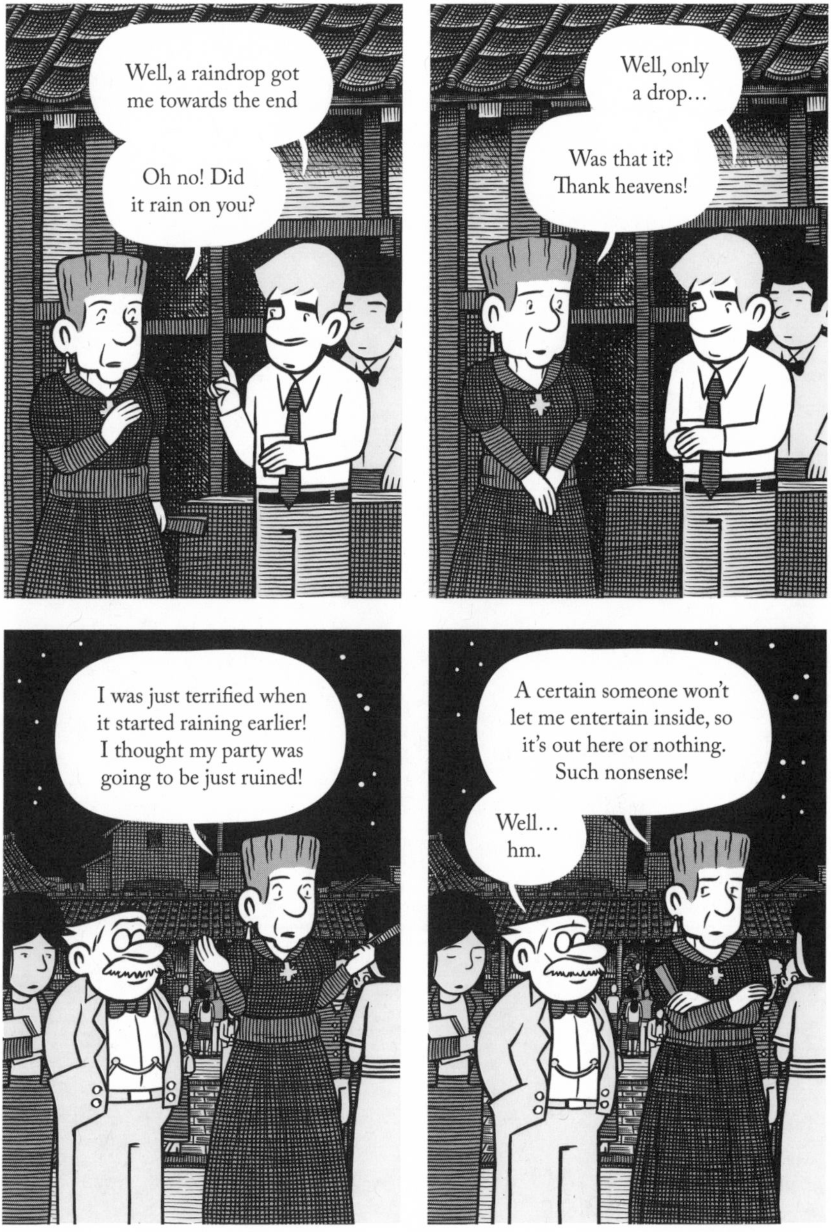
Well, a raindrop got me towards the end
Oh no! Did it rain on you?
Well, only a drop…
Was that it? Thank heavens!
I was just terrified when it started raining earlier! I thought my party was going to be just ruined!
A certain someone won't let me entertain inside, so it's out here or nothing. Such nonsense!
Well… hm.

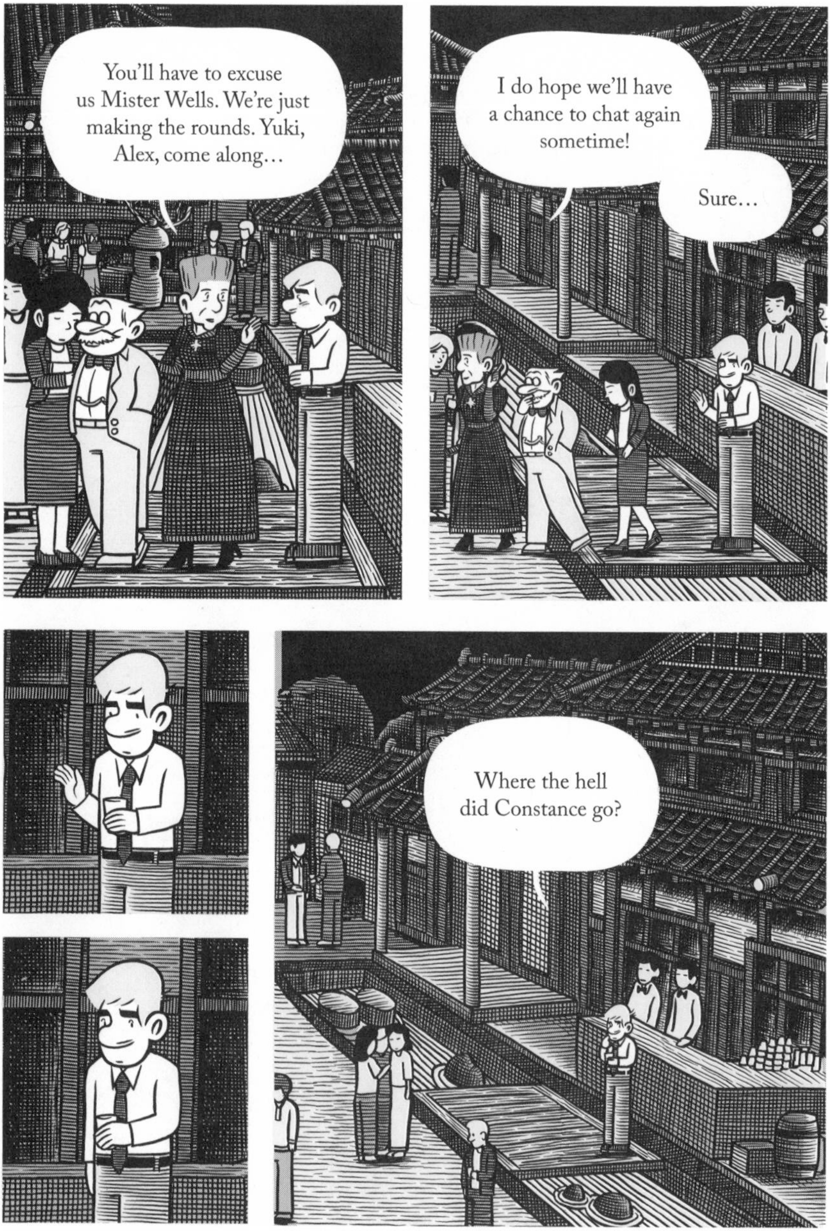
You'll have to excuse us Mister Wells. We're just making the rounds. Yuki, Alex, come along…
I do hope we'll have a chance to chat again sometime!
Sure…
Where the hell did Constance go?

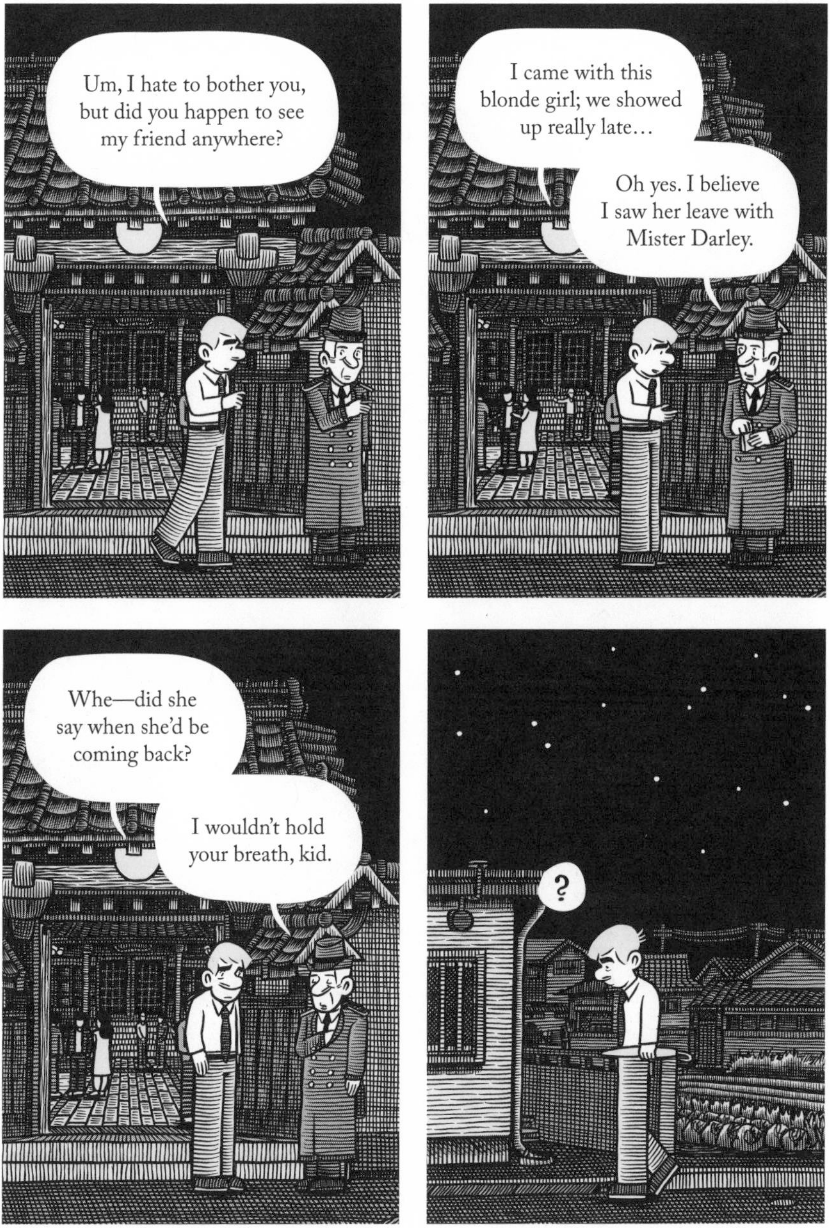
Um, I hate to bother you, but did you happen to see my friend anywhere?
I came with this blonde girl; we showed up really late…
Oh yes. I believe I saw her leave with Mister Darley.
Whe—did she say when she'd be coming back?
I wouldn't hold your breath, kid.
?

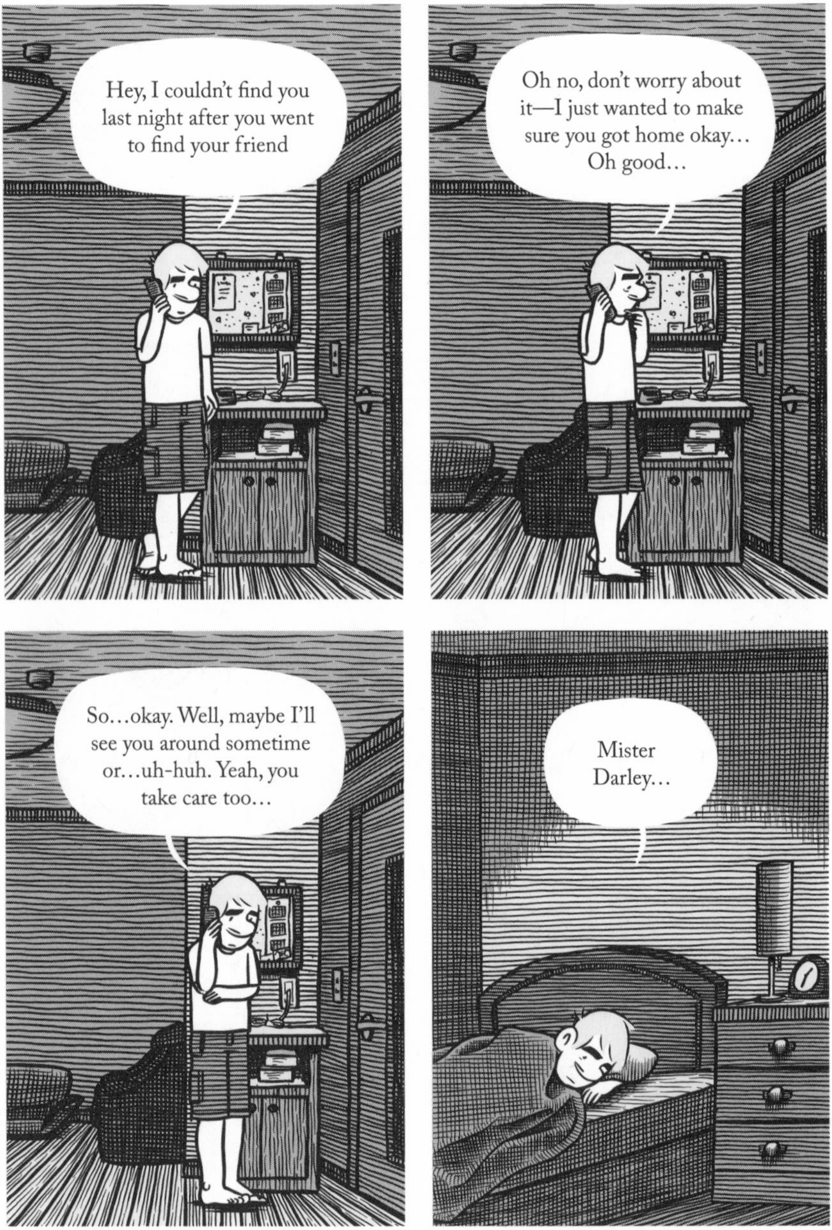
Hey, I couldn't find you last night after you went to find your friend
Oh no, don't worry about it—I just wanted to make sure you got home okay... Oh good...
So...okay. Well, maybe I'll see you around sometime or...uh-huh. Yeah, you take care too...
Mister Darley...

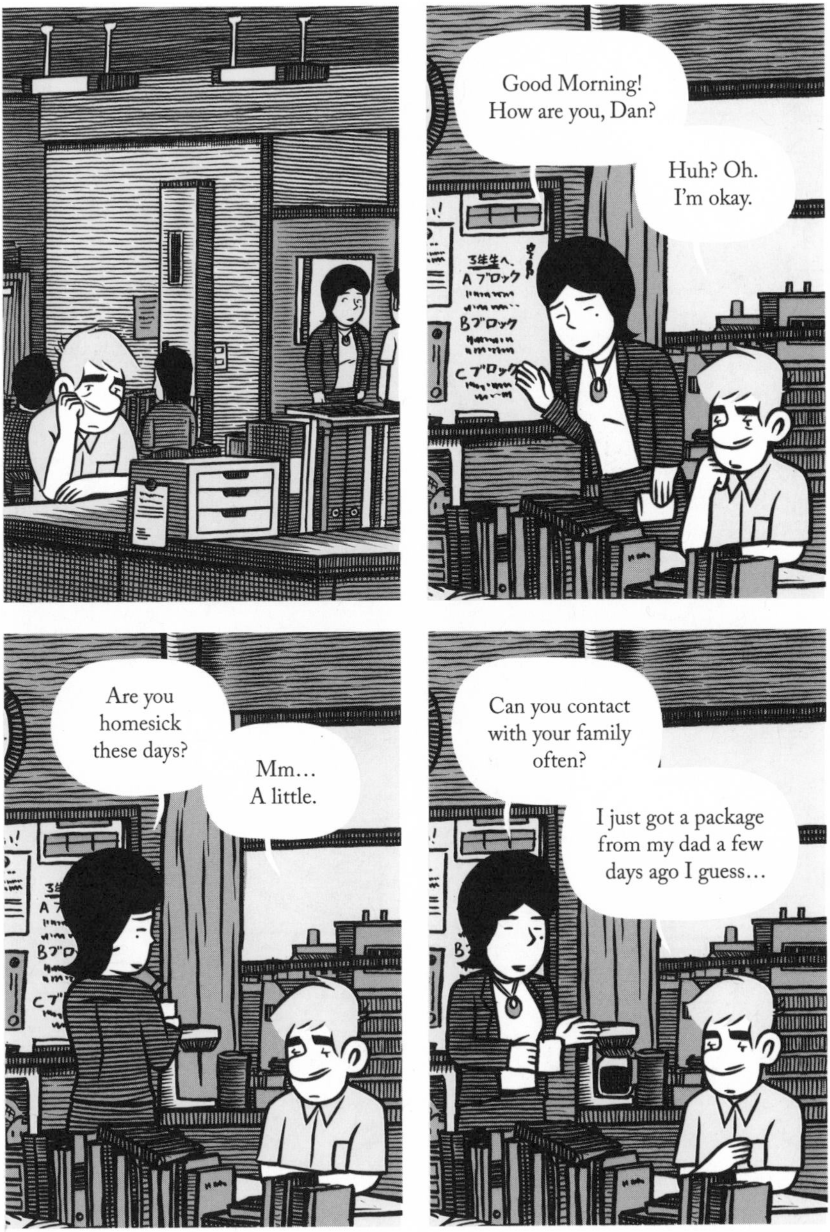
Good Morning!
How are you, Dan?
Huh? Oh.
I'm okay.
3年生へ、
Aブロック
Bブロック
Cブロック
Are you
homesick
these days?
Mm…
A little.
Can you contact
with your family
often?
I just got a package
from my dad a few
days ago I guess…

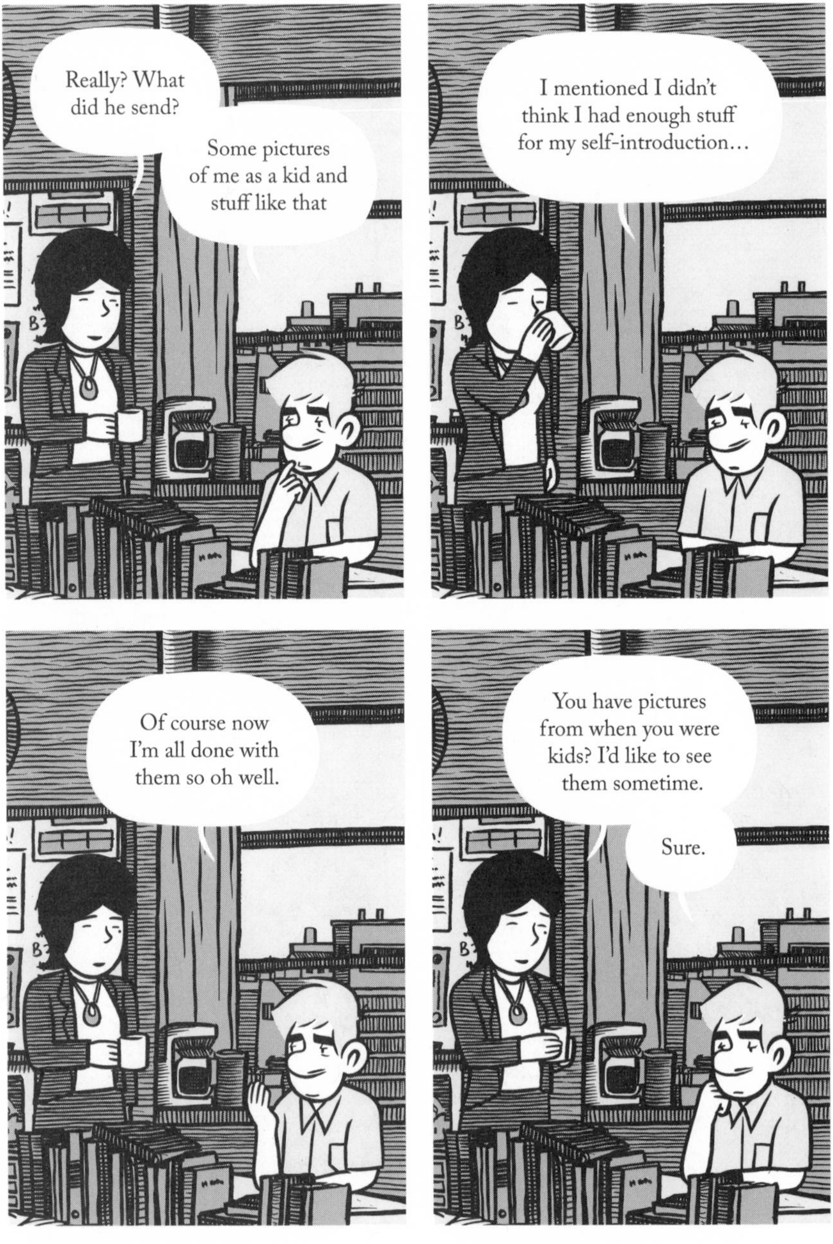
Really? What did he send?
Some pictures of me as a kid and stuff like that
I mentioned I didn't think I had enough stuff for my self-introduction...
Of course now I'm all done with them so oh well.
You have pictures from when you were kids? I'd like to see them sometime.
Sure.

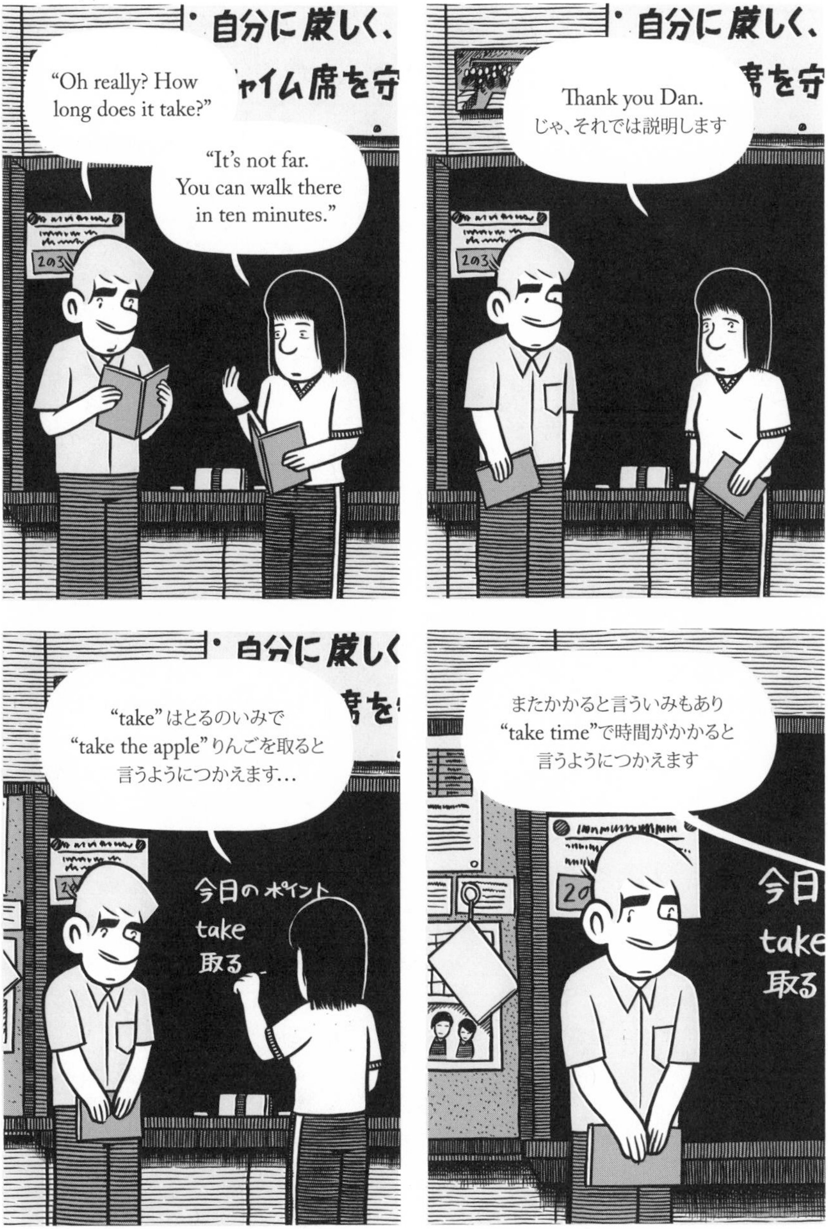

自分に厳しく、
“Oh really? How long does it take?”
“It’s not far. You can walk there in ten minutes.”
Thank you Dan.
じゃ、それでは説明します
“take”はとるのいみで
“take the apple”りんごを取ると
言うようにつかえます…
今日のポイント
take
取る
またかかると言ういみもあり
“take time”で時間がかかると
言うようにつかえます

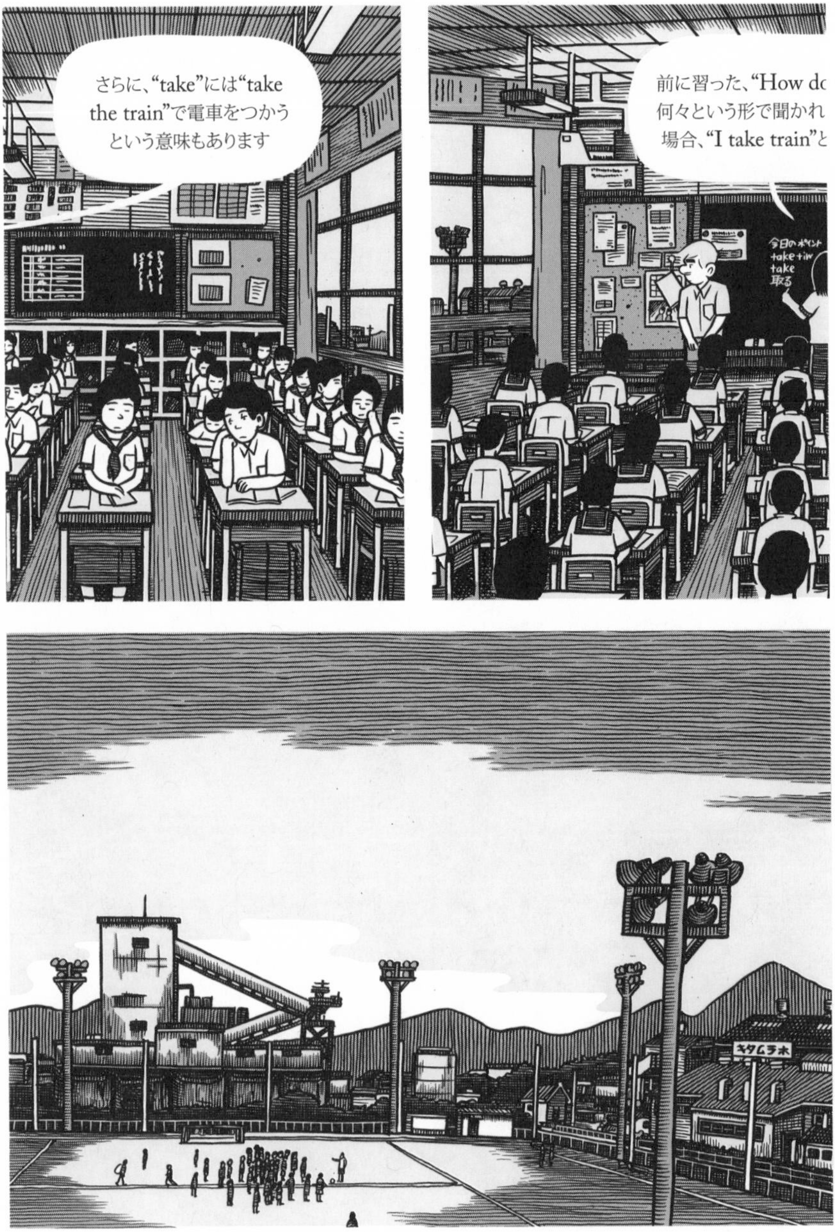
さらに、“take”には“take the train”で電車をつかうという意味もあります
前に習った、“How dc
何々という形で聞かれ
場合、“I take train”と
今日のポイント
take
取る
キタムラホ

Wholesalers, distributors, retailers and libraries can purchase copies of this and other Pliant Press books at discounted rates. Address inquiries to: chris@topshelfcomix.com

SECOND PRINTING AUGUST 2008

10 9 8 7 6 5 4 3 2

Publisher's Cataloging-in-Publication Data
Martinson, Lars
Tonoharu: Part One / Lars Martinson
p. cm.
ISBN 978-0-9801023-2-1 (acid-free paper)
I. Title
Library of Congress Control Number: 2007940522

ACKNOWLEDGMENTS

THE AUTHOR wishes to thank Japanese
cultural consultant C.W. Kelly for his advice
and insight. Thanks also go out to Mr. Chris
Ware for his willingness to indulge the
author's inane questions on the subject
of book production.

THIS GRAPHIC NOVEL is distributed
through an arrangement with Top Shelf
Productions. Thanks to Chris, Brett,
and Leigh for all their help.
TOPSHELFCOMIX.COM

A VERY SPECIAL THANKS goes to
Steve and Marci Martinson for all
their love and support over the years.

COLOPHON

THE FRONT COVER ILLUSTRATION,
Tōnoharu at Midday, is the first in a series
entitled *Four Views of Fukuoka-ken*. It was
informed by the works of Katsushika
Hokusai [北斎葛飾] (1760-1849).

THE ENDPAPERS are based on a Japanese
cosmetic box from the Heian Period, 12th
century. Original design in maki-e lacquer and
mother-of-pearl inlay. From the collection of
the Tokyo National Museum.

THIS GRAPHIC NOVEL is set in
Adobe Caslon and *Kozuka Mincho* [小塚朝月].

IN OUR NEXT INSTALLMENT

WINTER ARRIVES, and with it comes long-sleeved school uniforms, New Year's parties, and Spring Festival preparations. A new friend introduces Dan to the local nightlife. Mister Darley makes an appearance.

ABOUT THE AUTHOR

LARS MARTINSON was born in
Minnesota on Mother's Day, 1977.
He is a direct descendant of the first
king of Norway. He has met a princess,
seen a five-legged cow, and eaten raw
octopus eggs. From 2003 to 2006, he
worked as an assistant English
teacher in Fukuoka, Japan.

LARSMARTINSON.COM

Tōnoharu

BY LARS MARTINSON

PROLOGUE

PART ONE

PART TWO

PART THREE

APPENDICES

EPILOGUE

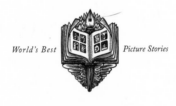

World's Best *Picture Stories*

PLIANT PRESS

For information about purchasing original art, and for news about *Tōnoharu: Part Two*, visit us online at:

PLIANTPRESS.COM